HEDGES and HEDGELAYING

A GUIDE TO PLANTING, MANAGEMENT AND CONSERVATION

HEDGES and HEDGELAYING

A GUIDE TO PLANTING, MANAGEMENT AND CONSERVATION

Murray Maclean

THE CROWOOD PRESS

First published in 2006 by
The Crowood Press Ltd
Ramsbury, Marlborough
Wiltshire SN8 2HR

www.crowood.com

This impression 2010

British Library Cataloguing-in-Publication Data
A catalogue record for this book is available from the British Library.

ISBN 978 1 86126 868 6

Disclaimer
Chainsaws and all other tools and equipment used in the management of hedges should be used in strict accordance with both the current health and safety regulations and the manufacturer's instructions. The author and publisher do not accept any responsibility in any manner whatsoever for any error or mission, or any loss, damage, injury, adverse outcome, or liability of any kind incurred as a result of the use of any of the information contained in this book, or reliance upon it.

Designed and typeset by Focus Publishing, Sevenoaks, Kent
Printed and bound in India by Replika Press

Contents

Acknowledgements

However much knowledge I have gained regarding hedges during my working life, I still continue to learn more. The discovery of new ideas and information continues to shape my understanding of our rich heritage of hedges and their role in the countryside.

In writing this new book on hedges and hedge laying, I have been helped by others who have specific knowledge or skills that have been invaluable to me, enabling me to present a more balanced and fuller coverage of the subject. My sincerest thanks go to the following:

Nigel Adams	Hedge layer
Janet Allen (ADAS)	Weed and disease control
Caroline Benson	Museum of English Rural Life, Reading: photographs
Carolyn Blackmore	Computer assistance
John Davison	Hollies
Chris Honeywell	Photographer
Gordon Maclean	Photographs (my father died in 1999)
Clive Leeke	Hedge layer and instructor
Valerie Petts	Line drawings
John Savings	Hedge layer and my instructor
Chris Tucker	Bomford Turner Ltd, hedge trimmers

I reserve my deepest gratitude for those who have given me the most consistent help throughout the preparation of this book, and without whose help this undertaking would have been much more difficult. My wife Joey has read carefully through all that has been written, and made corrections and suggestions that have been most welcome.

I have been involved with the growing and planting of hedges for many years, but I did not have the same deep understanding of the art of hedge laying; for practical training in this skill I have been extremely fortunate to have been able to turn to John Savings. John has taught me the basic skills, and has answered every question with the patience and good humour for which he is renowned. He is a skilled, professional hedge layer who has won many competitions and was honoured to instruct His Royal Highness The Prince of Wales (currently the patron of the National Hedge-laying Society).

Introduction

In recent years hedges have enjoyed a much greater level of public awareness and interest in their wellbeing, which has resulted in a greater appreciation of their beauty and benefit to us all.

In the years following the end of World War II our long heritage of hedgerows suffered in the drive to increase agricultural output to feed a nation that had lost many of its rural roots. Prior to the war, a burgeoning urban population had been increasingly fed by food imports from around the world. Shortages of food during the war galvanized the Ministry of Agriculture to increase home food production. This 'food from our own resources' programme continued until well into the late 1980s before enough questions were asked about the high cost of support for farmers and the increasingly detrimental effects this was having on the fabric of the countryside.

Farmers had responded to the wartime need for increased food production by embracing mechanization wholeheartedly. The horse as the main source of power on the land was almost completely replaced by the tractor within fifteen years following the end of the war. With the advent of the tractor came a vast array of new machinery that the tractor could pull and operate. Both became ever larger and more sophisticated, requiring bigger fields within which to work effectively.

So began the widespread removal of hedges across most arable counties of England. The Ministry of Agriculture encouraged this hedge removal with the payment of generous grants to clear and drain land to increase food production and improve efficiency. This drive for greater output enabled food to be produced at a lower cost. Food prices fell steadily in the decades following the war, to the inevitable point where farmers found themselves having to make even further cost savings in order to retain a modest profit from the production of their crops.

As we move into the twenty-first century farmers now face new demands from their masters in government. With cheap food imports once more supplying an increasing proportion of the nation's food requirement, the pressure to feed the people has been replaced by a need to restore and conserve the landscape for the enjoyment and recreation of an almost totally urban population.

The farmers' role has changed from being that of respected food producers to the custodians of our rural heritage. Grants for food production have been replaced with mountains of directives and forms extolling the virtues of every conceivable aspect of conservation. Hedges, ponds, woodlands, heath and moorland are all now the chosen beneficiaries of grant aid and other inducements to both conserve and extend them.

The implementation of all these new measures has brought with it opportunities for the revival of old country crafts such as hedge laying, hurdle making, coppicing and stone walling; the planting of hedges, copses and woodlands, together with the formation of field margins, are all designed to reverse the steep decline in wild bird and small mammal numbers.

In many areas there has already been a noticeable improvement in the diversity of animal and plant species to be seen and enjoyed by all. The overall length of hedges across the country and the areas of woodland planted are both increasing steadily once more. Wild bird numbers are improving, for raptor species in particular, which must signify that their food sources have also improved in recent years.

There is much more to be done, and this book will help to further a small part of this cause.

CHAPTER 1

The Evolution of the Hedge

THE ROMAN INVASION

We have to thank Julius Caesar for the first written reference to hedges. In his report on the battle for Gaul (northern Europe) in 57 BC he describes how the Nervii tribe, on the borders of Belgium and France, had constructed hedges by cutting and laying small trees and binding them with brambles and thorn to provide a stockproof barrier to keep their cattle safe from marauding local tribes and to thwart his cavalry. It is safe to assume that the Britons of the same era would also have developed similar barriers to contain their stock.

Julius Caesar also related that during his first exploratory 'invasion' of Britain in 55 BC his soldiers fed themselves by cutting corn grown by the Britons. In his second invasion he demanded corn from the local tribes to feed his troops. Tacitus, writing in 79 AD, recorded that the Britons had a flourishing trade with Gaul, selling them grain in exchange for other goods. The growing of corn in a lowland, wooded landscape would have required protection from the ravages of deer, wild boar and other animals; thus some form of protective enclosure would have been constructed either from light brush cut in the woods, or they could have dug up

An artist's impression of a Bronze Age settlement on the banks of a stream. The thatched round houses were a common sight across Britain, situated either on high ground for protection from other marauding tribes or, in settled times, on lower, level terrain near to a water supply and where easily workable land was to hand for growing crops and grazing cattle. The areas cleared in the native woodland for their primitive arable strip cultivations and the wattle enclosures for their livestock were the early beginnings of our field and hedgerow heritage.

small thorn and other 'hedge' plants to form a living fence, built in conjunction with posts and dead brushwood to protect the young hedge until it matured. We know that the walled enclosure of small fields had been in use as far back as the Neolithic period, particularly in upland areas, where stone was cleared from the land intended for cultivation or for stock retention.

The Romans brought to Britain all the trappings of their advanced civilization. They constructed an excellent network of roads to link their garrison towns and other communities, taking over land to build their villas and establish thriving farmsteads across lowland Britain. All this industry would not have been lost on the local tribal groups who embraced the Roman way of life and began to expand their own cropping, clearing more woodland and scrub on the drier, easy-working soils above the flood plains. The raising of cattle had been central to their way of life, but increasingly the cultivation of land gained in its importance to their economy.

THE ANGLO-SAXONS

At the beginning of the third century the Roman occupation came to an end as the Empire began to experience problems at home. Legions were withdrawn, leaving the Romano-British population to defend themselves from the increasing Saxon incursions across the North Sea. A period of increasingly unsettled times followed until the Norman Conquest in 1066.

The Saxon invaders soon began to settle the lands they originally came to conquer, to become known as the Anglo-Saxons. They continued the practice of clearance and cultivation of land across lowland Britain developing the village community as we know it today. Hedges feature in many of the Saxon land charters, and many of their field boundaries exist to this day in those parts of England not subjected to the wholesale hedge removal of the post World War II era.

THE NORMAN CONQUEST

William the Conqueror arrived in 1066, but it took him nearly twenty years to fully subjugate the Saxon population and deal with his own squabbling Norman barons. In 1086 he instigated a full survey and inventory of the whole of England to be compiled into the *Doomsday Book*, which remains a unique record of the way the country was governed and ordered, in addition to providing William with a census of the population as a basis to tax and control the kingdom.

The king took over the ownership of all land, redistributing it amongst his faithful barons and knights in recognition of their services to him. In addition large areas of mixed woodland were enclosed to form royal hunting forests, further depriving the rural population of their ability to grow their own crops. The feudal system was established, whereby the new baronial land-owning class became responsible to the king for the management of the lands vested in them, either employing men to work for them or sub-letting to tenant farmers. A period of stability ensued with the continuation of a rural economy.

Throughout the Saxon period a patchwork landscape continued to evolve as woodland and scrub were slowly cleared to make way for further arable cultivation. Much of this land was in the proximity of each village, where it formed large open fields, cultivated under a two- or three-field strip system. Each villager held long, narrow strips of land in each of the fields, ostensibly to divide the good and poorer soils up fairly between all the strip holders and to ensure an agreed rotation of crops each year in each field. Other land was held by tenant farmers, which they were able to enclose and farm as they wished.

THE BLACK DEATH

The relative peace of the eleventh to fourteenth centuries was marred by the Black Death in 1349, which claimed nearly half the population and led to a severe depression. With so few people left to cultivate the land, arable cropping diminished; hedges, fences and woodland fell into decay, which would continue until the next era of great change in Tudor times.

These centuries were also marked by wars, both at home and abroad. The Hundred Years war with France (1337—1453) required many men from the shires to fight for the king, further depleting the rural population. This was followed, in 1455, by the Wars of the Roses, a civil war between those of Lancastrian and Yorkist persuasion.

THE TUDOR REFORMATION

Henry VIII will always be remembered for his 'battles' with the Pope in Rome, who refused to grant him a divorce from his first wife; this forced him to declare himself to be the Supreme Head of the Church of England. The refusal of church leaders to agree to his demands led to the suppression of the monasteries. The king took control of all the church's extensive lands and property, redistributing them to his favourite courtiers. These courtiers had little respect for the church's tenant farmers, whom they in turn dispossessed of their land. They enclosed more land to provide secure pastures for the grazing of extra sheep. The price of wool had been high and stable for many years and continued to be so. These new 'wool barons' demonstrated their new-found wealth by building fine houses and renovating churches, notably in the Cotswolds.

In 1549 Robert Kett, a Norfolk farmer, led the last attempt by tenants and labourers to contain the power of the lords of the manors, who continued to enclose land wherever they could find some small justification, so dispossessing the cottagers from their strips and thereby adding to their hardship. Farming for the wealthy continued to prosper at the expense of the poor until the Civil War in 1642.

In the early sixteenth century the first agricultural writers of merit began to record their observations and make recommendations for the improvement of farming practices. Fitzherbert's *Booke of Husbandry* was published in 1523. He was a keen advocate of hedge enclosures:

> ...it is much better to have several closes and pastures to put his cattle in, which should be quick-setted (hawthorns planted), ditched, and hedged, so as to divide those of different ages as this was more profitable than to have his cattle go before the herdsman (in the common field).

He was followed by Thomas Tusser, whose writings became the handbook for the country gentleman farmer for the next two hundred years.

THOMAS TUSSER

In 1557 there appeared *A Hundred Good Pointes of Husbandrie* by Thomas Tusser, who went on to expand this celebrated book into *Five Hundred Pointes of Good Husbandrie* before his death in

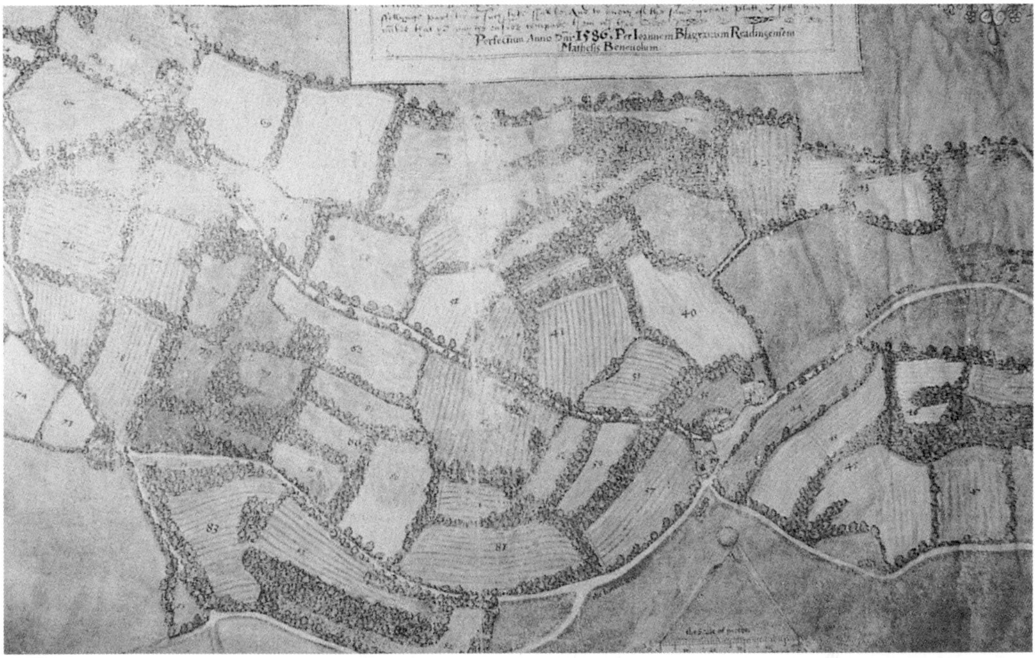

Harpsden village, near Henley-on-Thames, 1586. This coloured tithe map drawn on vellum by Mathesis Benevolum is held in the Oxfordshire Archives. The colours and detailed representation of this rural landscape show us the diversity of hedgerows and woodland strips that bordered the small arable and grass fields. The detail and shading have all the qualities of a good aerial photograph. Visiting the parish today reveals that some hedges have been removed to form larger fields, but the area retains its narrow, hedged lanes and wooded slopes. (Oxfordshire County Records Office)

1580. The books are written in rhyming verse and yet contain many wise observations on the best farming practices of the period. The book's continued popularity was ensured by William Mavor's updating of the original rhyming text in 1812. Mavor was a distinguished agricultural writer who realized the lasting value of Tusser's great work, and added extensive footnotes throughout in order to update the original text.

Tusser informs us that he was a keen advocate of enclosure, as opposed to open fields (formerly called 'Champion Country'), and his observations on the care and cultivation of hedges are as valid today as when he wrote them nearly 450 years ago!

October's husbandry
Sow acorns, ye owners that timber do love,
Sow haw and rye with them, the better to prove:
If cattle or coney (rabbit) may enter the crop,
Young oak is in danger of loosing his top.

Mavor's note: This advice is excellent, and it is to be lamented that so few acorns are sown. The first year a thin crop of rye will protect them, after which the plantation should be fenced against cattle and rabbits, even though the hawthorn are sown with them.

Where speedy quickset (hawthorn plants), for a fence you will draw,
To sow in the seed of the bramble and haw.

Map of the 'Manor of Winsly & Parsonage of Haugh', 1727. The village of Winsley is situated near Bradford-on-Avon in Wiltshire. The map shows an admirable mixture of freehold fields, woodland and pasture. There are arable strips in the field at the top left of the map, and many fields are shown to have hedge or old woodland strip boundaries. In the centre of the map is an excellent example of the formation of small fields by clearances made within a large wooded area. This area has now been totally cleared of woodland to provide open pasture on level land at the top of a hill. (The Museum of English Rural Life, The University of Reading)

Mavor's note: Brambles might be planted with advantage, and trained as vines, for their fruit. Haws, it is almost needless to say, are the fruits of the hawthorn.

> *January's husbandry*
> Leave grubbing or pulling of bushes, my son, Till timely thy fences require to be done. Then take of the best, for to furnish thy turn, And home with the rest, for the fier to burn.

Mavor's note: To leave a sufficiency of bushes, in order to fill up gaps in hedges, as occasion may require, is obviously right.

> In every green, if the fence be not thine,
> Now stub up the bushes, the grass be fine,
> Lest neighbour do daily so hack them, believe,
> That neither thy bushes, nor pasture can thrive.

Mavor's note: It would be a beneficial practice if hedges were constantly kept trimmed and clipped, at the height of four feet. Not only would the fences be more durable, but corn or grass would thrive better in their vicinity. A careless or slovenly farmer tempts his neighbour to trespass, *believe*, or in the night.

February's husbandry
Buy quickset at market, new gathered and small,
Buy bushes or willow, to fence it withal:
Set willow to grow, in the stead of a stake,
For cattle, in summer, a shadow to make.

Mavor's note: Quicksets (hawthorn plants) should not be too old before they are planted; and except in mending gaps, they are now secured by post and rails. It is judicious to plant willow-poles, instead of dead stakes, not only for durability but profit, where the situation is favourable, for the production of this valuable aquatic.

AN AGE OF CHANGE

The eighteenth century was to witness great changes in English agriculture. Open (common) field farming was in decline, and the enclosure movement was gaining momentum. The population of Britain was expanding fast as the seeds of the coming Industrial Revolution were being sown. Jethro Tull, from Shalbourne in Berkshire, invented the seed drill in about 1701, but did not publish his book *Horse-Hoeing Husbandry* until 1731. The ability to sow seeds in uniform lines and then be able to horse-hoe between them to control weeds was a remarkable leap forwards in the production of cereal crops. Such mechanization could not be imple-

An eighteenth-century round house beside the main Oxford to Swindon road (the A420) at Longworth. It may have been a tollhouse on the early Oxford to Bristol turnpike road. Nearby stands the 'Lamb and Flag' public house, which had been a coaching inn on the turnpike. The colour shades in the old hedge indicate a wide selection of species. It contains thirteen different species within a 400m (1,300ft) length, and eight species in random 30m (100ft) stretches, indicating that this hedge could have been beside the roadway for over 700 years, taking us back to the Middle Ages. In fields to the south of the road is situated Cherbury Camp, an impressive Iron Age fort with a large banked enclosure and three ring ditches.

mented in the increasingly out-dated strip-farming fields. Field sizes had to be increased and enclosed to protect the crops from wandering village stock if food production were to keep pace with an expanding economy.

The enclosure movement began slowly at the beginning of the century, the early enclosures being made by the agreement of all parties concerned. As the century progressed, so the rate of enclosure increased. The following list gives some indication of the speed of change:

Queen Anne	*1704—14* Two acts enclosing 1,439 acres (583ha)
George I	*1714—27* Sixteen acts enclosing 17,960 acres (7,271ha)
George II	*1727—60* 220 acts enclosing 318,778 acres (129,060ha)
George III	*1760—97* 1,532 acts enclosing 2,804,197 acres (1,135,302ha)

When an act of enclosure was granted, it was binding in law; many were passed without the willing agreement of all the small villagers, who had held strips in the old open-field system. Many of these dispossessed labourers either had to seek employment with the new landowners, or move away to work in the towns and cities.

Enclosure was a turbulent era for agriculture, but time would show that it was necessary if the nation were to be able to feed itself adequately as it moved steadily towards its industrial destiny. At the end of the eighteenth century the nation was at war with France once more, this time against the armies of Napoleon Bonaparte, who had declared that England was 'a nation of shop-keepers' that could be starved into submission by blockading its ports. But he miscalculated the strength of the Navy under Nelson, and the ability of the English farmer to respond to the need for increased output from their 'improved' lands.

THE INDUSTRIAL REVOLUTION

The old winding, rutted roads and the wide drovers' tracks were becoming anachronisms in an increasingly busy and ordered countryside. The Duke of Bridgewater commissioned the first canal from Manchester to Worsley in 1755, to be followed by the works of Thomas Telford, the famous canal and road builder. In 1819 a Scotsman named Macadam first introduced the use of compacted, broken stone to form the basis of the roads we know today.

The heyday of canal building lasted from 1760 to 1830, by which time over 3,000 miles (5,000km) of inland waterways linked all the main industrial towns of the North and Midlands, carrying coal and goods to supply the booming steel and cotton industries.

The canals, and later the railways, cut straight across the open countryside, changing field shapes, which required new hedging and fencing. As the pace of canal building began to slacken the railway era began, with great engineers such as George Stephenson and Isambard Kingdom Brunel building lines to connect all major centres of industry. These two great men were to transform transport, and their impact on the countryside will remain for ever.

By the end of the nineteenth century nearly every town in the country was linked by either a main or a branch line; most important centres of trade were also served by the canal system. All these transport arteries were hedged and fenced to keep farm stock from wandering on to the track or into the canals. In common with the enclosure hedges of the eighteenth century, most of these new hedges were of hawthorn and some blackthorn. W. J. Malden, writing in the 1899 *Journal of the RASE*, provided a detailed specification for the Midland Railway hedges:

> Double rows are planted in parallel lines, the lines being 4 inches apart and the plants 8 inches from one to the other in the rows. The planting is done so that one row breaks joint (is staggered) with the other. 100 plants to the chain (22yds or 20 metres) – 3 year old Quicks (hawthorn) are purchased at 11 shillings (55p) per 1000. The quicks are cut back at planting, left untrimmed till they attain a height of 6—8 feet (2.5m), when they are layered, being subsequently trimmed in late autumn/ early winter.

This description indicates the high standard and density necessary to quickly provide a thick stock-proof hedge capable of ensuring the safety of rail travellers from wandering farm animals.

THE FIRST AGRICULTURAL CENSUS

Accurate information on agricultural output should have been a government priority with the expansion of farming in the early eighteenth century, but it was not until 1793 that the efforts of Sir John Sinclair MP persuaded the government to establish the Board of Agriculture to gather statistical information and instigate improvements in farming practices through a series of county surveys, still of great value to those engaged in historical rural research. In 1866 a bill was introduced empowering the Board of Trade to collect information on crop production from all farmers. These records show the changing pattern of farm crops to this day.

There is no comparable information on the planting or removal of hedges. The enclosure awards rarely gave any detail of the amount of hedges planted. Similarly, the Ministry of Agriculture (now called the Department for the Environment, Food & Rural Affairs, or DEFRA) is unwilling to release statistics on the amount of grant-aided hedge removal following World War II, grants that were available up to the early 1990s.

The overall amount of hedgerow planting and removal during the period 1860 to 1940 is likely to have been in balance; a time of some agricultural progress interspersed with years of depression.

The examination of enclosure awards can be most rewarding to the trained eye; a wider understanding of these documents can be gained from regular research allied to a practical knowledge of local field patterns. It should not be assumed that all these maps were correctly drawn up, as can be illustrated by a detailed map of Frilford parish in Oxfordshire, dated 1846, owned by the author. The map was drawn up by Commissioner Edward Driver to indicate the line of a new road to bypass the main part of the hamlet. It shows a field boundary to the north of the 'West Field', which is in existence to this day. Yet in 1860 when Edward Driver's nephew was appointed commissioner to draw up the Frilford Enclosure Award, he copied from the same map but omitted this hedge and ditch line. The moral of this tale is that research from old maps must be corroborated by evidence on the ground and from other maps, wherever possible.

Aerial photographs or visual surveys can reveal the line of old hedges, ditches and roads, especially if the photograph is taken when the ground has been freshly ploughed, or during summer drought conditions under a grass or cereal crop.

Photography was invented in 1835, so from the latter part of the nineteenth century we have an excellent photographic record of farming practices and country scenery.

TWO WORLD WARS

The events of the twentieth century were dominated by World Wars I and II, wars that had an immense impact on every aspect of the British way of life and its countryside. Prior to the start of World War I, the English landscape had remained almost untouched since the enclosure movement two hundred years earlier.

The methods of cultivation had changed little since Jethro Tull's invention of the seed drill, and the horse remained the motive power on the land. The advent of steam power made little impact on the majority of farms, except for the annual visit of the threshing team, which was powered by a thirsty steam engine. The field size on most farms was too small to accept the steam-ploughing sets, designed to work efficiently in the large open fields of the eastern counties.

The demands for factory workers in the munitions and supply factories of the Great War led to a further drift of labour from the land, as well as the many young men who went 'to fight for king and country' in the mud of Flanders fields, many never to return. Farmers were left short of staff, and yet witnessed the potential of the new tractors, which the government supplied during the war years to bridge the labour shortage gap. Those farmers who embraced mechanization realized its potential to increase crop production, but it was to be a repeat performance twenty years later when the storm clouds gathered to herald in World War II that finally set the seal on mechanization on the land. Government support for farming after World War I had been short-lived, with many thousands of acres becoming derelict throughout the depression of the twenties and early thirties. Hedges and ditches fell into disrepair, as there was insufficient income to do more than 'dog-and-stick' farming.

In the late thirties the government took heed of the warning signs, and began actively to encourage farmers to increase food production. At the outbreak of war there were approximately 2.5 million acres (1 million hectares) less land in arable cultivation than in 1914. Unlike the First War, the management of agricultural production was firmly controlled from the start of the war by the establishment of the County War Agricultural Committees, or 'War Ags' as they became known. They undertook the task of increasing output by the reclamation of derelict land and by directing production. In Leicestershire the percentage of arable land went up from 15 to 50 per cent in four years, and nationally it was increased by 4,500,000 acres (1,821,860 ha); however, whilst much scrubland was brought back into cropping, there was little direct hedge removal as part of the restoration of arable cropping.

The construction of airfields for the Royal Air Force and USAAF, and training camps for the two armies, consumed thousands of acres of prime farmland right across southern and eastern England. C. S. Orwin in his book *The Future of Farming* (1930) illustrated the ease of hedgerow removal by citing the consequences of building a new aerodrome at Abingdon in Oxfordshire, where 2.5 miles of hedgerow were removed to clear the necessary 432 acres (175ha). At the nearby Grove airfield, 5 miles of hedgerow were grubbed out to convert 272 acres (110ha) of prime milk-producing vale land into an open expanse for the three runways.

Across southern, central and eastern counties of England airfields were constructed in such numbers that US pilots joked that they '...could taxi the whole length of the island without leaving a runway!' The construction of all these operational airfields, together with their satellite airfields built nearby (in case the main runways were bombed while the squadrons were airborne) resulted in the need for substantial areas of prime farmland, with thousands of miles of hedges being removed from the landscape.

By the end of the war there were over 600 airfields covering 360,000 acres (145,750ha). In addition, nearly 4,500 army camps had been built to shelter the troops in the run-up to D-Day. Since the end of the war, few of these sites have been fully returned to agricultural use. Some have become industrial parks, while others remain to this day as bleak, wind-swept areas of corn and concrete.

POST-WAR MECHANIZATION

After the end of the war the Ministry of Agriculture gave farmers every possible encouragement to continue increasing production. The grants for the purchase of new machinery and the erection of new buildings went hand in hand with drainage schemes and the grant-aided removal of hedges to allow for the ever-increasing size of tractors and machinery to be used effectively in larger fields. The Countryside Commission calculated that between 1947 and 1985 about 155,000km of hedgerows were lost, representing a reduction of almost a quarter of the nation's stock of hedges – or a length of hedgerow sufficient to girdle the earth four times!

Another wartime introduction was the widespread use of herbicides and insecticides, which played a dramatic part in increasing the yield and quality of arable and horticultural crops; but it became apparent by the 1970s that the extensive use of these pesticides was taking a heavy toll on all forms of wildlife. Rachael Carson's book *Silent Spring*, published in 1962, was greeted with scorn by some, yet with alarm by many more. She was the first of many to raise public awareness of the damaging side-effects from widespread pesticide use. We move into the twenty-first century with both the government and numerous conservation groups that sprang up as a direct result of public concern, now working hard to reverse the damage done to wildlife.

The hedge has now assumed an important new role in the countryside, one that was previously not acknowledged, that of being the single greatest benefit to the survival and recovery of many animal and plant species, which have suffered from the loss of their habitat and food sources over the past fifty years.

In the coming chapters we will show how hedges can fulfil both their traditional roles and, when allied to field margins, offer an opportunity to restore the diversity and richness of animal and plant life that was once typical of rural England.

CHAPTER 2

The Choice of Trees and Shrubs

There are numerous reasons why people choose to plant hedges, so it is worth looking at their possible reasons, and the requirements that lead to such a decision:

- To mark a boundary line between one's own land and that of a neighbour.
- To act as a screen to prevent other people looking on to one's own property.
- To form a screen around an unsightly building, a machinery or vehicle park, a rubbish disposal site, or any other reason falling into the category of 'screening from view something that is unsightly'.
- To provide both shelter and containment for livestock.
- As a windbreak to protect high-value horticultural field-grown crops.
- To divide one part of a garden from another, or to act as a windbreak for sensitive garden plants.
- To form an attractive feature beside a road or leading up to a property.
- To prevent soil erosion on light sandy soils, especially where vulnerable spring-sown crops are grown.
- As a conservation hedge, to join up other existing hedges or woodland in order to provide a sheltered passage for the safe movement of wildlife across the countryside.

The decision to plant a hedge must be followed by an appraisal of all the considerations that can influence its physical make-up and mature appearance. W. J. Malden, writing in the RASE journal of 1899, provided an excellent list of important points to be considered. Some of these are not so pertinent to hedge planting today, but they are worth being aware of; thus Malden recommends that a hedge should:

- be stock-proof reasonably quickly;
- be uniform in its vigour of growth;
- be easily kept within bounds;
- present a compact front;
- be strong enough to resist the efforts of animals to escape; this will be made easier if thorny species are chosen (hawthorn, wild rose, blackthorn);
- choose plants suited to the soil type;
- contain species that are frost hardy, or in coastal regions, able to withstand salt-laden winds;
- Shelter animals from cold winds;
- produce shoots close to the ground, so containing both small and large animals;
- be resistant to fungal diseases (especially mildew on hawthorn, wild roses and crab);
- not produce suckers that can spread into adjoining fields (blackthorn);
- not be edibly attractive to the animals within the field, or to game sheltering in the hedge;
- if it is intended to coppice or lay the hedge at a later date, contain species that will re-grow vigorously from a close-cut stump.

TREES AND SHRUBS SUITABLE FOR HEDGEROW USE

The following list provides a description of all the trees and shrubs suitable for hedgerow use. It is followed by a short list of those species that should *not* be chosen, and why they are to be avoided. The trees and shrubs are listed in order according to their scientific (Latin) names.

Field Maple *(Acer campestre)*

A small- to medium-sized tree, growing to 5–10m (16–33ft), most commonly found as a hedgerow shrub. It grows strongly in a wide range of soils and is very tolerant of dry, sandy conditions where it is at risk of becoming too dominant in a hedge. It responds well to trimming, although its shoots are somewhat brittle and tough. The field maple is a native species, commonly found growing in hedges throughout England.

The leaves have three to five unequal-sized, toothed lobes and are a dull green colour with a reddish stalk, which turns bright yellow-orange in the autumn.

It carries small, yellow-green flowers hidden within the developing foliage. The flowers develop into pairs of winged seeds (called 'keys'), which stretch out horizontally to look like a bird in flight.

The young and older bark is sandy-brown in colour with flaky, longitudinal fissures that have a reddish edge when the bark is young.

Barberry *(Berberis Vulgare)*

The wild barberry is an uncommon hedgerow shrub, not a true native but introduced in ancient times. It forms a compact, small bush of not more than 3m (9–10ft), and is thus an ideal addition to a mixed species, or to a stock-proof hedge because of its dense spiny branches.

It has small oval to ovate, mid-green leaves that spring from spiny branch axils and are arranged in alternate clusters. The lower leaf surface is a downy whitish-green, and has a spiny edge.

The barberry carries hanging clusters

Field maple.

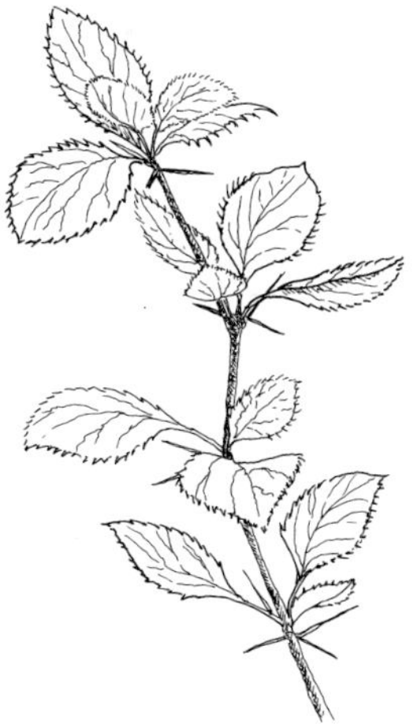

Wild barberry.

of small yellow flowers that can turn to clusters of oblong bright red berries in the autumn.

The bark is a pale grey-brown, becoming darker with age.

Hornbeam *(Carpinus betulus)*

An attractive tree growing up to 20m (66ft) in height, with a rounded, bushy crown. It is native to Europe and south-east England. It is now more commonly planted as an alternative hedge choice to beech, holding its leaves well into winter. It responds well to trimming, but can be somewhat 'ragged' in its growth in early years.

The leaves are ovate to oblong, bright green turning bright yellow in autumn. There are prominent ribbed veins on the underside of the leaves, which have serrated edges.

It flowers in March with male and female catkins, the male (2.5cm/1in plus) being twice as long as the female (1.25cm/1/2in plus). Fruiting catkins mature into hanging clusters of thin seed bracts.

The bark is grey and smooth, and is vertically fluted or corrugated as it matures.

Hornbeam grows well on heavy to loamy, moist soils in central southern England, but does not like dry or frost-prone sites. It prefers neutral to acid soils.

Hornbeam.

Dogwood.

Common Dogwood *(Cornus sanguinea)*

A small, dense hedgerow shrub found in southern England, now a regular constituent of newly planted, mixed species hedges. It is less common in older hedges and thus an indicator of hedge age.

The leaves are dark, dull green, smooth-edged, oval and pointed. They are borne opposite to each other on purplish stems.

Clusters of cream to white flowers are carried on older wood in May to become bunches of white berries turning black in the autumn.

Its blood-red young shoot growth becomes greenish-brown as the bark ages.

Common dogwood has a vigorous and fibrous root system that prefers moist clay to loamy soil conditions. It grows well, but more slowly, on limestone soils, and is widely distributed in England. It will produce sucker growth if not controlled.

Hazel *(Corrylus avellana)*

A widely distributed, native hedgerow plant found throughout Britain. A plant with many uses, from gardeners' beanpoles, thatchers' spars to the hedge layer's stakes and binders. Historically it had many other

Hazel.

uses, including lathes for wattle-and-daub walls, basketwork, hurdle making and walking sticks.

Its round to oval leaves are heart-shaped, slightly pointed and have a serrated edge. They are softly hairy on both sides, being a paler green on the underside.

In late February, before its leaves appear, the male catkins shed their pollen on to adjacent little red female tassels, and if pollinated, form edible nut fruits in the autumn.

The bark is smooth and shiny, pale grey-brown to greenish brown, according to age, with horizontal lenticels (aeration pores) up the stems.

Hazel naturally forms a multi-stem bush that regenerates vigorously when coppiced; thus it is a very common and valuable hedgerow plant. It prefers a moisture-retentive, acid to neutral soil, but is nevertheless found growing on a wide range of soil types.

Hawthorn *(Crataegus monogyna)*

A native thorny shrub that can grow into a small, gnarled tree 10m (33ft) high with age, if provided with the freedom of a scrubland setting.

A very tough hardy plant that will colonize and survive on derelict land. It is found across a wide range of soil types. Centuries of use have proved it to be the finest plant for stock-proof hedges.

The hawthorn has shiny bright to dark green lobed leaves. The lobes vary in number and shape according to the many different strains, but there are usually three to five, and they can be finely serrated.

Its bark is greenish grey when young, becoming a dark grey, and cracking into browner fissures, with age. It bears many thorns on both shoots and branches.

Dense clusters of small white flowers appear in early May; these become bunches of blood-red, oval berries in the autumn, each berry containing one hard-shelled seed.

The Midland hawthorn *(Crataegus laevigata)*, also native to Britain, bears flowers with two to three styles, and berries with two seeds. It can be distinguished from the common hawthorn by its leaves, which usually have only three lobes and are less serrated, giving them a broader look.

The hawthorn must be regarded as the 'king' of the hedgerow, as it meets every important requirement of the landowner. Its qualities as stock-proof barrier, shelterbelt and screen have meant that it has become synonymous with the English countryside.

Hawthorn.

Spindle Tree *(Euonymus europaeus)*

Spindle tree.

This tree is normally seen as a small, sparsely furnished bush, but it can grow into a small 5m (16ft) tree when situated in a woodland edge setting. It is found throughout England as a slow-growing native woodland and hedgerow shrub. It adapts well to a wide range of soils, having a very fibrous root system. It is unfortunate in being a well known host plant for the black bean aphid, so has not been popular with farmers for hedgerow planting until recently; but changes in agricultural cropping have reduced their concern for this disadvantage.

The leaves stem opposite one another, being oblong to oval in shape, pointed and spear-like, with finely serrated margins; the bright to dark green leaf colour turns to an attractive reddish yellow in the autumn.

The spindle bears small, yellow-green flowers in the leaf axils during May and June that become distinctive, bright pink berries in the autumn. Each berry contains four bright yellow seeds.

The stem is another distinctive feature, being angular in shape, with grey and green corky bark and rough-lined ridges along its length.

This is a shrub that should be planted, in small numbers, into both old and new hedges.

Common Beech *(Fagus silvatica)*

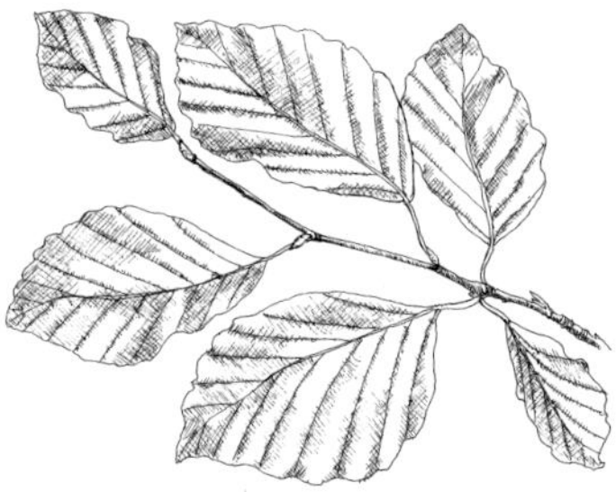

Common beech.

The beech has long been cultivated as a large, native timber tree growing to a height of 30m (100ft); yet it is equally well known for its qualities as a garden and country hedge. Beech responds well to chalk upland or moister limestone soils, but will not tolerate very dry or wet sites. It likes to grow in well drained soils where there is good summer rainfall. It is not to be recommended for use in a hedge where livestock are present as they will browse on its tender foliage.

The leaves are broad, shiny, smooth and ovate in shape, pointed with a wavy edge. The foliage is a bright green in early summer, becoming darker later in the summer before turning brown and yellow in the autumn. Beech retains its leaves throughout winter to be replaced by the fresh spring growth.

In May the beech bears clusters of small, pale green, mainly female flowers, with fewer clusters of male flowers hanging in long tassel bunches. The fruit (seed) is the familiar 'mast', a rough case containing two small, triangular nuts borne in the late autumn.

The bark is smooth, and grey to silver in colour.

Sea Buckthorn *(Hippophae rhamnoides)*

Sea buckthorn.

A hardy maritime shrub, commonly found on sandy foreshores or in coastal gardens, because of its tolerance of salt-laden, windy sites. It forms an attractive bushy windbreak for exposed sites. It will grow well in dry, sandy conditions.

It has distinctive long, thin, silvery grey-green leaves that stem from sharp, spiny shoots. The buckthorn produces many small, yellow-green flowers in late April. Female and male flowers are carried on separate plants, and when pollinated will form clusters of bright orange berries in the autumn. Being a single sex plant, male plants must be planted with female ones in a ratio of one to five to ensure good pollination.

The bark is silvery grey and scaly, becoming grey and rougher with age. Sea buckthorn will produce suckers from which further plants can be established.

Holly *(Ilex aquafolium)*

Holly.

A slow-growing, small evergreen tree that will make an excellent hedge for those who are patient and prepared to wait for the worthwhile result. It is a native to Britain found growing on a wide range of soil types, but it prefers a neutral, moist and shaded site. It grows well in a woodland setting.

Its dark green, glossy leaves are firm and leathery, oval-to-oblong with deep undulating edges that carry spiky points, which makes holly an ideal shrub for inclusion in a stock-proof hedge.

White female and male flowers are to be found on separate trees and appear in May within the leaf axil. The flowers, when pollinated, will become bright red berries (seeds) in the autumn, and are an excellent food source for a wide range of birds. Holly is a single sex plant, so known male and female plants must be grown together to obtain regular crops of berried growth for sale. If berried holly is required for the

Christmas decoration trade, the trees must be netted early in the autumn to prevent bird damage.

The young shoots are dark green and smooth; as the bark ages it becomes grey-green, but remains smooth. The wood of mature trees is hard, fine-grained and white, making it valuable for use in carving, turnery and inlay work.

Wild Privet *(Ligustrum vulgare)*

A semi-deciduous native shrub growing to a height of 6m (18ft) and found in hedges and scrubland sites. It prefers calcareous, lighter soils with some moisture. The evergreen form *(Ligustrum ovalifolium)* is more commonly seen, and used for garden hedges.

Its oblong oval, spear-shaped leaves are dull green, smooth with pointed tips, and stem opposite each other from smooth, pale brown shoots.

It produces a mass of small white flowers with a somewhat unpleasant scent; these become shiny black berries in the autumn, providing a good food source for birds and small mammals. The berries are poisonous to humans, especially to children, so ensure that they do not touch or pick them. The bark is smooth, light brown on young shoots, becoming darker and duller with age.

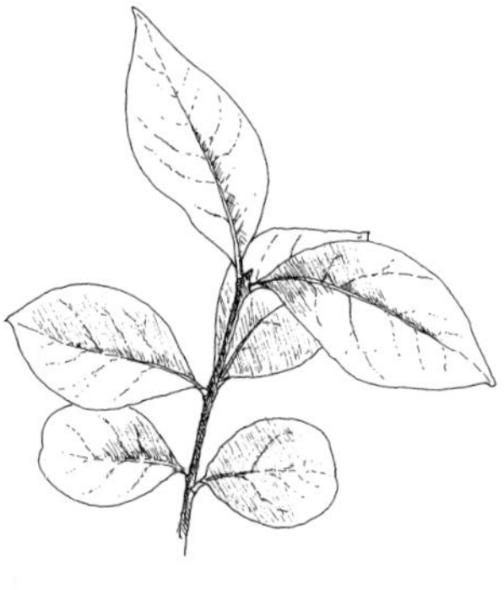

Wild privet.

Privet responds well to trimming to provide a thick, semi-evergreen, hedge that is easy to maintain and provides good game cover in a woodland setting. It has a vigorous and fibrous root system that grows well in a wide range of soils, surviving in dry, poor conditions and thriving in moist ground. It will tolerate polluted, salty and wind-swept sites.

Crab Apple or Wild Crab *(Malus silvestris)*

The true wild crab is a comparatively uncommon native tree. Many of the crab apples found growing in hedges and woods are the result of discarded apple cores. Unfortunately some recent commercial seed has come from the pressings of apples for juice and cider making, which makes the resulting plants raised from this seed much more susceptible to mildew infection, as they will be closely related to their dessert apple parentage.

The crab grows into a small compact tree 5m (16ft) tall, and is best suited to a woodland edge or for inclusion in a mixed species hedgerow. Its leaves are elliptic to oval in shape, with a serrated edge, dark green on the upper surface and pale grey-green, 'felted', on the underside.

Crab apple.

The flowers are typical of 'apple blossom', being open, pink-white with distinctive yellow stamens; they are in full bloom during late April to early May. The fruits are the familiar small, inedible crab apples of late summer, which can be collected to make crab-apple jelly and jams.

The tree bark is a reddish brown when young, becoming grey-brown, rough, furrowed and flaky as it ages.

Cherry or Wild Plum *(Prunus cerasifera)*

This is the most common form of wild plum found in Britain. It is native to southern England, although probably introduced by the Romans. Some wild plums are edible, others are not! The cultivated forms include damsons and gages. It will grow upright to form a small 6m (20ft) tree, but is commonly found as a hedgerow shrub. In central southern England there are some pure plum hedges.

Like the blackthorn, it has a tendency to sucker around the base. It will thrive in a wide range of soils, and is suitable for planting in exposed or rough ground sites.

The wild plum produces solitary white flowers, that appear in late February just before its bright green leaves. The flowers, if pollinated, become red or yellow fruits in late summer.

The glossy, dark green leaves are flat, long, oval to spear-shaped, tapering at each end with a deep main rib and a finely serrated edge.

It carries some long thorns on the reddish-green young growth and on the rougher, grey mature wood.

Blackthorn or Sloe *(Prunus spinosa)*

A hardy and robust native shrub or small bushy tree, second only to hawthorn for use in stock-proof hedges. It is widely grown and especially suited to coastal and exposed sites because of its ability to withstand salt-laden and windy conditions. It will grow in a wide range of soils, and responds well to trimming to produce a thick hedge.

Blackthorn has two major disadvantages: it suckers very freely, so beware of this when using it in a hedge that will not be required for stock management (cattle browsing will contain the sucker growth); and secondly, the thorns are very 'aggressive' and can cause septicaemia if the thorn is not quickly removed and the skin wound treated to prevent infection. I do

Cherry or wild plum.

Blackthorn or sloe.

not recommend blackthorn for use in any mixed species hedge that is to be planted in a public place, beside a footpath, or a children's play area.

Its broad, oblong, pointed mid-green leaves, with serrated edges, spring from green to purple shoots. A mass of white flowers appears in March before any leaves, and if pollinated, will form small, dark blue, damson-like fruits in late summer. The fruits are excellent when pricked with a skewer and left to soak in gin, with added sugar, to make the rich liqueur 'sloe gin'.

The blackthorn's multi-branched older wood has dark grey-brown, smooth bark. It is popular with makers of walking sticks because the straight young wood is hard, and its bark is smooth and has an attractive, dark maroon-black sheen.

Purging Buckthorn *(Rhamnus cathartica)*

A bushy shrub that can grow into a small 5m (16ft) tree, commonly found in hedgerows, on scrubland, or beside streams. It prefers calcareous to neutral soils, but is found on a wide range of soil types that retain some moisture in dry seasons.

Purging buckthorn.

It has broad, 'egg'-shaped leaves that stem opposite each other; these are a matt mid-green colour, smooth with a finely serrated edge, and they turn yellow in late summer.

The purging buckthorn bears yellow-green flowers in late May, which become clusters of poisonous black berries in the autumn: this species is therefore not suitable for stock-proof hedges. Its pale grey-brown shoots can carry small thorns, and they in turn stem from a trunk with darker brown bark that becomes fissured and 'sooty' with age.

The buckthorn is recommended for mixed species hedges because it is a food plant for the brimstone butterfly.

Alder Buckthorn *(Rhamnus frangula)*

A small woodland shrub that can grow into a small delicate tree no more than 6m (20ft) tall. It is usually found in damp open woodland sites or beside ditches and streams. It is an attractive addition to a hedge grown on a damp site.

Alder buckthorn.

It has small, oval, alder-like leaves that are bright shiny green with a smooth edge. The leaves stem from dark brown to violet hairy twigs.

In May-June the alder buckthorn produces clusters of greenish-cream flowers that later turn into small red berry fruits, which darken upon maturity to become almost black.

Its bark is smooth and purple-brown with white corky cells when young; it becomes grey-brown as it matures, but still retains pale markings.

Dog Rose *(Rosa canina)*

The dog rose *(R. canina)* is the most common of the UK's four native wild roses, the others being the field rose *(R. arvensis)*, the sweet briar *(R. rubiginosa)*, and the downy rose *(R. tomentosa)*.

It is a long-stemmed, rambling native shrub that needs the support of adjacent hedge plants to prevent it spreading, rather than growing upwards. It will grow on all soil types and in every situation, however inhospitable, making it an acceptable choice for most types of hedge – which it will probably colonize in due course if not chosen at the outset!

The dog rose has oval to elliptical, dull grey-green leaves with finely toothed edges. Its attractive pink to white flowers bloom steadily throughout early summer to become long, lobed red 'hips' (berries) in the autumn, each containing numerous seeds in a pulpy centre.

Its stems carry many hooked, spiky thorns. The young wood is smooth and green, but it becomes grey, tough and fissured with age.

Ramanas Rose *(Rosa rugosa)*

This rose is a relatively recent introduction from Japan, which has found a useful role as a tough, attractive, compact hedge plant for amenity and domestic hedge use. It is a dense, compact plant that will form a low-growing hedge, but will sucker if given the opportunity.

It has large, oval, bright green, paired leaves that are hairy on the underside. It produces either pink or white flowers that turn into clusters of bright red, oval to globular hips in early autumn, each of which contains many seeds in a pulpy centre.

Dog rose.

Ramanas rose.

The young shoots are creamy grey and covered with many small hairy thorns; as the stems age, they become grey.

Gorse *(Ulex europaeus)*

A fast-growing, dense, spiny bushy shrub introduced from Europe to become widespread across Britain. Its ability to grow in the poorest conditions, withstand drought and tolerate salt-laden winds has ensured its widespread use as a hedge plant.

Gorse has long been used on top of West Country soil and stone hedge-banks, and it is also found growing on heath and moorland, wherever it can colonize and spread unhindered. It rarely grows higher than 1.5 to 2.0m (5 to 6ft), preferring to spread as a low bush.

Its leaves are no more than small, narrow, soft, pale green spines, and only found on lush young growth, which is not common. Most mature plants carry very little new growth, remaining green branches with grey-black hairs and long, stiff, sharp spines.

Gorse bears a profusion of bright yellow pea-like flowers that first appear in February and continue through to June, making it an early and enduring food source for bees and other insects.

Wayfaring Tree *(Viburnum lantana)*

A non-native, bushy, deciduous shrub found in hedges and on the chalk and limestone soils of southern England and in Wales; it is uncommon in northern Britain. It has distinctive large, oval, dull green leaves with finely toothed margins and a whiter, downy, rough underside. The leaves turn a bruise-red in the autumn.

This tree bears large, dense clusters of creamy-white flowers in May, which become bright red berries in the autumn; these later turn black.

The young shoots are a downy oatmeal colour that becomes light brown and smooth as the stems age.

Its name has no known connection to wayfarers, and in fact there are many commoner wayside shrubs that would be more worthy of the name!

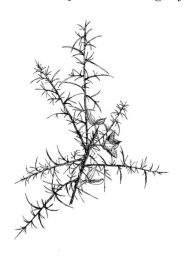

Gorse.

Wayfaring tree.

Guelder Rose *(Viburnum opulus)*

Another member of the non-native viburnum family that is a much loved English hedgerow plant. A slow-growing, bushy shrub that prefers a damp site; it is therefore usually seen on a ditch bank, near to water, or in a damp woodland margin.

It has green, maple-like leaves with lobed edges, which stem opposite one another. It bears broad clusters of pure white flowers that form an outer ring around a centre core of dull, creamy-white fertile flowers; in the autumn these flowers form bunches of blood-red berries, and the leaves turn a deep crimson and cream colour.

The guelder rose has smooth, thin grey twigs and similar bark; neither of the viburnums grows to more than 4 to 6m (12 to 18ft) high.

This completes the list of shrubs commonly found growing in hedges. However, there are some shrubs that must be avoided in your selection of suitable hedgerow plants.

Guelder rose.

SPECIES TO BE AVOIDED IN COUNTRYSIDE HEDGES

Box *(Buxus sempervirens)*

This plant has been used as a garden hedge plant since Roman times. Archaeologists working on a Roman villa site at Winterton in Lincolnshire found box clippings that had survived in a saturated waste pit. Trenches, probably for ornamental box hedges, were discovered at the Roman palace in Fishbourne (Sussex).

Box is commonly used as a small border hedge in old walled kitchen gardens and around formal borders.

It is not suitable for hedges where animals are present, not only because of its slow growth, but primarily because its foliage is poisonous to cattle, especially if withered prunings are left after hedge trimming.

Broom *(Cytisus scorparius)*

This is a common heathland shrub thriving on dry sandy banks and open woodland. It is extensively used on golf courses.

Broom is not recommended for general hedgerow use because its foliage is dangerous to animals, being diuretic; if eaten in any quantity, it causes hallucination.

Laburnum *(Laburnum vulgare)*

A hardy shrub or small tree growing to a height of 5 to 6m (16 to 20ft) and often chosen as a popular garden tree. It is also found in old hedgerows throughout Wales, especially in Cardiganshire, for which there is no known explanation in view of its toxicity to stock animals. The pea-like seedpods, if eaten, are poisonous to both humans and livestock.

It bears cascades of yellow flowers in spring, which are a valuable source of nectar for bees; this is a possible reason for their abundance in hedgerows, as well as their earlier use for fine furniture veneers.

Rhododendron *(Rhododendron)*

A plant family with many species, mostly evergreen. It was discovered in the Himalayas in the mid-seventeenth century, but it was not until the mid-nineteenth century that a wide range of different varieties was brought back to England by Sir Joseph Hooper, who popularized their use for parkland planting. They became all the rage, and were extensively planted on many estates throughout the country.

The rhododendron has become associated with the driveways and wooded grounds of large estates, thriving in the mild, moister climate of the West Country. It prefers an acid soil, growing well in the shade of firs and pine trees.

Its foliage is poisonous to livestock, so it is not commonly grown as a hedge. It has recently been identified as a host plant for the serious fungal pathogen causing the death of oaks in parts of the USA: 'sudden oak death' is now a notifiable disease, so the control and elimination of rhododendron in areas of potential infection is recommended.

Common Elder *(Sambucus nigra)*

A very vigorous and invasive hedgerow shrub or small tree, also found in woods and on scrubland. Its many seeds are spread by birds, and they can germinate readily to grow quickly, dominating their position if left unchecked.

It will grow to become a small tree and then often dies back slowly to leave an unsightly gap, especially if growing in an established hedge.

The gap caused by decaying elder bushes in an otherwise good early nineteenth-century enclosure hedge that has been allowed to grow taller to provide greater wind protection for adjacent horticultural crops. It will be difficult to fill the gap without removing all of the elder and its roots. The introduction of some fresh soil for planting may help the replacement plants to compete with the mature hedge and establish themselves quickly.

The elder does not have many virtues, but it can be useful as a quick cover or screen for planting on waste sites or on poor reclaimed land. It is loved by birds and home-made wine makers for its abundant bunches of purple-black berries, providing food for the former and elderberry wine for the latter.

Yew *(Taxus bacata)*

A fine evergreen tree that makes an excellent hedge when kept trimmed regularly; it is also a noted churchyard tree. It is associated with the bowmen of the Middle Ages, who used its strong and supple wood to make their longbows.

The yew will tolerate most soils; although slow-growing, it will grow steadily over many centuries to become one of Britain's longest lived trees. Yew makes a superb dense and attractive garden hedge, and can grow to a great height, with regular and careful trimming, without becoming bare at its base when it reaches maturity.

Its foliage and seeds are poisonous to most livestock, making it unsuitable for planting in any position accessible to horses, cattle or sheep.

Common Elm *(Ulmus procera)*

The English elm was a dominant feature of our lowland landscape until the devastating effects of Dutch elm disease in the early 1970s reduced the population to no more than hedgerow shrubs. All the fine trees were killed, although they quickly re-grew from suckers to form young trees; but as soon as these reached a certain age

The continuing problem with elms. A forest of suckers has sprung up from the stumps of a few mature Jersey elms that died in 1976. These suckers will grow a little taller before the Dutch Elm beetle will strike again to kill them all off.

Since this photograph was taken in 1990 the sucker growth has been attacked and has died off once; it has re-grown, but is being attacked by the beetles yet again!

and height, the Dutch elm beetle reappeared to kill off the tree once more. The beetle is a carrier of the fungus *Graphium ulmi* or *Ceratocystis ulmi*, which are the true killers.

Only where the young growth is contained by regular trimming in a hedge form does the elm survive, sadly no longer able to grow into the majestic trees they once were. It appears that the beetle does not attack the small young growth associated with a regularly trimmed and contained hedge.

However fine a mature elm looked, it was not admired by farmers. Its broad, spreading canopy greatly reduced crop yields within its shadow, and it has the ability to produce a multitude of suckers that soon surround each tree, forming a thicket that further affects the yield of adjacent crops, and requires regular removal or cutting to contain their spread.

Nurserymen have made no attempts to encourage the elm's revival because of Dutch elm disease and its undesirable suckering habit. A tree that died or was felled many decades ago will continue to make its presence felt through the constant re-growth of numerous suckers for years to come.

TYPES OF HEDGE

The selection of plants for hedge planting will depend on the purpose of the hedge, and on the element of personal preference in plant selection. When deciding upon the choice of species to use in a new hedge there can be no better guide than to examine the range of plant species to be found growing in local hedges, especially on a similar soil type. Those species that are flourishing should be seriously considered for selection.

A Boundary Hedge

A wide variety of plants can be chosen according to preference, as well as noting the range of plants found growing well in your own locality. Hawthorn should be the main variety, representing no less than 60 per cent of the total to ensure good, dense growth. Blackthorn would be a second choice, if there were a need to keep a neighbour's livestock at bay! At least 30 per cent of the hedge could include other such plants as field maple, hazel and common dogwood, plus smaller quantities of purging buckthorn, dog rose and holly.

A Conservation Hedge

The choice of plants in a hedge of this purpose will depend on several requirements, but mainly its ability to attract, shelter and sustain wildlife as it moves about the countryside. A wide range of species will be needed to meet these demands. Hawthorn is still the main contender, as it can produce plenty of edible fruits that are popular with birds in the winter months. Squirrels and mice are attracted to hazel nuts and beech mast. Many species of bird will also feed upon blackthorn sloes, rose hips and other berried fruits.

The flowering time for common hedgerow shrubs in order of blossoming is as follows (allow for variations in timing according to seasonal weather conditions and geographical location):

- January — Wild plum, or bullace
- February — Hazel catkins
- March — Blackthorn
- April — Crab apple
- May — Hawthorn, spindle, wayfaring tree
- June — Wild privet, guelder rose
- June/July — Dog rose

Most of these flowering plants form fruits in the autumn, providing a valuable and safely accessible food source throughout the long winter months. When their fruits fall to the ground or are dropped by birds, they provide food for mice and other mammals living in the shelter of the bottom of the hedge.

A good conservation hedge of native species needs to combine cover, protection and a ready supply of food for the range of wildlife that chooses to live within the hedge during the nesting season or throughout the year. The following mixture of shrubs is suggested for new hedges being planted with wildlife conservation as the main objective:

- Hawthorn, 60 per cent
- Field maple, 5 per cent
- Common dogwood, 5 per cent
- Hazel, 10 per cent
- Blackthorn, 10 per cent
- Purging buckthorn, 5 per cent
- Dog rose, 5 per cent

Hawthorn should not be reduced below 50 per cent as its natural growth is so much better than all other hedgerow plants at producing the hedge density and structure necessary.

Field maple, common dogwood, buckthorn and dog rose can be reduced, or exchanged, to make way for other suitable species such as wild crab, grey sallow, wayfaring tree and guelder rose. The final selection must take into consideration the range of animal and bird life to be encouraged; and don't forget to take careful note of the different hedge species to be found growing in nearby hedges, both to complement and add to this indigenous selection. Some butterflies and other animals have a particular affinity with specific hedge plants; this subject, together with the conservation of wildlife, will be discussed in Chapter 4.

Coastal Hedges

The need to protect property, gardens or growing crops from the fury of strong salt-laden winds requires the use of a smaller range of tough hedge species that can tolerate these harsher conditions. Firstly, take a walk around the neighbourhood to examine other established hedges for ideas and confirmation of the ability of each species to grow adequately and so provide the necessary protection required.

The following species have a good record for survival and growth in coastal regions:

- Hawthorn *(Crataegus monogyna)*
- Broom *(Cytisus scoparius)*
- Sea buckthorn *(Hippophae rhamnoides)*
- Holly *(Ilex aquafolium)*
- Wild plum *(Prunus cerasifera)*
- Blackthorn *(Prunus spinosa)*
- Dog rose *(Rosa canina)*
- Gorse *(Ulex europaeus)*

Screening Hedges

Planting a hedge for the specific purpose of screening one's garden or other property from the prying eyes of neighbours or passers-by will require the selection of a suitable species that is evergreen, or retains its leaves for most of the winter months.

The choice of true evergreens is limited to the slow-growing holly, holm oak or yew. Hornbeam, wild privet, garden privet and beech retain their leaves well into winter, with beech being alone in its ability to retain its leaves until the old ones are 'pushed off" by the appearance of new leaves in spring.

If an evergreen screen is required urgently there are few other successful options than to use the unpopular Leyland cypress *(Cupressocyparis leylandii)*, or the more acceptable Western red cedar *(Thuja plicata)*, which I have not described so far because they are neither native plants nor ones that complement the rural surroundings. There is no denying that the Leyland cypress has been, and will continue to be, planted to provide a quick screen for some building or view that requires to be hidden, because of its proven record of growing quickly to provide a dense cover on most soil types or in an exposed or unfavourable environment. The Western red cedar is visually less obtrusive, however, and its growth characteristics are similar. Both conifers trim well and can form an excellent dense, tall screen in a much shorter time than normal countryside hedge plants.

I would prefer the use of plants that are in harmony with the surrounding rural scenery, so that they blend into the landscape, rather than standing out as being obvious screening. Try to use native hedge species mixed with some of the evergreens mentioned above to achieve a good cover that is partially evergreen. Choose fast-growing plants such as field maple, hazel, hawthorn and wild plum as the main constituents, adding either wild *(L. Vulgare)* or evergreen privet *(L. Ovalifolium)* – the last-named is neither a native nor a true rural species, but it retains its leaves longer that its wild form, and does not look too out of place in a mixed hedge.

All the species mentioned above will stand mechanical pruning to retain good bushy growth; this is especially necessary when using deciduous hedge plants, as they will need a good density in order to provide a visual screen in winter.

A dense and vigorous young hawthorn hedge that offers good wind protection and will be secure against livestock. It is advisable to erect some form of light fencing to minimize browsing damage to the hedge and so ensure that it remains stockproof.

A Stockproof Hedge

Long before the Enclosures Movement began, farmers and landowners knew there were only two hedge species that time had proved suitable to contain livestock: hawthorn and, to a lesser degree, blackthorn. Both have a bushy and vigorous growth habit, and carry an abundance of sharp thorns, which deter animal browsing and escape attempts!

Hawthorn is the most commonly used species suitable for hedging to contain livestock without the need to erect barbed-wire fencing. An exception to its universal use was in the county of Kent where growers of apples and pears

A shelterbelt of Italian alders in the spring. Although planted at quite a wide spacing, these trees offer a good permeable windbreak during the summer months. Some side-branch pruning has been done to encourage fresh growth closer to the main trunk of each tree. Alders have a compact, non-invasive root system that will not detrimentally affect the growth of adjacent crops; in addition they are able to fix their own nitrogen needs on their roots.

would often substitute their hawthorn hedges with alder windbreaks, because hawthorn is susceptible to the bacterial disease 'fireblight' that can also seriously affect fruit trees.

Blackthorn will produce a good thorny barrier, but it tends to produce sucker growth from the base that can quickly spread into the adjacent field and is rarely fully controlled by livestock grazing. It also has the disadvantage that the thorns are liable to cause septicaemia unless they are quickly removed. Another problem with blackthorn is its susceptibility to 'silverleaf', a bacterial disease affecting *Prunus* species. So once again, growers of plums will avoid its use for orchard hedges.

Other species that can be mixed with hawthorn and blackthorn to provide a thorny barrier are barberry, holly, wild crab and purging buckthorn, all of which carry some barbs to deter browsing. Holly has the added benefit that it is evergreen, giving colour to an otherwise leafless winter appearance.

A suggested mix of species for a stockproof hedge should consist of 80 per cent hawthorn, plus 10 per cent blackthorn, with 10 per cent of other species to add a little colour and contrast. The overriding requirement is to ensure a secure hedge that can be easily trimmed to keep the growth tight to form an impenetrable barrier; this is best achieved with hawthorn.

A Windbreak for Crop or Livestock Protection

The choice of plant species must reflect the reality that they will probably have to endure windy conditions while they are growing to maturity themselves, before they can offer protection to others!

The emphasis must be on plants that grow vigorously and have a strong and extensive root system. Shrub species such as field maple, hazel and wild plum, as well as hawthorn, will provide the necessary growth. If height is more important than density you will have to resort to the use of traditional shelterbelt tree species, such as the alder varieties: *Alnus Cordata* (Italian alder), *Alnus Glutinosa* (common alder), and *Alnus Incana* (grey alder). The former is favoured by fruit growers because it leafs up earlier in the spring than the other two, but it is not so well rooted. All three alder varieties can be trimmed to provide a quick-growing, compact, hedge-type windbreak. All alders have the benefit of root systems that can fix nitrogen in the soil, so they do not compete with any adjacent crop for their nitrogen needs.

Poplars have been used extensively for windbreaks, but they create problems in the longer term. The varieties of poplar used for windbreaks include *Populus Robusta* (a common poplar clone); *Populus canescens* (grey poplar), *Populus nigra Italica* (Lombardy poplar), and the hybrid variety *Populus* TxT 32. All are noted for their fast growth, which is welcomed in the first ten years; thereafter they continue to grow at a similar rate to become large timber trees, which is not a characteristic that is required for a windbreak screen. Unlike alders, poplars do not have a compact nitrogen-fixing root system; on the contrary their roots are large and invasive, soon causing problems as they compete with adjacent crops for available nutrients and water.

All the hedge species mentioned above will grow to a height accessible to modern hedge trimmers, and will retain dense growth over their full height if they are trimmed regularly. Field maple and hazel will need annual trimming to avoid the lower part of the plant becoming bare-stemmed. Hawthorn and wild plum will retain smaller shoot growth at lower levels more readily.

PLANT PROVENANCE

During the past decade a greater awareness has arisen regarding the origins of the hedge plants being offered for sale. Conservation bodies are now strongly recommending that all new plantings should be with plants that have a 'local provenance' – by which they mean that the individual plant species should have been raised from locally collected seed or cuttings from local mother plants.

The Forestry Commission Technical Paper 31 – 'Genetic Variation and Conservation of British Native Trees and Shrubs' – sets out their current knowledge and the policy implications leading on from the information gathered. However, it is important to understand what is meant by the words 'native', 'origin' and 'provenance' before discussing what is becoming a confused situation.

Native: The dictionary refers to a 'native' plant as being one that originated in a certain country, or area within that country; that is, it is indigenous.

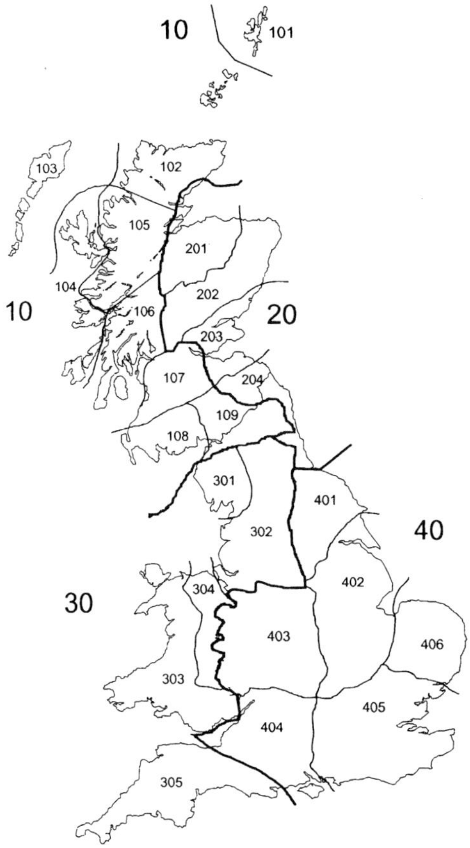

A map of seed zones in Britain, showing the regional divisions and zones for seed and plant collection identification. There are four large regional divisions (10 – 20 – 30 – 40) that are subdivided into smaller zones for more localized provenance identification. (The Forestry Commission)

Origin: Again, the dictionary states that 'origin' refers to the place where something existed from the first: a starting point.

Provenance: This is the place from which a particular plant, or seed, was found; it may not be referring to its true 'native origin', but simply to where that plant came from – that is, it could refer to seed collected from plants on the side of a new motorway. Such plants would have come from another source prior to being planted on the side of the new road, so they cannot be regarded as being of 'native origin'.

The Forestry Commission devised a mapping system for seed zones throughout the British Isles to enable foresters and all those involved in plant material sourcing to be able to provide provenance data on any seed or plant collections. The country is divided initially into four main regions: eastern and western zones within northern and southern divisions. These are identified as Regions 10, 20, 30 and 40. Each region is sub-divided into four or more zones.

The seed zone map provides a degree of control on the sourcing and subsequent use of seed lots within a chosen area; for example, conservation groups can specify that the plants they wish to buy must have a seed origin of 'Zone 403', which is as near as possible to covering the heart of England, and thus would satisfy planting needs for 'native origin' plants into central Wales and central southern England.

The collection of seeds or plant material within a designated zone does not mean that the collected seed is native to that zone, nor that the seed originated in the zone. The seed collector must carry out searches in the chosen area to verify the historical provenance of the trees from which he proposes to collect seed or plant material; for example, where seed is collected from plants on the verge of a motorway, the collector can rightly claim that the seed has been collected within a designated zone, and that it is of British *provenance*. But everyone knows that motorways have only been in existence for a maximum of fifty years, so the true *origin* of those plants is not the site upon which they are growing. In fact it is very likely that they came from Europe, because at the time a higher proportion of plants used for early motorway planting were imported from nurseries on the continent. British nurserymen still cannot fully match the cheaper production costs of their counterparts in Belgium, Holland and especially in Eastern Europe.

It is estimated that nearly half the trees and shrubs planted in the British countryside are still imported from the continent, the majority of plants coming from specialist nurserymen in Belgium and Holland. These nurserymen source their seed from a wide range of countries, some from the UK and some from their own certified seed sources, and a large quantity is collected in eastern Europe, where labour costs for seed collection are much lower than in western Europe.

At this point I would like to illustrate the history of the use of seeds and plants from non-native origins to show the scale of the problem facing those who wish to see a greater use of true native seed and planting stock. I quote from William Marshall's book *Planting and Ornamental Gardening* of 1785, where he describes the methods of raising hawthorn plants: '...the practise of the London Nurserymen is this: the strongest of the seed-bed plants having been drawn at two or three years old for sale, they clear the beds entirely.'

This statement implies that they are selling plants across the country, and I would guess that they were not so concerned about the provenance of the original seed as some people are today; it would have come from the cheapest and/or the most accessible sources. This is illustrated in another quotation from the same book, where the author discusses the use of 'furze' (gorse) for sowing on hedge-banks:

> If the Furze be made use of as an assistant Hedge-wood, it is better to sow the seed on the *back* of the bank than upon the *top* of it; for in this case it is more apt to overhang the young plants in the face of the bank; whilst in the other it is better situated to answer the purpose intended; namely, guarding the back of the bank, as well as preventing its being torn down by cattle. ...One pound of seed will sow about forty statute rods (220 yards/ 203 metres). The French seed is the best, as the plants from this seldom mature their seed in this country, and consequently are less liable to spread over the adjoining enclosure. It may be had at the seed-shops in London for about fifteen pence a-pound.

These statements indicate that the London seed houses would purchase their seed requirements from wherever it was available, to sell on to their customers across the country. At this time many country gentlemen had town residences, which they would visit regularly for both social and business reasons. Some of them would have purchased seed to be sent down to their country estates for raising to carry out their own tree and shrub planting. So, the international movement of both seed and plants was an established business by the late eighteenth century, and there can be little doubt that it was a necessity if landowners were to be able to purchase adequate seed or planting material to meet the needs for enclosing fields on the scale witnessed during this period and well into the nineteenth century.

M. D. Hooper (co-author of *Hedges*, The New Naturalist series) wrote in the magazine The Local Historian Vol. 11, No. 2, 1974:

I have, myself, tried to discover the sources of the immense number of hawthorns required for enclosure hedges, and have had only one minor success: the Huntingdon Record Office has typescript extracts from the day book of John and James Wood who ran a nursery at Brampton. These extracts record the sales of thousands of quicks and many trees, of which Elm is far the most frequent. Most of these sales took place after 1762.

It is dangerous to speculate upon where their seed came from and to whom the subsequent plants were sold, but if their nursery specialized in selling hedge and woodland plants, they would have sold over a wide local area at the very least. Were they buying their seed from the London seed houses mentioned above?

Some references to the source of plants used in planting enclosure hedges can be found in Sir John Sinclair's *General Report on Enclosures* drawn up by order of the Board of Agriculture and published in 1808. In the extensive appendix section of the book are the following references to plant sources:

1. Salop: 'When the fence (hedge) was so far advanced, young hawthorns, or hollies, or their berries, were put between the stems of the old quick...Of between two and three miles of fencing (hedging) made in this manner...and the rude manner in which they were transplanted, by being stocked out of old wood-land...As the value of most coppice woodland is daily declining, I look upon this as a valuable appropriation of it, wherever it can be done; one lot of ground is cleared, and another is enclosed.'

2. Salop: 'When the line of fence (hedge) was marked out, a trench was dug of considerable width and depth. Strong bushes of hazel, willow, hawthorn, or whatever could be met with in a neighbouring wood...'

[These are interesting observations on two counts: one, because it confirms the practice of digging up young plants from nearby woodland; and secondly, because it throws into doubt the origins of some old hedges that learned persons have attributed to being the remnant of an ancient woodland !]

3. York: 'The prevailing hedge wood is white-thorn. Formerly it was in this, as in other places, gathered in the woods and the rough grounds. But at present, and for some years past, "garden quickwood" (nursery-raised plants) has been pretty generally, though not yet universally planted.'

Here is further proof that the enclosure hedges were planted with stock that was dug up locally where possible, but increasingly landowners had to resort to buying the larger numbers of plants needed from nurserymen further afield.

Here is a quote taken from the August 1936 issue of *Agriculture*, the journal of the Ministry of Agriculture, from an article entitled 'The Hawthorn plant and the selection of "quick" for hedging':

> The slowness of growth from seed and the cheapness of one-year-old imported quick, which are bigger and stronger than those grown in this country, have considerably reduced the amount of quick grown at home from seed, and practically all the young plants grown today, in this country, are of Italian, German or Dutch origin. The one-year-old imported quick are planted out in nurseries, where they remain for one or two years, during which time they are once or twice transplanted. The quick are then sold according to size, with no distinction of variety or suitability for various soil or climatic conditions.

This statement shows due concern for what was going on, but does not attempt to offer any recommendation to do otherwise. The Ministry was aware of the problems: farming had been in a parlous state ever since World War I, thus they would have been pleased to see any attempts to restore or plant hedges, and not been unduly concerned at the minor detail of the provenance of the planting stock. In many ways the situation remains unchanged: farming is in the doldrums once more, and farmers need every encouragement to continue replanting hedges and woodland removed during the post-World War II years of exhortation to 'grow more food from our own resources'.

Nurserymen in the UK are still unable to meet the need for all the plants required, for the same historical reason: the costs of production on the continent still remain lower than in Britain.

NATIVE TREE AND SHRUB SPECIES

For those wishing to use plant species of known native origin, I have listed here shrub species, and tree species that are likely to be planted into new hedges.

Shrubs	Trees
Field maple	Common alder
Box	White birch
Hornbeam	Hornbeam*
Common dogwood	Beech*
Hazel	Ash
Common hawthorn	Holly*
Midland hawthorn	Wild crab
Broom	Aspen
Spindle	Wild cherry
Beech	Sessile oak
Holly	English oak
Wild privet	Goat willow
Wild crab	Grey sallow*
Blackthorn	Common osier
Purging buckthorn	Mountain ash
Dog rose	Yew*
Field rose	
Grey sallow	
Gorse	
Yew	
Wayfaring tree	
Guelder rose	

The tree species marked with an asterix (*) denotes that they are also listed in the hedge shrub list as being plants that have a dual use: regular pruning and clipping will keep them as excellent hedge forms. A few willow varieties also have a dual use, but do not respond very well to the constraints of a trimmed hedge.

There are other shrub and tree species that have native origins but are not listed above because they are not commonly regarded as hedgerow trees, especially in newer plantings. The final choice will always be influenced by personal choice that, hopefully, will have been made after taking due account of those species that are commonly found in the locality and so represent the character of the area.

Regional Variations in the Choice of Species

The following observations are the result of a questionnaire sent out to regional FWAG offices several years ago; the information remains a useful guide to local conditions and variations in plant species used for hedging:

Berkshire, Buckinghamshire and Oxfordshire: Three arable counties with declining dairy and stock farming. Sheep are still to be found in most areas.

The planting of double-row hedges is recommended, with mixed species now more prominent in farm conservation and management plans.

Hawthorn continues to be the dominant species, followed by blackthorn, hazel, field maple, dog rose and one of the viburnums, usually guelder rose, to make up the hedge mix. Holly is more evident on the moister soils of the Chiltern Hills.

Avon and Gloucestershire: These counties feature both lowland and hilly areas, again with declining numbers of dairy and stock farms. Conservation plays an increasing part in future farm plans, with the same sort of hedge mixes as indicated above, except for the greater use of holly in areas where it is already a common hedgerow plant.

Hampshire: An arable county with large areas of both open downland, the New Forest and its gentle coastline. Hawthorn remains the most common species, but with much more hazel than in the Midland counties. A wide variety of species is to be found in both existing and new farm hedges.

Hereford and Shropshire: Two counties with good and enduring mixed farming traditions. The large areas of high-grade soils support strong hedges, with many different species to be found. Hawthorn, blackthorn, hazel, holly, field maple, the viburnums and wild rose varieties all feature commonly.

Somerset: With higher rainfall in many parts, this county remains a stronghold for dairy farming. The exposed hill fields are usually contained by stone walls, but there are good stockproof hedges of hawthorn and blackthorn. Newer amenity hedges now contain good mixes of the usual species, with hawthorn as the basis.

Devon and Cornwall: Two dairy and stock-rearing counties, with a predominance of earth and stone hedge-banks around its familiar small fields, and along its many narrow lanes. These hedge-banks are topped with hawthorn, gorse, blackthorn and dog rose, with smaller amounts of hazel and field maple.

Essex and East Anglia: The flat, open landscape of large parts of these counties has become associated with sizable arable enterprises cropping very large open fields that would benefit from more hedgerows. Hedges were removed in this region as a result of wartime airfield construction, but historically the area has had more open fields than other parts of the country. New hedge planting features a wider selection of species over the normal hawthorn-based hedges.

North and South Wales: Dairy, stock and sheep farming remain the prime farming enterprises in the lush landscape. Heavier rainfall and milder weather along the south-western coastline ensures good growth of the prominent early potato crop, which benefits from the wind protection provided by earth- and stone-banked field boundaries, common throughout the country. These hedge-banks are usually topped with hawthorn, blackthorn and gorse; the latter two species survive the salt-laden coastal winds better than hawthorn. In sheltered valleys hazel is a common addition, together with holly, dog rose, common dogwood and some field maple.

Lancashire: A good arable, stock and mixed farming county. Moving north does not change the common ingredients of a good hedge, namely hawthorn, blackthorn, hazel plus some guelder rose and field maple, the latter two being recommended to broaden the species' range in new hedges. Earth hedge-banks are suggested as being a way to obtain better growth on poor reclaimed land such as coal pits and other old industrial sites.

Cumbria: An important livestock landscape, its fields bordered by many miles of stone walling constructed from the clearance of fields on the slopes and in the shadows of its hilly terrain.

There are some earth and stone hedge-banks, together with traditional hedges in the flat valley lands. New hedges will feature a wider selection of species as seen in most counties wishing to encourage wildlife conservation.

Yorkshire: An arable and stock county, many of its fields are bordered with stone walls as well as traditional hedges. Hawthorn and blackthorn remain the dominant species for stock control. Sea buckthorn is used in coastal areas, otherwise the choice is wide open, and dictated by preference: hazel, purging buckthorn, dog rose, common dogwood, guelder rose and field maple. Encouragement is given to establish a perennial grass sward beside the hedge for the provision of cover for game and nesting birds as well as the control of annual weed.

Dumfriesshire and Galloway: Crossing the border into the rolling hills and dales of the Scottish lowlands, hawthorn remains the most common hedge species, but on some older estates beech hedges remain common.

The traditional Galloway 'hedge' is the combination of a stone wall with the hedge planted to grow out from the base of the wall. This style is no longer being followed because of the high cost of wall-building.

Fencing is placed around new hedges to prevent damage by sheep and rabbits. There is also a keen interest in the sowing of field margins to provide the rough grass favoured by barn owls to hunt along.

The above regional notes are very sketchy, being based on the limited data returned. It would take a whole book to cover in any detail the salient features of every county in the country that had a good stock of hedges. The notes provide an approach to recognizing both local and regional differences in the composition of hedges. It is important to select a range of species for a new hedge that reflects the ancient, pre-enclosure hedges within the immediate locality. This will broaden the conservation value of the hedge as well as restoring to the area some of its richer hedgerow heritage.

CHAPTER 3

The Influence of the Landscape and Soil Types

J. C. Beddall summed up the value of hedges in the opening paragraph of his book *Hedges for Farm and Garden*, published in 1950:

> Who can think of England without thinking of a land of fields and hedges? Nowhere else are there hedges quite like our English ones, nowhere else are they such a feature of the landscape, for the hedges hold the very spirit of our countryside. Like the mesh of a far-flung net, they frame the pattern of our fields, that maze of meadow and arable, orchard and copse which lie over hill and vale in this fair and lovely land...

The variety of the English landscape is an asset we must continue to cherish, conserve and enjoy to the full. Many will board an aircraft for their annual holiday, to be whisked away to some location that the travel brochures have told them is 'exotic – romantic – alluring – breath-taking...'; yet they leave behind a land that can offer a variety of scenery unmatched for such a small country, scenery that many will rarely attempt to get to know because it has to be sought out and found to be appreciated, something that many holiday brochures don't set out to do for our island home.

The pleasure of our landscape is in its infinite variety. A closer examination of this diversity will reveal that

The Vale of the White Horse in Oxfordshire, as seen from the Ridgeway; a prehistoric cross-country route. It looks down on to a patchwork of irregular fields, woodland and winding roads, all remnants of 'ancient' countryside. Note the curved woodland edge in the foreground and the thin long field to the left, beyond the large open field; both are features of a pre-enclosure landscape.

Planned countryside. This is an excellent example of the late eighteenth-century land surveyor's 'art' in the Cotswolds, forming the enclosure fields that transformed the landscape of lowland England – a precise layout of regular shaped fields bounded by hawthorn hedges or stone walls. It is easy to see that these fields would have been much easier to plough and cultivate at the 'dawn' of mechanized farming following on from the development of the corn drill by Jethro Tull.

lowland England can be divided into two distinctive types: ancient countryside, and planned countryside.

Ancient countryside: This consists of patches of woodland and pasture with little villages, narrow winding roads and small irregular-shaped fields enclosed by either earth banks, hedges or stone walls. In Normandy (France) such landscape is called the *bocage*, and to travel through it gives one a better idea of how much of lowland England looked before the advent of the enclosure movement in the eighteenth century.

Planned countryside: This consists of larger, regular-shaped fields, mostly bordered by compact, single species hawthorn hedges; it was originally called 'champion' country, with larger villages joined by better, straighter roads also edged by similar hawthorn hedges or stone walls. This was the result of the surveyor's work during the heyday of the enclosure movement throughout the eighteenth and early half of the nineteenth centuries.

The boom years for agriculture following World War II accelerated the earlier enclosure movement's enthusiasm for enlarging field sizes, by the removal of many miles of hedges, and particularly the grubbing out of valuable mixed species historic hedges to form the extensive fields that now typify areas of the eastern counties, as well as other parts of central and southern England, especially where land had been cleared during the last war to build airfields and other military training areas. The enlargement of field sizes went on with the blessing of successive governments up to the early 1990s, when grants for the removal of hedges were finally stopped and replaced by grants to replace the same hedges!

No invading army may have reached our shores since the Normans in 1066, but the effects of two world wars during the twentieth century dramatically transformed our landscape for ever. The need to grow more food during those war years was followed by the postwar corn boom that left its mark on the eastern counties of Essex, Suffolk, Norfolk and Lincolnshire, together with parts of Hampshire and Wiltshire, opening up fields that were already larger than average for traditional *planned countryside*.

Fortunately there are regions of Britain that have retained much of their historic landscape, regions where the undulating and more rugged terrain was not so inviting to the arable farmer's large plough and combine. Counties such as Cornwall, Devon, Somerset, Dorset, parts of Sussex and Kent and the Welsh counties have retained many of the characteristics of *ancient countryside*.

Farming continued to be the primary use of land up to the end of the twentieth century; but as we move into the new century, farmers are being encouraged to become better custodians of the flora and fauna of the landscape, as well as meeting the need for food supplies, which will be sourced from those who can supply the country's needs at the lowest cost. This will mean ever-increasing quantities of food being imported into Britain from eastern Europe, in particular.

The changes being introduced by the government will stimulate farmers to revise the way they view their farms, encouraging them to introduce a wide range of conservation measures to restore lost habitats, to turn back the clock somewhat to a landscape associated with areas of *ancient countryside*.

The restoration of hedges together with associated field margins is an important element of proposed measures to conserve and enhance wildlife habitats. The choice of plants selected for new hedges will be influenced by the soil type and the surrounding topography. The best choice of plants should be made after examining the growth and vigour of local old hedges. This will include the common plants such as hawthorn, blackthorn, hazel and field maple, but look carefully for the more unusual plants that have found their way into these hedges, species that will vary according to differing soils.

Soil types can vary considerably within one field, yet the locality may well be classified as being predominantly only one type. Set out below are hedge species found on a range of soils:

Free-draining light sandy loams and gravel soils: Field maple, hawthorn, gorse, blackthorn, wild plum, yew.

Chalk and limestone soils: Beech, common dogwood, hazel, hawthorn, holly, field maple, wild privet, spindle, yew, wayfaring tree, guelder rose.

Heavier loams and silt soils: Beech, blackthorn, wild crab, hawthorn, hazel, hornbeam, holly, wild plum, common dogwood.

Damp and boggy sites: Common dogwood, purging buckthorn, alder buckthorn, willows (of all types).

Clay soils: Hawthorn, holly, wild crab, blackthorn, wild plum.

Windy and exposed/coastal sites: Blackthorn, hawthorn, sea buckthorn, holly, gorse, wild privet.

Hawthorn and blackthorn should be regarded as the dominant and universal species for a 'working' hedge; thereafter the choice will be influenced by regional or soil type variations. There are no hard and fast rules, but increasingly, conservation considerations will influence the mixture of species in a particular hedge (*see* Chapter 4).

Farmers and landowners have access to soil maps of their land to help with cropping decisions. The Ordnance Survey carried out a nationwide soil survey in England and Wales during 1967—8. Each area map covers an area approximately 10 miles (16km) by 15 miles (24km) to a scale of one inch to

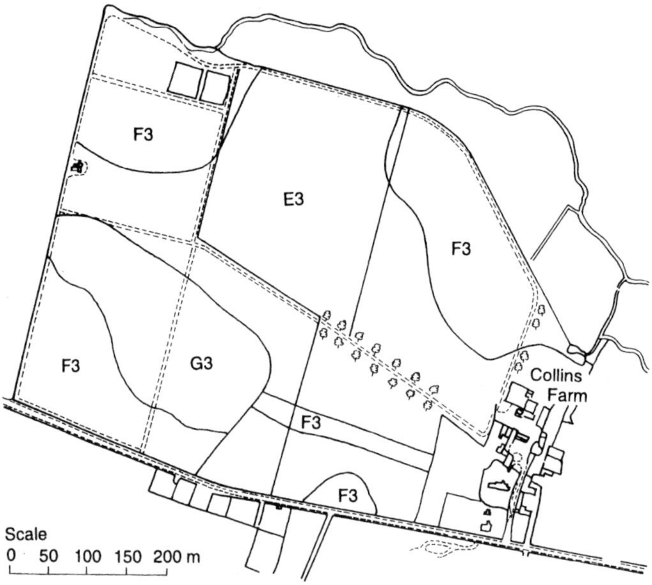

A detailed soil map of the author's 30-hectare (75-acre) farm at Frilford, in Oxfordshire. The map was drawn up by Irrigation Management Services Ltd to show the variations in the sandy loam soil, indicating differences in the 'Available Water Capacity'. Such knowledge ensures the economic use of irrigation and influences the rotation of crops. The farm grows a range of high-value horticultural crops that require irrigation to obtain their full potential.

the mile. These highly coloured maps provide excellent detail of the variations in soil type in any chosen area. Your local map will indicate your own soils, and will enable you to identify other similar soil types in your locality, which may provide confirmation of suitable hedge species.

Access to satellite plotting now allows farmers to have all their fields very precisely surveyed for their suitability for specific cropping. Areas of poor soil can be identified and possibly taken out of cropping to be planted to woodland, or hedged to allow for an alternative conservation use.

On my own small, intensively cropped farm I commissioned a specialist irrigation management company to carry out a detailed soil examination, plotting all the small but significant changes in the moisture-holding ability of the light sandy loam. The resulting map has been of great value in the selection of suitable ground for the range of crops grown. One piece of very poor soil has been taken out of production and planted to a woodland strip, to provide a valuable windbreak for those crops grown on the better adjoining ground. The allocation of land according to its inherent fertility can bring greater benefits, rather than continuing to grow unsuitable crops without due consideration for the soil's potential. It is no longer economic, nor good farming practice, to pour extra fertilizer on to land that is not suited to a proposed crop.

Returning to the detailed soil map for my own farm (see above), the blanket definition of a 'light sandy loam' revealed three distinct variations in available water capacity, which has been acknowledged by the way the land is now cropped. Water-hungry crops such as potatoes are planted on the more moisture-retentive soils, marked on the map in the area 'E3', leaving the dryer land for cropping with vegetable crops such as asparagus and sweetcorn, marked on the map in the areas 'F3' and 'G3'.

With the present encouragement to replant hedgerows, it is a good time to look at re-dividing larger fields back into smaller blocks according to the soil type and its moisture retention. Any small pockets of thin, rocky or saturated ground can be converted to woodland, hedge or flower-rich field margin rather than continuing to struggle with such pieces in adverse conditions.

The planting of new hedges can provide some surprises if one is not aware of the finer points of the soil structure upon which it is planted. The constant close trimming of old hedges may have removed most of the visible variations in growth due to soil factors, but a new hedge planted nearby may show interesting differences in growth vigour due to the soil type or the suitability of one or more of the chosen plant species.

WIND PROTECTION

The concentration of hedge-banked fields in the West Country, Wales and in some other coastal regions stems from earlier enclosure in a landscape that requires protection from the wind and driving rain coming in from the English Channel to the south or the Bristol Channel and the Atlantic Ocean in the north.

A good hedge or hedge-bank on level terrain will provide full wind protection for a distance equal to five times its height. Thus a 3m (10ft) high, semi-permeable hedge will give 15m (50ft) of full protection from wind on its leeward side. Thereafter the level of protection declines steadily until the full wind speed is restored at a distance equivalent to twelve times the height of the hedge – at 36m (118ft).

Protection from the strength and chilling factors of high winds in exposed fields not only provides welcome shelter for livestock, but also aids the establishment of early crops in springtime, such as bulbs and early potatoes in Cornwall, Devon and South Wales.

A Cornish hedge-bank with oak and hawthorn showing the effects of constant exposure to the prevailing high winds from the Atlantic. A greenhouse has been erected in the lee of the hedge-bank to gain valuable protection from the hostile climate. (The Museum of English Rural Life, The University of Reading)

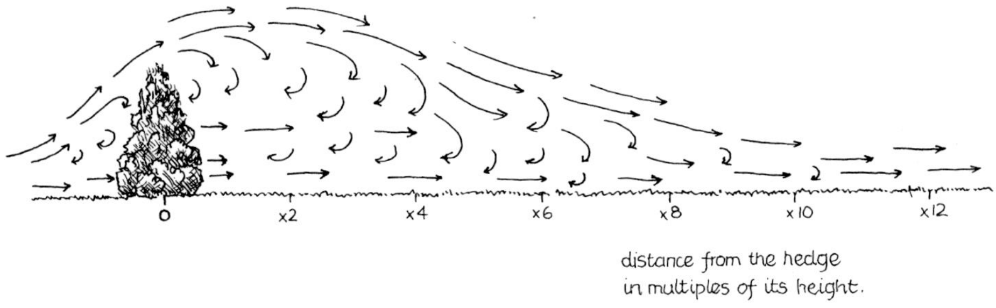

The diagram shows the shelter value of a semi-permeable hedge according to its height. The height of the hedge is very important in obtaining the greatest area of protection in its lee.

All arable and especially valuable vegetable crops benefit from wind protection. There will be a small crop loss close to the hedge, unless a field margin has been established, but from a distance of about twice the height of the hedge out into the crop, to a distance equal to twelve times the hedge height, there will be some gain in both yield and quality above the overall field average.

There is a direct benefit to both crops, livestock and to wildlife from allowing hedges to grow taller. Modern hydraulic hedge trimmers are very versatile and can cope with heights above 3m (10ft). Consider the potential benefits to your own crops, livestock or even the garden by allowing your own hedges to grow gradually up to the safe maximum trim height. The low 1.5m (5ft) enclosure hedges have less value to farming today, because most now contain strands of barbed wire to keep the stock in the field; so let the hedge grow up to offer greater shelter, as well as provide benefits to wildlife (discussed in the next chapter).

A hawthorn hedge trimmed at the maximum height of the machine to give wind protection to the pole- and trellis-work of a hop garden. The hop bines are very vulnerable to wind damage when the crop has grown to the top of the wires in midsummer, and are heavy with the crop of hops. A high wind can easily do extensive damage to the whole garden if not adequately protected.

CHAPTER 4

Wildlife Conservation

For a greater part of the twentieth century farmers had little regard for the advocates of hedge planting, who were unaware of the problems caused by birds and rabbits hiding in, and protected by, hedges. Rabbits grazed heavily into the edges of cornfields, and flocks of small birds fed on the heads of grain at harvest time. Numerous hedges were grubbed out in order to get rid of the maze of warrens, and thus the source of damage to adjacent crops from the plague of rabbits that were endemic until the arrival of myxomatosis in the late 1950s. The recent return of rabbits has given cause for concern once more, but it seems that as soon as their populations build up to a certain point, the disease returns and numbers are reduced once again to manageable levels.

Small hedgerow birds no longer cause problems for farmers. There is no need for cage traps or the earlier (nineteenth-century) practice of scaring birds into catch nets – quite the reverse, in fact; indeed, there has been such a dramatic decline in the number and variety of birds to be found in hedges today that the notion of having to trap them seems inconceivable to us now. The Royal Society for the Protection of Birds has initiated surveys in recent years to trace the causes for the regrettable decline in the number of hedgerow birds.

These surveys point to possible causes for the decline of specific species. In general terms the problems stem from the changes and increased efficiency of modern agriculture. Gone are the diversity of arable crops and the pattern of pasture and meadow associated with mixed farming up to the 1950s. Since that era, farming has experienced a revolution, brought about by the development of the tractor and all its related machinery to complete in half the time all the work hitherto done by man and horse.

The post-war introduction of herbicides to control crop weeds, closely followed by insecticides to deal with every possible pest, combined to remove most of the food sources for many farmland birds, and this wholesale cleansing of the farmer's crops has led to an imbalance in the life cycle of the flora and fauna of the hedgerow. Furthermore the move towards mono-cropping in many arable areas has resulted in an absence of weeds in cereal crops, so those insect species associated with particular weeds have declined, as have the birds that fed upon those insects. The demise of arable weeds has also reduced the amount of weed seeds upon which many birds fed in winter, further reducing bird populations. The use of broad-spectrum insecticides has also had a serious effect upon 'beneficial' insects, those that feed on the insects the farmer wishes to control – they, too, have been eliminated.

Fortunately farmers and their agronomists are now aware of the need to choose narrow-spectrum pesticides that do not harm beneficial insects, and there is an increased awareness of the damage inflicted upon wildlife in general. Alongside

A tall and overgrown wild plum hedge in flower with other hedgerow shrubs below, providing the diversity of cover that will benefit a wide range of bird species as well as supplying a valuable source of food throughout the year, especially from the autumn fruits.

this realization are new restrictions on the range of pesticides in use on farm crops. Many pesticides that are known to be harmful to the environment are now being withdrawn from approved use. The revocation of so many arable chemicals may reach a point where farmers will be forced to return to a better balance of mixed cropping to help reduce particular problem weeds or insect pests in their crops.

BIRDS

A mature hedge should be able to provide adequate nest sites for a wide range of farmland birds, but it will need to have a good mixture of plant species and have a margin of vegetation on either side to provide a good source of insects and weed seeds upon which these birds and their ravenous offspring can feed in safety. In its turn the insect population will need adequate host plants to feed on. So a simple life cycle has to exist within the hedge for all its 'inhabitants' to survive and thrive in this environment.

The presence of trees within a hedgerow will provide a nesting site and habitat for birds that would not normally be found in a hedge, such as crows, rooks and some raptor species: buzzard, kestrel and sparrowhawk; though the latter may not be welcome, as they prey upon small birds and their young offspring.

The form of the hedge influences the range of birds to found within it; for instance hedge sparrows, robins and wrens prefer a hedge that is thick at the base because this will provide the cover they like for scratching about in the darker recesses for insects, especially in winter when the surrounding open ground is frozen hard. The thickness of the hedge will also provide valuable shelter from the cold weather. The bottom of the hedge, with its carpet of dead leaves and fallen fruits, will remain unfrozen to offer a much needed food source at a time when all wild animals need extra food simply to maintain their body temperature for survival.

Songbirds such as the blackbird and thrush sing from the top of the hedge, nest in the middle of it, and join the others scratching about in the bottom for seeds,

The Value of Hedges for Common Birds

Bird	Nesting Site	Feeding Area	Shelter
Hedge and tree sparrows	*	*	*
Robin	/	/	*
Blackbird	*	*	*
Wren	*	*	*
Blue and great tits	*	*	*
Greenfinch and goldfinch	/	*	*
Bullfinch and chaffinch	/	*	*
Starling	/	/	/
Linnet	*	*	*
Skylark	/	/	/
Thrush	*	*	*
Cuckoo	*in other birds nests	/	/
Pigeon	*tall hedges	*	*
Magpie	*tall hedges	*	*
Yellow hammer	*	*	*
Collard dove	*tall hedges	/	/

snails, grubs and worms: each according to taste. Small bushy trees growing in a hedge, such as wild crab, plum and holly, provide the higher vantage points and nest sites preferred by woodpigeon and ring doves.

Game birds, and especially pheasants, will use the cover of a hedge with a good wide base to shelter under, and so they can pop out into the adjacent field to feed; they will also enjoy the warmer conditions in the lee of the hedge. The Game Conservancy has produced a compact little booklet setting out the management of hedges and field margins for game conservation.

Many of the above birds are equally at home in woodland margins, where a mixture of bushes, scrub and smaller trees offers a similar amount of cover and shade with safe access to their food sources, be it on the woodland floor, out in the fields, or within the grass margins beside the field.

Modern farming practices have greatly reduced the abundance of wildlife that was associated with hedgerows from Victorian times and into the early half of

Mixed species hedges bordering an old lane. Two distinctive hedges: on the left a tall, untrimmed one; and on the right, one that has been trimmed tight and low. Between them they offer a diversity of habitat, which when added to the wide untrimmed margin in between, provides an ideal environment for wildlife that will not be found within the adjacent cropping fields.

the twentieth century. The author owns a late nineteenth-century bird-catching net that was used by farm lads to catch or disperse the flocks of hedge sparrows from damaging farm crops.

A large piece of fine mesh netting was attached to two 3.5m (12ft) long bamboo poles, joined at the tapered end with a leather thong to form a tall hinged arch. The thick ends of the poles were held upright by one man, the outstretched arched net held aloft like a full sail. He proceeded to walk up one side of the hedge while another man carried a similar open net on the other side of the hedge. As they walked up the hedge, one or more men would be walking down the hedge from the other end towards them, beating the hedge with sticks, and shouting or whirling a wooden rattle to scare the sparrows, finches, linnets and other small birds out of the hedge.

The frightened birds would fly forwards down the line of the hedge in short-flight 'hops' until, unwittingly, they would find themselves caught in the nets; whereupon the two men holding

The Victorian bird-catching net fully extended, showing the frame of two long bamboo poles joined at the top by a leather thong that acts as a hinge when the net is folded inwards to trap the birds that have been driven into it.

The diagram shows how the nets are deployed either side of a hedge and positioned open to catch the sparrows and other small birds that are driven into them by a beater with a rattle.

the nets would swiftly close them up, like a book, trapping the birds inside. The birds would be killed to earn a reward from the farmer, and were probably eaten – this was a time when farm labourers could rarely afford to eat meat and were often forbidden from catching a rabbit for the pot.

The 3.5m (12ft) length of the bamboo poles makes it likely that these trap nets were used for working along the overgrown, unmanaged hedges that were common during the depressed farming period from the late nineteenth century until the early 1930s. During and after World War II, hedgerow grubbing, or restoration, removed many such overgrown hedges, and close trimming has become the norm with the advent of hedge cutters and flail trimmers. Some larger hedges remain in the more intensive dairy regions where shelter from the elements is still valued.

The presence of a variety of birds in a hedgerow is the visible sign of a thriving ecology, but what is less obvious to the human eye will be the range of insects, invertebrates and small mammals colonizing the hedge bottom.

MAMMALS

Before the arrival of myxomatosis in the 1950s the rabbit was a serious pest of the hedgerow, living in deep burrows that had often turned the hedge bottom into a bare mound, undermining and destroying the hedge. The serious damage to both the hedge and adjacent crops was ample justification for the widespread grubbing out of thousands of miles of hedges; these were bulldozed out and burned on site to form larger fields, free of rabbits, with no longer any need to maintain the aged, overgrown hedge growth.

The hedgehog may have originally acquired its name because of an association with hedges, but it is now more frequently seen in gardens and overgrown sites that can provide its diet of beetles, grubs and small invertebrates. The more common hedgerow mammals are mice, shrews, voles and moles. All have a diet of insects or worms that can be found in, or under, the leaf litter. Moles will seek their food from shallow runs below the ground, while voles feed at ground level. Mice are capable of climbing up into the hedge to reach the berries of dog rose, hawthorn and other such seeds. Along with squirrels, mice are attracted by the larger hazel nuts during late summer.

All these hedgerow inhabitants are preyed upon by kestrels and buzzards hovering overhead or perched in the trees awaiting any movement in the hedge below. The vole will not venture from the shade, but mice and shrews will forage out in the field margin and into the crops of grain or pulses.

One unwelcome inhabitant is the brown rat. Increasingly banished from the farmyard, it has extended its territory to include hedge bottoms, where it will burrow into the hedge or ditch bank. However, increasing numbers of all these smaller mammals are providing food for larger birds such as owls and the raptors already mentioned.

Stoats and weasels are regular hedgerow visitors in their search for food, feeding on mice, voles and the chicks of game birds, the latter making them the enemies of the gamekeeper.

Banked hedges on warmer sandy or heathland soils provide a home for native species of lizards and snakes. The lizard lives on a diet of insects and spiders, while snakes are carnivorous, feeding on small frogs, mice and any small bird unfortunate enough to be caught on the ground.

Hedges provide all these inhabitants and visitors with cover and shade within which to feed, breed, roost and even to hibernate.

INVERTEBRATES

The single largest group to live within the hedgerow and its environs are the invertebrates, and these include a wide range of aphids, beetles, flies, insects and mites that are a very important link in the life cycle of the hedge. This group causes nearly as much concern to farmers as does the field-edge reservoir of 'misplaced plants', commonly called weeds! This is because many of these invertebrates feed on these same plants, and so all are invaluable elements of the hedge's ecology.

As we have already observed, the farmer's reliance upon his spraying machine as a panacea for all pest and weed problems has, over the past forty years, led to a serious imbalance in the flora and fauna of the hedgerow. However, the current cost of pesticides, combined with falling product prices, is leading to a fresh appraisal of the potential benefits of reducing the use of sprays in general and, more specifically, adopting instead carefully targeted sprays that will not harm other forms of wildlife, leading to an improved situation for the future.

The ability of beneficial insects to help with the control of farm pests can be illustrated by the known contribution made by the larvae of a number of hoverflies and of ladybirds that feed upon aphids and can make a considerable impression upon aphid numbers. The green lacewing will also help with the control of aphids. In some instances, where aphids are known to be carriers of a damaging virus infection such as leaf roll and mosaic viruses of potato seed crops, it will be necessary to use a selective pesticide spray to save the crop, rather than wait for the slower control from localized colonies of hoverflies and ladybirds.

The removal of hedges across lowland Britain has led to increased crop infestations from some pests that were neither so important nor so aggressive in earlier decades when hedgerows contained a greater diversity of habitat to sustain larger predator numbers. A good mixed species hedge with an uncropped and unsprayed grass and wild flower margin on each side will provide an excellent habitat for predator insects that can move into the growing crop in the summer to feed and multiply upon any incoming pest, be they aphids, caterpillars or mites. The anthocorid bug is an excellent predator of the fruit-tree red spider mite, as is the ladybird.

The earlier use of broad-spectrum insecticides, such as the widespread use of DDT in the postwar years, had a devastating effect upon numerous beneficial insects. The larvae of the rove beetle would help control cabbage root fly, but were seriously affected by DDT; likewise bird populations were reduced by feeding upon the insects affected by these insecticides. Our understanding of these problems is now such that the situation is continually being improved by the withdrawal of an ever-increasing number of pesticides that have been found to be a danger to wildlife and the environment.

Some farmers and growers are following the example of glasshouse growers, who have been introducing predator insects to control specific crop pests for many years. It requires a detailed understanding of both the pest and its environment to be able to select and introduce the right predator at the correct stage to gain the full potential for integrated pest control. The hedgerow can provide the environment for the introduction of many beneficial insects (pest predators) to help control farm crop pests.

The most noticeable invertebrates in a hedgerow are butterflies and moths, which will be found where there is an abundance of flowering plants in the mixed species hedge with associated established grass margins. Single-species hedges of hawthorn or blackthorn can only harbour those few insects that are known to have an affinity for them. Increasing the selection of hedgerow species will ensure an equally diverse ground flora, and a greater diversity of invertebrates will follow. The ermine moth caterpillar is to be found feeding on the young spring leaves of hawthorn. The brimstone butterfly feeds on the flowers of buckthorn, but many other butterflies and moths will be attracted to the flowering plants in the hedge bottom. Even the flowers of the hedge ivy attract numerous moths and flies.

There are several other smaller insects and mites that colonize hedgerows. We may not see them, but birds and other small animals in their search for food will be well aware of any potential 'dinner' lurking in the depths of a hedge. They will gain the protection of the hedge canopy as they search and feed in safety, hidden from larger predators. The list below indicates the number of insects and mites that can be found feeding and living upon common hedgerow shrubs:

Hawthorn	209
Blackthorn	153
Wild crab	118
Wild rose	107
Hazel	106
Beech	98
Field maple	51
Hornbeam	51
Honeysuckle	48
Spindle	19
Holly	10

The above list was gleaned from *Farming & Wildlife, a Practical Management Handbook* published by the RSPB, which contains much valuable information on how modern farming can work to conserve wildlife in the countryside.

Peacock, comma, red admiral and tortoiseshell butterflies feed on the flowers of the annual nettle. The brown hairstreak butterfly has an intimate association with blackthorn, while the hedge brown feeds on grasses, and the orange tip on garlic mustard. The caterpillars of the small ermine moth eat the leaves of spindle, which is

A large patch of garlic mustard, also commonly known as Jack-by-the-hedge, growing in an old hedge bottom. This is a common hedgerow plant that needs an undisturbed margin in which to grow and spread. With more verges being left untrimmed and farmers being encouraged to leave grass margins beside their hedges, such plants will be able to thrive and extend their habitat.

associated with older hedges. So the environment immediately adjacent to a hedge is as important as the hedge itself in achieving the full potential of the hedgerow to provide a habitat for so many animal forms.

Prior to the widespread use of inorganic fertilizers and pesticides of every description to cope with all the problems that arise in modern farming, farmers had no choice but to work in harmony with nature to obtain good yields from their crops. Many of their methods, which we now describe as 'conservation measures', were simply inbred good husbandry techniques, honed over the centuries from the experience of successive generations. Thus much of the advice now being offered to farmers is simply making them aware once more of the part that nature can play in obtaining good crops.

A view looking down on to a tightly trimmed hedge, showing how the field of corn, to the right, has been drilled tight up to its base, offering no habitat for wildlife. On the left is an untrimmed roadside verge with wild flowers growing. This is not an ideal habitat because of its proximity to the busy road. Farmers are now being actively encouraged to form margins around all fields, so hopefully this field will soon have a wildlife-friendly grass margin between the hedge and the crop.

FIELD MARGINS

A hedge can be described as a thin strip of woodland, and the adjacent grass margins can be called a strip of meadow. These analogies draw our attention to the combined environment one is attempting to create within the restricted area between adjacent fields of arable crops.

The formation of field margins – an uncultivated strip of land between a crop and field boundary that is rich in perennial grasses and flowering plants – is a key part in the establishment of wildlife corridors across the landscape; these not only offer a habitat for a wide range of animal and plant species, but also provide a safe passage for the movement of wildlife from one habitat to another. The recent practice of cultivating a field right up close to its boundary or to a hedge has removed the reservoir of wild plants that were there in former decades.

The use of herbicides to control 'weeds' in arable crops has also greatly reduced the selection of dormant wild flower seeds capable of germinating naturally at the field edge, even if given the chance by the establishment of a strip free from cropping. Natural regeneration is unlikely to provide the full range of wild flower species desirable, because there is a risk that aggressive perennial grasses and weed species will quickly dominate the nutrient-rich soil.

FWAG, DEFRA and other conservation advisers are available to offer sound advice on the establishment of a well balanced seed mix of wild flowers and grasses suited to a particular soil type or locality. Most new field-margin soils will suffer from being rich in nutrients, following years of intensive arable cultivation. To reduce this fertility it will be necessary not to use herbicides and fertilizers, and to remove the residues from all grass cutting for several years to reduce the soil fertility as quickly as possible, so providing the necessary conditions for the establishment and spread of wild flowers.

If fertilizers and herbicides are not carefully excluded from a new field margin, the establishment of aggressive weeds such as cleavers, couch, sterile brome, thistles and docks will take control at the expense of more fragile plants such as cornflower, daisy and yellow rattle, to name but a few.

The use of pesticides on adjacent crops must be carefully controlled and preferably kept at a safe distance from the margin, even if this means a crop strip remaining unsprayed – either switch off the spray boom end section, or blank off boom-end jets on the first bout around the field to preserve the flora and fauna at the field edge. It is a pointless exercise trying to establish a field or hedgerow margin if one does not take adequate care to exclude all herbicides and insecticides for the well-being of all elements of the field-edge ecology.

Changing attitudes and a greater awareness of our rich rural landscape heritage now offer the best chance for the future survival of hedges and their associated field margins than at any time since the end of World War II. Farming practices will continue to adapt, not only to satisfy the nation's need for food, but also because of the desire to see a rich and varied landscape that is maintained for the enjoyment of future generations.

CHAPTER 5

The Preparation and Planting of Hedges

PLANNING

The decision to plant a new hedge should be the result of careful thought because the outcome of one's labours could survive for centuries. We appreciate the beauty and benefits of old hedges that were planted by our predecessors, so we need to be aware that future generations will, hopefully, be grateful for the efforts we now plan to make.

Before proceeding with the work, check on the current availability of grants towards the cost of planting and maintenance. The range and level of grant payments varies according to which scheme is currently available. Contact the offices of your local Farming and Wildlife Advisory Group (FWAG) or the Department for Environment, Food and Rural Affairs (DEFRA) for details, and possibly a visit by them to the proposed site. Some grants are also available from local councils. These latter grants will vary greatly in both scope and finance according to the policies of the council; rural councils will naturally be more interested in rural well-being than an urban council.

Having decided to plant a hedge, make a list of the shrub species that you wish to use, according to the purpose of the new hedge. Take note of the range of plants to be found in other such local hedges, and how the plants have grown on a similar soil type.

The next decision is the choice of a suitable nursery from which to purchase the required plants, together with any guards and canes that may be necessary because of local rabbit or hare problems, or because the grant conditions specify that the plants must be protected. If you are not familiar with the quality of the plant supplier, it is worth going to see the plants growing on the nursery. Don't be mean with the *quality* of planting stock; it may cost a few more pence to obtain strong, well rooted transplants, but the benefits from improved establishment and subsequent vigorous growth are well worth the extra investment.

Plant Size and Quality

There are national standards for the sizes and basic quality of plants; these are set out in a table of options under the British Standards Number BS3936.

The specification and options for both tree growers and the end user are extensive; an understanding of the age and sizes of plants available will help with the decision on the ultimate aim for the hedge. A planting calculator will help calculate the number of plants required according to the length of hedge.

The best results will be obtained by using a 'transplant', a one-year-old seedling that has been transplanted and

Distance between plants in row	Length of hedge in metres 1	2	3	4	5	6	7	8	9	10	20	30	40	50	60	70	80	90	100	200	300	400	500	600	700	800	900	1 km
15 cm (6 in)	6	13	20	26	33	40	46	53	60	66	133	200	266	333	400	466	533	600	666	1333	2000	2666	3333	4000	4666	5333	6000	6666
30 cm (12 in)	3	6	10	13	16	20	23	26	30	33	66	100	133	166	200	233	266	300	333	666	1000	1333	1666	2000	2333	2666	3000	3333
45 cm (18 in)	2	4	6	8	11	12	15	17	18	22	44	66	88	111	133	155	177	200	222	444	666	888	1111	1333	1555	1777	2000	2222
60 cm (24 in)	1	3	5	6	8	10	11	13	15	16	33	50	66	83	100	116	133	150	166	333	500	666	833	1000	1666	1333	1500	1666
75 cm (30 in)	1	2	4	5	6	8	9	10	12	13	26	40	53	66	80	93	106	120	133	266	400	533	666	800	933	1066	1200	1333
90 cm (36 in)	1	2	3	4	5	6	7	8	10	11	22	33	44	55	66	77	88	100	111	222	333	444	555	666	777	999	1000	1111

* To calculate the number of plants required for a length of hedge, simply take the length units and add together:

For example, 655 m of hedge with plants spaced 30 cm (12 in) apart:

600 m = 2000 plants
50 m = 166 plants
5 m = 16 plants

Thus, 2,182 plants are required for 655 m of hedge.

A planting calculator. To find out the quantity of plants required according to your chosen spacing, simply choose the line relating to the 'distance between the plants in each row', and move along it until you meet the known hedge length – see top line. Read off the number where the two cross.

grown on for a further (second) year to become a sturdy transplant (=1+1). It will be much better able to cope with variable ground conditions, and will have a larger and better developed root system than a one-year-old seedling, which will enable it to better withstand drought and weed competition.

It needs to be emphasized that one should not buy transplants expecting them to grow vigorously if they become smothered in weed and have not been watered in times of drought. Transplants, like all new plants, need to be cared for during their early years of growth, to enable them to reach a point where they will be able to look after themselves sooner than if left unattended. If the young plants are not cared for they will either not grow at all, or will take many years to become a worthwhile hedge. A little care will reap dividends, and ensure that the hedge becomes a benefit to its location within three to four years.

The cost of good quality transplants will vary between suppliers. It is best to try and buy direct from the producer to ensure that you get the plants that you may have seen growing on the nursery in the summer. Buying from a reputable nursery should mean that you can buy from the catalogue knowing that the plants will be of a uniform high quality, without the need to see the plants growing beforehand.

There are usually three sizes of hedgerow transplants offered for sale:

30–40/45cm (12—16/18in): These are the smallest and cheapest available, but the risk is that some plants of this size may be genetic 'runts', small specimens that may never get going properly. However, in most cases they may not have grown taller for a variety of cultural reasons, such as late planting, shortage of nutrients or water, or simply cool and dull growing conditions during the summer. So if price is an issue, this size is acceptable.

40/45–60cm (16/18–24in): This is the optimum size to choose for hedge planting. It is the half-way point in terms of cost and quality. At this size the plants have grown well from a seedling and put on good root growth, and are a manageable size for planting at a fair price.

60–90cm (24–36in): This is the largest size recommended for hedge planting. The plants are much more robust, and have a greater visual impact when planted out. As this size will cost more, it is usually only selected for garden or commercial sites where the customer is prepared to pay a premium to get an instant result. The larger plants have a bigger root system, which will require a bigger planting hole: a further addition to the planting cost. For farm and other rural planting sites the smaller 40/45–60cm size is to be preferred.

Site Preparation

There are a number of ways to prepare the ground in advance of planting; these will vary according to soil type and ground cover. The best course of action is to plan well ahead to ensure that the site will be in an ideal condition for planting in the autumn. Do *not* leave preparations to the last minute or until late in the planting season, as both will result in poor establishment and subsequent slow growth.

The site may be an arable field with the proposed planting line within the present cropping area. Prepare and drill the crop, including the proposed hedge site, with the intended autumn-sown cereal crop of winter barley, wheat or oats – but not oilseed rape. Later, in the early winter, hand or machine plant the new hedge directly into the young cereal crop, which will grow up to nurse and protect the young plants throughout the following spring and summer from the extremes of heat, drought and wind. The taller growing corn also encourages the young hedge plants to grow upwards to the light.

Where heavy soils discourage prior cultivations, prepare a clean site by regular mowing or the use of herbicides, such as Glyphosate. Following this surface clearance, spread a mulch of wood chippings, rotted straw, farmyard manure or other material to prevent weed re-growth and to provide extra humus to be incorporated prior to planting.

Alternatively, on heavy soils, plough along the proposed planting line in the dry summer months and thereafter keep the ploughed land clean with a contact or translocated herbicide to prevent weed re-growth. In the following months the soil along the ploughed strip will break down to become more friable and so produce a better tilth for autumn planting.

It may not be possible to carry out prior cultivations; for instance, the site may be too close to other physical objects such as a neighbour's wall or fence to allow for the use of machinery. Cut down any rank grass or weed cover, and keep the cleared site weed free by the application of herbicides or simply by further regular mowing.

A black polythene strip can be used whether or not the land has been cultivated. Mow down any weed cover, lay the polythene sheet (200-gauge thickness) to cover the full width of the planting line, and dig in the edge of the sheet. Ensure that the sheet is wide enough to be securely dug in.

At planting time lift one side of the film to expose the full width of the planting area and roll the film to one side. Plant the hedge as planned, be it a single or a staggered double line of plants. After planting, cut off the top growth of all the plants to a height of 15cm (6in) above the ground. Re-lay the black polythene sheet across, and over, the cut-back hedge plants, and dig the edge back into the same position as before. Finally, walk along the covered line of trimmed plants pushing the cut stems through the polythene. This reveals the plants but none of the underlying soil is exposed to light, so preventing weed growth and conserving moisture. The cut back plants will grow away vigorously in the spring without the check from weeds and with retained soil moisture.

Having paid a higher price for robust transplants it may seem a waste to cut off most of the top growth that one paid for, but experience has shown that this method is the best way to obtain stronger, upright growth in the first year. The nineteenth-century hedge planters cut back all their plants in this manner to obtain healthy and strong growth in the shortest possible time, especially where they were unable to control weeds after planting.

The Planting Season

Planting can commence as soon as the transplants are dormant and fit for lifting in the nursery, which is normally at the end of October or early November. The nurseryman will let you know how early he can lift plants, according to the season. Planting can then continue until early March at the latest. Don't plant any later than this in case there is a dry spell in late March or April; the newly planted transplants will not have been able to become established in such a short time, before the end of their winter dormancy and subsequent bud break in April. The optimum period for planting is from early November to the end of January inclusive, and if it is carried out then, there will be sufficient time for the roots to become established in the soil and to have begun to send out new root growth to supply the plant with its water and nutrient needs before the onset of spring growth.

It will not be possible to plant on all winter days. Do not plant during frosty conditions (below 0°C/ 32°F), nor on very wet or windy days. Wet soil can puddle when firming up around the plants with one's feet, causing anaerobic conditions around the roots, which prevents them from 'breathing' and so reduces new growth.

In windy weather there is a risk that the tender bare roots could be desiccated before being planted if adequate care is not taken to ensure that they are kept well covered right up to the moment of planting. Do not lay the plants out on the ground in advance of planting; keep them damp in the shelter of the planting bags until it is their turn to be planted.

Potted evergreen plants such as holly, laurel and green privet should not be planted when there is a risk of severe frosts; plant early in the planting season (November) or later in early spring to minimize the risk of frost scorch to their leaves, which may occur if such plants have not been hardened off in the same way as a field-grown transplant.

Hedge Site

Having decided on the position of the new hedge, allow adequate space for the hedge to grow to its anticipated mature height and width. A mature hedge can spread to cover a width of nearly 2m (6.5ft) for single-line planting or up to 3m (10ft) if planted as a staggered double line. If the hedge is to be planted on a roadside verge or bordering a lane, ensure that it is sited sufficiently back from the roadway to allow for the safe passage of vehicles, or wider harvesting machinery if on a farm road. Leave wide accesses for entrances into fields, and provide the necessary sight lines for vehicles exiting the property entrance, field or lane.

Do not plant hedges close to existing fences or walls, where later growth could damage the foundations or become entangled in the fencing.

Always keep one's neighbours informed about plans to plant a new hedge, and preferably consult them about your choice of plants and the plan for its longer term care and maintenance, especially if one side of the new hedge borders their property. We are all aware of the bad publicity in recent years from the thoughtless planting of the very vigorous Cypress Leylandii to screen one neighbour from another. All too soon it results in a lot of ill-feeling from the neighbours as the hedge quickly grows too tall and becomes a nightmare to control, shading their gardens from their share of sunlight and affecting the growth of plants on their side of the hedge.

The marking out of the proposed planting line can be achieved in several ways:-

- If the hedge line has been cultivated in advance, this should be done as straight as possible, so that the cultivator tine marks can act as line indicators.
- Planting into a ploughed furrow should again provide the straight line required.
- For planting into a strip desiccated by herbicides you will have to lay a line if the dead sward is not an adequately straight marker.
- If any of the above aids to providing a straight line do not exist, there will be no alternative but to lay a string or cord line, stretched tight and held in place with canes hooked into the line at regular intervals.

Care of Plants Before and During Planting

Choose a collection date for the plants that is as close as possible to the day/s when you intend to do the planting. Examine the plants upon collection to ensure that they are freshly lifted, the roots are moist, and that the different variety bundles are adequately labelled. If the roots have dried in transit, give them a good soaking in a water trough, or water them with a fine hose, placing them back into clean, strong, black plastic bags. Tie the neck of the bags tightly to prevent the roots from drying out, and store the bags in a dark, cool, frost-free room ready for planting within a few days.

If you take delivery of the plants and are unable to plant them all within a few days, it is advisable to dig a small trench and 'heel in' the bundles of plants close together with their roots well covered with soil to prevent drying or frost damage, ensuring that all are labelled so that you know the different varieties and quantities of each. Once heeled in, the pressure is not so great to proceed immediately with the planting; one can lift as many bundles as required and plant according to the time available. Do not plant in frosty or wet conditions, and

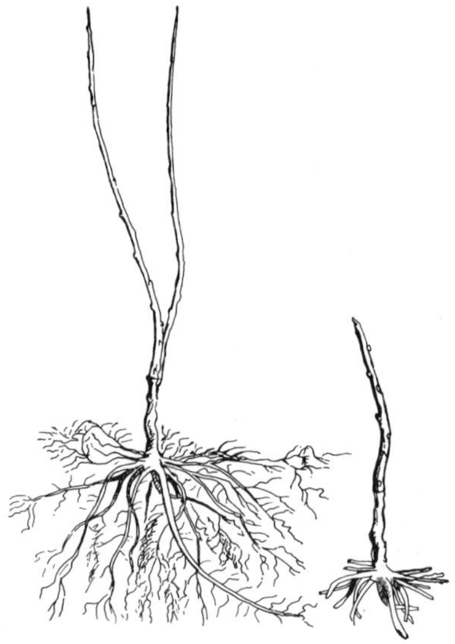

The illustration from William Cobbett's book The Woodlands (1825), showing how he wished to see sturdy transplants trimmed back before planting. This is an excellent illustration of how it should still be done to ensure good establishment and growth after planting.

take care if collecting plants during frosty weather; ensure that the bundles of plants are well covered in transit.

William Cobbett, writing in 1825, recommended the practice of cutting back the tops of the plants prior to planting. Pruning both the top and the roots is still regarded as being the best way to stimulate fresh, vigorous new growth. Depending upon the size of plants purchased, cut off at least a quarter of the total root and also cut back the tops by a quarter to encourage the formation of new young roots and vigorous top growth the following year.

Most nurserymen still practise pruning back the tops and roots of young seedlings or transplants prior to planting out in the

Bundles of wild crab (left) and common dogwood (right) transplants, trimmed and ready for planting. Note the difference in the amount of root on the two species. The wild crab has a compact root system that is common to many other species, but the dogwood is much more fibrous and bulky, requiring a bigger hole or a much wider slit to accommodate it adequately.

nursery to form stronger plants in the following growing season. We must never be too proud to acknowledge the good planting practices of our predecessors from the eighteenth and nineteenth centuries. The majority of our mature hedgerows date from these times, and remain a testament to the enduring quality of their work.

Marking Out

Prior cultivations, such as plough furrows or cultivator tine marks, may provide the straight line mark required for planting.

Some of the following suggested planting methods will provide the straight line necessary, but if not, there is no alternative but to lay out a string line. The line should be stretched tight and straight and held in place by canes hooked into the line at regular intervals. It will need two people to lay a line straight – one to sight from one end to the other, while the other positions the intermediate canes.

SINGLE ROW PLANTING

Cultivated Ground

Most of the old enclosure hedges from the late eighteenth and nineteenth centuries were closely planted single rows of hawthorn and some of blackthorn. The planting of single rows is still very acceptable, so long as adequate numbers of plants are used to ensure a good, dense stand that will keep livestock or the weather at bay.

Cultivate a strip of ground a metre wide to a depth of a spade, about half a metre, to provide friable, weed-free soil for good easy planting. Strong two-year-old transplants should be lined out at 20cm (8in) intervals, and after planting, cut the hawthorn and other plants back to 45cm (18in) above the ground.

Ploughed Trench

The use of a single-furrow plough to 'dig' out a planting trench not only speeds up the work when planting long lengths of hedge, it provides a straight line to work to, and the open furrow allows for a good root run between the lined-out plants. Line the plants against the furrow wall, and simply replace the soil, firming up the plants well; ensure the replaced soil between the plants is also level and firm.

Planting into a ploughed trench. Note how the furrow wall provides a straight planting line. Once each plant is positioned, simply draw friable earth from the adjacent ploughed furrow, and firm up around the plant. Note the plants in the white storage bag; keeping the plants in the bag right up to the moment of planting keeps them moist: do not allow them to dry out by laying them out in advance. Always place the open end of the bag away from the wind to prevent the plants drying in the bag.

Ploughed-up Ridge

For areas with limited topsoil depth, poor drainage or adverse soil conditions, it may be worth considering using the ploughed ridge or crown method of planting.

In the summer prior to planting, mow down all grass and weed cover before using a plough to make a traditional opening and return pass to form a 'crown', or soil 'cairn' as it is termed in North Wales. Keep this ploughed ridge free of weeds with herbicides until planting the single line of plants into the ridge in the autumn before wet winter weather.

The plough-inverted turf will rot down in the late summer to provide better drainage and planting conditions on heavier soils in the early autumn. The weed-free, ridged soil will also become more friable with drying and weathering in the late summer, making it easier to plant into in the autumn.

Notch (or Slit) Planting

Notch or slit planting is the cheapest and quickest planting method, but can only be achieved by using seedlings (1+0), or the smallest size of transplants (1+1) with a reduced root system that will fit into the narrow confines of the slit opened up by a spade. These seedlings will require trimming back in the same way that transplants are trimmed.

Insert the spade into the soil to its full depth, and then move it vigorously backwards and forwards to open a slot wide enough to accommodate the root, spreading them out before heeling up firmly. A variation of the single slit is to cut two slits in the shape of a 'T', placing the plant into the junction of the two slits. This provides a bigger area into which to place the root, but it is still only really suitable for the planting of small

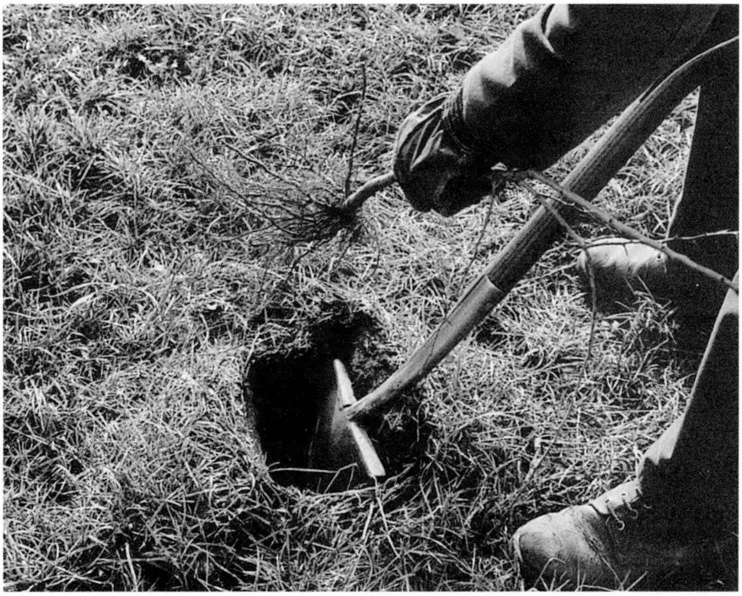

Notch, or slit, planting. A wide slit is opened by working the spade back and forwards to an adequate depth, according to the length of the roots. Place the plant into the opening behind the spade, ensuring that the roots are spread out before allowing the earth, or turf, to fall back as the spade is withdrawn.

seedling plants; smaller two-year-old transplants can be planted by this method.

Spacing

A single-line hedge needs to be spaced closely, at 20cm (8in) apart, to ensure that any gaps from dead or slow-growing plants can be filled by extra growth from adjacent plants. The line should be planted with bushy and vigorous species to provide adequate growth to achieve the required density from the mature hedge; use hawthorn, blackthorn, wild plum, hazel and possibly field maple.

A minimum of 60 per cent of the plants should be either hawthorn or blackthorn, with the other species mixed in for variety. A suggested mix is 60 per cent hawthorn, 10 per cent blackthorn, 10 per cent hazel, 10 per cent field maple and 10 per cent wild plum. There are numerous combinations of different species and different percentages according to soil type, local species suitability, individual hedge requirements, and personal preferences. All these factors are dealt with in other parts of the book (*see* Chapter 2).

DOUBLE ROW PLANTING

Cultivated Ground

As with single row planting, the best results are achieved by prior cultivation or ploughing to prepare weed-free, easy planting conditions that will ensure the roots of the young plants have the right environment to establish quickly and grow away strongly in the spring.

Ploughed Trench

The use of a two- or three-furrow plough is preferable for providing a wide enough cultivated strip to accommodate the two rows that are usually spaced half a metre (18in) apart. There will be more soil to move and level off after planting the two rows on either side of the ploughed strip because the plants are spaced at wider intervals in each row, but the physical work is likely to be achieved more quickly than digging each hole by hand into uncultivated land.

Plant each row at a spacing of 40cm (16in) between plants, staggering the plants in the second row, placing them between the positions of those in the first row.

Pit planting. Dig out a hole that is of adequate size and depth to accept the root easily, placing the soil close to the side of the hole. Stand the plant in the hole and spread the root out before replacing the soil carefully around the roots. Tread the soil down firmly without too much pressure, which could result in compaction

The tractor wheel marks or the ring roller lines, across the cultivated ground, can be used as a planting line, in the absence of any other marker.

Pit Planting

Use a clean, sharp garden spade fitted with foot treads for digging the holes. Each hole should be dug to the depth and the width of the blade. Place the soil close to the edge of the hole and loosen the compacted soil in the bottom of the hole. Place the plant into the hole, spreading its roots out evenly and fully.

As the soil is replaced around the roots, gently shake the plant up and down in short strokes to ensure that the soil percolates in amongst the roots. Finally, replace the rest of the soil and firm by treading gently around the stem. Take care not to puddle the soil if conditions are wet.

If the soil dug from the hole is of poor quality or lacking in organic matter, import some better, nutrient-rich topsoil from the edge of an adjacent arable field. The use of commercial planting composts is not recommended for farm or country hedge planting; the plants should be capable of establishment in most farm soils without such an added expense.

Tine or Subsoiler 'Slot' Planting

A tine cultivator or sub-soiler can be drawn through the soil to open and loosen the soil along the proposed planting lines. Two passes in opposite directions, returning along the same line as the first pass, will provide marked lines with the soil nicely loosened to make hole digging much easier, as well as obviating the need for marking the line. The resulting slots should require less effort to open up with a spade to the required size for planting.

Remember to spread the roots out evenly and firm around each plant. Also firm the ground between the plants to close the tine channel lines; this will remove any remaining air pockets, which would prevent the roots from growing properly. The underground effect of the tine's passage will have loosened the compacted soil on either side of each plant, so making it easier for the young roots to grow out into their immediate surroundings.

Notch, or Slit Planting

This method is normally only used for planting small seedlings and so is not recommended unless the ground has been well prepared, making it easy to open up a wide enough slot to be able to spread out the bigger root system of normal transplants (1+1), which are recommended for all garden or field hedge planting.

The potential problems with slit/notch planting are these:

- The slit may not be big enough to accommodate the roots properly, even when using the 'T' double slit method.
- The sides of the slit may be smeared or compacted by the spade in the opening process.
- An open slit in heavy or clay soils may not close up fully around the roots, leaving an air pocket and probably smeared sides, both of which will prevent growth. This can stunt growth or cause the plant to die from lack of root development.
- Slit planting by its very nature is a quick and potentially easier way to plant. It is used more by contract planters than by those doing the work themselves, because the former are probably on an agreed price for planting, which does not allow adequately for a decent job to be done.

Speed should not be allowed to influence the quality of the work. If the work is done in a hurry it will result in higher plant losses and poor growth, which means that the dead ones will have to be replanted next season and the rest will not make as much growth as they would if they had been carefully pit-planted. A year's growth could be lost and the hedge will take longer to reach maturity than it would if the work had been done with greater care at the outset.

For both pit and slit planting, the ground should be cultivated beforehand to provide good soil conditions. It is not recommended to plant into a compacted grass sward, even if the area has been cleared of weed by mowing or desiccation with a herbicide. Compacted soil may not kill the plants, but it will stunt growth, which is nearly as bad. The hedge could take several years to overcome the effects of initial soil compaction.

Machine Planting

Purpose-built tree planters for mounting on the back of a tractor are available, and worth considering for those planning to plant long stretches of hedges over a number of years. An alternative is to buy an old vegetable transplant machine, which can be easily adapted to plant transplants very successfully. Similar machines are used by commercial tree growers for their planting work.

Hand-fed machines speed up the work, improve the quality of planting, regulate plant spacing, and help to maintain straight-line working, without the need for markers or tape lines.

Hand planting remains the most common way to plant hedges, but those involved in commercial hedgerow planting, or those committed to a long-term planting programme, should seriously consider either buying, making or borrowing a suitable machine to be able to gain all the benefits from machine planting, which include savings on labour and time costs.

It may be possible to hire a suitable machine from a local nurseryman or vegetable grower, who would not be using it much during the winter months. Another option is to purchase such a machine second-hand.

Not all hedges can be planted by machine because there may not be adequate space for tractor access. The proposed hedge may be too close to a fence, a wall or a roadside verge, or on a steep slope, or some other physical obstacles may require planting to be done by hand.

The author's experiences over a number of years indicates that where machine planting is possible, worthwhile savings on labour costs will pay for the purchase or hire of the machine. It is hard to accurately define the savings possible because there are so many variable factors influencing the speed and efficiency of the work to be done, such as soil type, weather conditions, available staff, site preparation plus the mixture and size of plants to be used.

Machine planting requires a team of at least three people to get the best from the process: a driver for the tractor, who can keep a straight line while proceeding at a very slow speed; an operator to sit on the planter; and one other person to supply the individual plants to the operator in the correct sequence, or to hand the bundles to him at the right moment to enable the tractor to proceed at a steady, uninterrupted pace along the row.

The operator on the planting machine will not have the time to select the different plants for a mixed species hedge: this work must be done by the other person, who must hand him the correct plants in the right sequence. If a fourth person were

Machine planting a mixed species hedge. The tractor driver ensures a straight line and sets the speed of work. One person (hidden from view) is sitting on the planter placing each plant into the furrow opened by the planter share. Another person selects the sequence of plants, handing each one in turn to the planter. The fourth person checks that the plants are upright and completes the firming up as the machine moves forwards quickly along the row. The other person in the picture was on hand to fetch and carry bags of plants; a non-essential luxury, but it ensured that the planting proceeded quickly without any stops to reload.

A view down on to the back of the planter, showing the operator placing plants into the share opening. Soil flowing around the share is guided back by a pair of coverers to fill in the planting slot. The pair of metal press wheels consolidates the ground once more. A final straightening of each plant and a little extra manual firming of the soil is necessary to finish off the planting to a high standard.

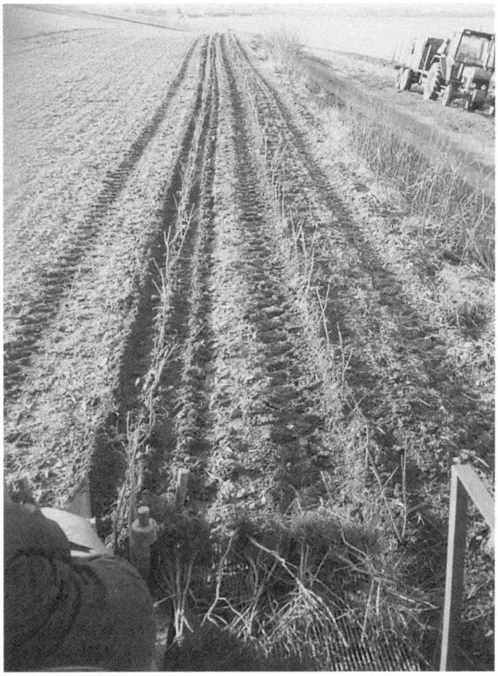

Looking back on the completed planting of two wide-spaced rows of a conservation hedge that will provide plenty of cover in the bottom of the mature hedge for wildlife. The hedge has been planted into a young crop of winter wheat that will provide some cover for the unguarded plants.

available, he would be able to help with the supply of plants, and then tread up the planted row with his feet to ensure that the plants were firmly held in the soil and that the machine share slit was also firmly trodden down between the plants.

Spacing

Double line planting requires that the plants are staggered in each line to provide the necessary even distribution along the finished hedge line. Spacing within each line may vary between 22cm and 45cm (9in and 18in), according to the type of hedge required. A stock-proof hedge will require a high proportion of hawthorn and/or blackthorn set at a spacing of 22cm (9in) in each row, to give a dense hedge at maturity that will keep cattle or sheep at bay; this equates to nine plants per metre run.

A conservation hedge, with a greater selection of species, should be allowed to grow up with minimal trimming to become a much wider based and open hedge. This will give the desired conditions for wildlife colonization. The plants should be set at 40cm (16in) centres in each row, to give five plants per metre run. The distance between each row should be at least 45cm (18in) according to the way the hedge will be managed. If the hedge is to be allowed to grow up with the minimum of trimming, then the spacing between the two rows can be set wider, at 60cm (24in), or even more if it is desired, especially if the hedge is required to provide game cover.

Mixing the Species at Planting

There are several ways to mix the species as you plant out each row, according to how you feel the hedge should look, but it is better to try and replicate the appearance of an older hedge so that the young hedge will grow up to look similar to old hedges nearby.

If the hedge is to be a stock-proof hedge that will contain mostly hawthorn with as few as 10 per cent of other species mixed in, then plant all the hawthorn with the other species planted at random, or as one in every ten plants at a regular spacing.

Where there is to be a greater mixture of species, as in a conservation hedge, more consideration must be given to placing the non-hawthorn species to present a natural effect. Some people like the 'block' planting approach, whereby the smaller percentages are planted in groups of three or four plants of one species. The problems with this approach are that it does not look like an old hedge that has evolved over the centuries, and it makes it harder for hedge layers to lay the hedge in the future.

The photograph shows a hedge with a 'block' of dog rose planted into a stretch of hawthorn. The thin and weaker growth of the dog rose will not provide enough material for the hedge layer to fill the gap adequately between adjacent stretches of thicker hawthorn. If the dog rose had been spaced out, or 'dotted' about in the hedge, it would be much easier for the hedge layer to accommodate the odd plants as he came upon them, leaving no visible gaps in the finished work.

Block planting of single species can cause problems for hedge layers, especially when there is a long section of dog rose that offers little self support. It is always advisable to mix the different species when planting a new hedge to avoid such a problem and to reduce the risk of disease spread. Note the thin section of laid dog rose in relation to the thick and vigorous pleachers of hawthorn beyond.

Assuming that the mixed species hedge is to contain over 50 per cent hawthorn and other species in 5 to 10 per cent batches, it is possible to work out a planting plan that offers a natural feel to the final plant mix. Set out below is a suggested approach to the mixing of plants in a conservation hedge containing the following mix of species:

60% hawthorn	= 1 in 2 plants + an extra 1 in 10 plants. (see actual layout list below)
10% hazel	= 1 in 10 plants
10% blackthorn	= 1 in10 plants
5% field maple	= 1 in 20 plants
5% common dogwood	= 1 in 20 plants
5% purging buckthorn	= 1 in 20 plants
5% dog rose	= 1 in 20 plants

This simple analysis enables the planter to draw up a planting list of the first twenty plants that can be repeated along the planting line, easing the layout and ensuring that the plants are well mixed to present as natural a look as possible for such a selection of species. The order of planting list could read as follows:

1. hawthorn
2. hazel
3. hawthorn
4. field maple
5. hawthorn
6. common dogwood
7. hawthorn
8. blackthorn
9. hawthorn
10. hawthorn
11. hawthorn
12. hazel
13. hawthorn
14. purging buckthorn
15. hawthorn
16. blackthorn
17. hawthorn
18. dog rose
19. hawthorn
20. hawthorn

The hawthorn are placed as every other plant, plus the extra two equally spaced out in the mix along with all the other species. It is uniform, giving the planters a usable pattern to work by that can be repeated, and it can be sure of using up all the plants correctly. The minor species do not appear that often, so avoiding an appearance of repetition.

CARE AFTER PLANTING

Weed Control

The control of weeds is essential for the survival and subsequent growth of the hedge. If the new hedge is planted into an old grass sward or other mixed sward, it will be necessary to control spring re-growth if no chemical weed control was carried out before planting. Desiccate the weed cover with 'Glyphosate' using a guarded spray jet around each plant, carefully following the instructions provided on the manufacturer's label.

Measures must be taken to control weed growth after planting to ensure good establishment of the vulnerable young hedge. Chapter 9 sets out all the options for the use of both chemical weed control and nurse crops to achieve this end.

DEFRA and FWAG can also offer the latest recommendations regarding the conservation options on weed control, which may differ from the commercial approach to controlling weeds for large planting schemes on farms or estates; such enterprises will have staff trained to undertake herbicide applications or to operate strimmers.

Should you decide to avoid using a herbicide to control re-growth, trim back the grass and weed cover with a powered strimmer or the careful use of a hand sickle. This 'no herbicide' approach will require repeating several times during the growing season, according to the weather and its effect on the growth of the weeds.

The new hedge will be capable of competing with other vegetation after two to three years of good, weed-free, establishment growth, but must be kept totally clear of competing vegetation to ensure good root formation and top growth.

Whichever weed control route one chooses to take, it is important to keep an eye on the young hedge at regular intervals throughout the summer to ensure that all weed competition is prevented, so enabling the hedge to establish a good root system from which good top growth can be achieved early in the first year, thus setting the hedge on a quick growth path to maturity.

At the end of each growing year, cut back at least a third of the year's new hedge growth to help stimulate next year's growth. Repeat the pruning process each winter until the hedge reaches its mature height, after which it is recommended to trim the hedge every two years unless it is required for stock control; in this case trimming every year is still recommended to keep the hedge growth tight and compact.

Watering

Watering is most important during the first two years of growth following planting. It is vital to be ready to water the new hedge as soon as any prolonged period of dry, hot weather arises in the spring or summer; the former is the most critical, as the newly planted hedge will not have formed enough new root growth capable of finding its own water needs in the surrounding soil.

There are various ways to apply water to the plants:

- A water bowser, which some farms possess for watering stock.
- A crop sprayer, an item that most farms will have; but take care to ensure that the tank is clean. The water can be gravity fed to the plants, or a hose/ lance can be rigged up to provide a more regulated and accurate application of water.
- An open-top tank on a trailer, with buckets to apply the water.
- Lay a polythene 'seep hose' from a nearby mains water supply, which will only require turning on at the tap for a set time to provide an adequate watering.

PROTECTIVE CLOTHING

Little has been written about suitable clothing to be worn when planting hedges. It is not simply a matter of choosing hard-wearing, protective clothing for outdoor work; the planting of hedges in the countryside involves handling prickly plants that can tear or snag on unsuitable clothes, and the thorny plants will also prick one's hands and legs if adequate preventative measures are not taken.

The choice of clothing has to meet several criteria: it must ensure that the wearer is kept:

- dry in wet weather;
- warm in cold weather;
- cool in mild conditions;
- free from perspiration even when fully protected against prickly plants or inclement weather;
- free to move without bulky clothing being a constraint;
- unburdened by weighty clothing;

- confident that the choice of clothes will withstand reasonable 'wear and tear', and be washable.

All these requirements can be met in most cases by the following range of protective clothing:

A one-piece cotton/polyester boiler-suit: This remains universal wear for most outdoor manual work. Cotton/ polyester is hardwearing, provides good protection against dirt, and is easy to wash. The fabric breathes well, so minimizing the problem of perspiration. Boiler suits are available in a wide range of styles, sizes and colours. They are not expensive for the wear that they will take during their useful life.

A pair of good quality leather boots: Dr Martens 'Air-Wair' boots have a long-standing reputation for providing a good, lighter-weight workboot. The cushioned sole, and the strong yet supple leather upper, offers comfort and freedom of movement. The sole is strong enough to withstand spadework. The uppers will benefit from being cleaned regularly and treated with 'Dubbin' or a suitable leather preservative compound to keep the leather both supple and waterproof. For those who prefer an even more robust boot with a reinforced/steel toecap, then the 'Caterpillar' brand is recommended.

A pair of quality rubber Wellington boots: These will be necessary in wet weather conditions. There are numerous brands, styles and different materials to choose from. Avoid boots made from plastic; they do not withstand prolonged spadework, and are more vulnerable to punctures from thorns or from the edge of the spade tread.

A pair of robust yet supple gloves: These are necessary to protect the hands from blisters, from cold or wet weather, and to deter the thorns of blackthorn and hawthorn. Cheap and lightweight cotton gloves may be adequate for digging work but offer no protection from thorns. Leather gloves provide better protection from thorns, but are liable to become hard when dried following use in wet conditions. Higher quality quilted leather gloves feel warm and remain waterproof for longer, but the extra thickness of the quilted lining restricts the movement of the fingers, especially when holding a spade or secateurs for long periods, and this can lead to cramp or hand strain.

Some expensive gloves have a 'Gortex' backing to reduce weight and provide better ventilation for longer periods of use.

The more recent introduction of a range of latex- or gristle-covered, cotton-based gardening gloves offers a good compromise between ease of use and durability, whilst providing waterproofing into the design. The cotton back of the glove is not latex impregnated, in order to provide ventilation and enable better hand movement. They give good protection from thorns. (*See* the illustration of different gloves in Chapter 13, 'Hedge Laying'.)

Forearm protectors: These are not readily available from protective clothing shops, so will have to be made up oneself, or made to order by a local manufacturer of lorry load sheets. They should be made of a close, hardwearing, cotton or thin canvas, tapered from the elbow to the wrist with elasticated ends to keep the protector in place on the forearm – a strong outdoor version of the casino croupier's black sleeves! These will keep the boilersuit arms clean, dry and free from thorn penetration. They will not restrict movement of the arms: on the contrary, they give better arm movement than from wearing a coat with thick, long sleeves.

A sleeveless, waxed cotton, lined 'body warmer': This garment offers maximum freedom of movement, body warmth, and protection from wind, light rain and cold conditions.

A set of plastic-coated canvas, or waxed cotton, leggings: Hung from the waist by a leather belt, these provide good protection from thorns, keep out the weather, and do not restrict movement as compared to wearing plastic over-trousers. Leggings allow one to move freely and kneel down more easily, and they offer better body ventilation when working actively.

A cap: Most people are unaware that up to 15 per cent of body heat can be lost from the head. Fewer hats are worn these days, but it is important to keep warm when working in cold weather in order to keep the muscles working freely. Not only does it conserve heat, but a cap will give both physiological and physical protection from the misery of working in the rain, if this cannot be avoided!

Those of us faced with constantly working outdoors should give a little more careful thought to the choice of suitable clothing for specific manual tasks that require ease of movement, and protection from the elements and against the prickly nature of some of the plants to be handled. The work will go much better if one is dressed correctly. Chainsaw operators are required by law to wear a range of protective clothing to reduce the dangers of their work, and to a lesser degree hedge planters need to be suitably dressed for their work, too.

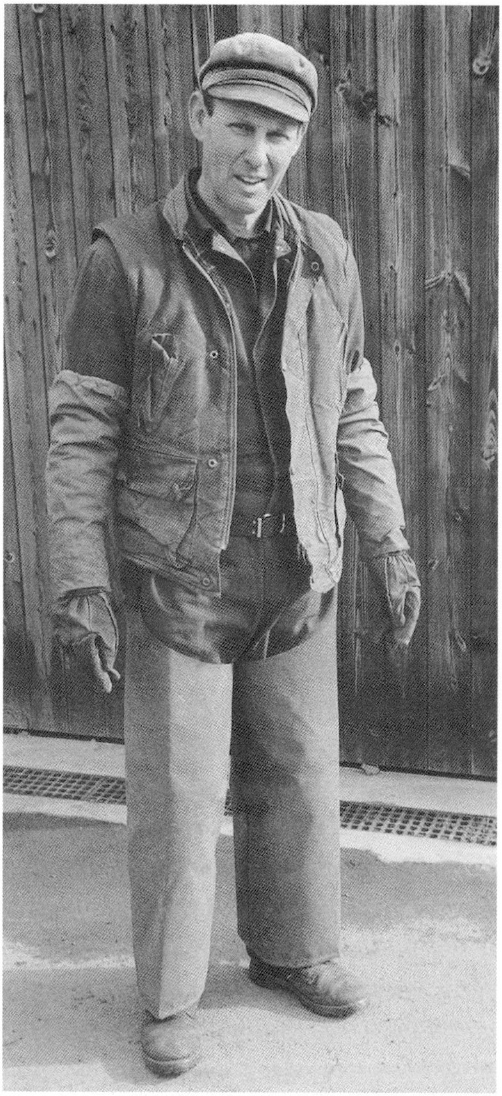

The author suitably attired for the prickly work of planting a hawthorn hedge. Plasticized, canvas leggings, worn over cotton overalls, protects against thorns and wet weather as well as allowing the wearer to kneel down if necessary. Gortex-backed leather gloves, forearm protectors and a short-sleeved jerkin also protect the wearer from the elements and the thorns, without restricting body movements. Some form of hat is recommended for outdoor work in cold weather; it has been calculated that up to 15 per cent of body heat can be lost from an uncovered head.

CHAPTER 6

Regional and Alternative Hedge Forms

Hawthorn and mixed species hedges planted to enclose arable and pasture fields are very common throughout England, but there are many regional variations of enclosure that have evolved to suit local conditions. The Cotswold and Mendip hill fields are bordered with stone walls, as are many lowland fields in Gloucestershire, Oxfordshire and Somerset. Stone was used because it was abundantly available from clearing the fields or by shallow quarrying close by. It may have been more expensive and time-consuming at the outset to build stone walls, but it offered a more secure boundary and was cheaper to maintain in the longer term when compared to the annual and regular work of gapping up, trimming or the laying of hedges, the latter being done every eight to nine years before the advent of mechanical hedge trimmers.

Cornwall, Devon, much of Wales and some of the adjoining counties feature stone-faced or turf-bank hedges, built to provide better protection for crops and livestock exposed to the strong winds coming in from the Atlantic.

By the 1970s conservationists were becoming concerned at the gradual loss of hedge-banks as a result of road widening and improvements. This led to the development of a new form of hedge-bank designed by Len Wade, a county council

A newly completed section of a Devonwade hedge-bank at Newport, Dyfed, showing the galvanized wire skeleton with its turf lining and turfed on top to prevent erosion. Also visible is an unfilled mesh extension prepared to form a banked gateway recess into the field.

surveyor at South Molton in North Devon. He designed a simpler and cheaper way of building hedge-banks.

He chose a galvanized, heavy duty wire mesh designed for the prevention of coastal erosion, and formed it into a narrow-necked, U-shaped 'basket' framework. The inner face of the mesh basket was lined with turfs, the rest of the basket being filled with earth and some small stone, all of which were usually available near to the road works site. The galvanized mesh framework provided the shape and stability for the new earth bank at a much lower cost than building it by traditional methods.

Len Wade's idea led to the widespread adoption of the 'Devonwade' hedge-bank throughout the South West and into South Wales, wherever new road alterations and widening schemes required the reinstatement of the original earth hedge-banks.

A view outside the cage, showing the steel formers and heavy braced boarding necessary to support the flimsy wire mesh until it is turf lined and filled with topsoil.

Building a Devonwade hedge-bank. A turf-lined section has been completed, and they are progressing with another section. Note the barrow-load of large turfs in the foreground awaiting use to line the inner sides as the section is filled.

THE DEVONWADE HEDGE-BANK

The foundation for a new hedge-bank simply needs to be compact and level ground; no preparatory footings are required. Galvanized 'weldmesh' (BRC No. 3610) or a similar approved fabric with a mesh size of 150mm x 75mm x 10mm SWG in sheets 3.75m (12ft) wide are bent to form an open-topped, tapered neck U-shape with a base width of 1.35m (4ft) and sides 1.2m (3ft 9in) high.

A closer view into the basket showing the steel formers in place on the outside of the cage, with three inner wire cross-ties to hold the bank shape in place once the cage is filled and the formers are removed. These are then moved forwards to support the next section to be filled.

A length of the basket cage is fabricated on site along the line of the proposed bank. Two large metal plate formers are fixed on the outside of the mesh cage to support the floppy mesh and hold it in position, like a pair of bookends, while that section is filled. Turfs are placed on the inner face of the cage with the grass side facing outwards to provide a 'living' liner, which will retain all the loose soil and any small stone core material. The core soil is placed into the cage by a digger bucket as the turf lining is built up the inside of the mesh basket. Early banks built by this method used topsoil for the filling, but this proved to be very unsatisfactory because the light and friable texture of the topsoil caused it to sink very quickly, and the bank collapsed. The problem has now been solved by using a heavier clay subsoil for the core filling, which does not sink, so remaining a good compact support for the turf outer lining. Clay soil retains its moisture better in dry summer conditions and does not 'wash out' in very wet weather.

A close-up of the filled hedge-bank; the turfs are already growing out through the wire mesh. Once the bank is completed the top of the bank will also be turfed to seal the top from erosion.

Galvanized wire ties of 8 SWG wire are fitted horizontally across the cage at close, regular intervals along the basket line to hold the filled cage in its correct shape once the former plates are removed and fitted to the next section. It requires a four-man team to construct the caged bank at a reasonable speed, one man on each side of the cage fitting the turfs up the inner wall faces, the digger driver filling the core with soil,

The same hedge-bank as in the photo on page 75, a year after its construction. Note the well established and vigorous growth of grass that is protecting the earth core. As the grass roots penetrate into the core they will be adding to the stability and strength of the bank. A hedge will be planted on the top in a year or so.

The same hedge-bank, as in the photo on page 77, in 2005, fourteen years after its construction, now with a mature hawthorn hedge established on the top of the bank and looking as if it has been there for a long time.

Severe erosion on the sides of a relatively new Devonwade hedge-bank, probably because the texture of the soil filling was too light; thus the turfs died from lack of moisture, leaving the sides vulnerable to the elements. In a high rainfall area it is imperative that every precaution is taken to reduce the risk of erosion. It also appears that the side of the bank is too steep, which would have aggravated the erosion problem.

and the fourth man working either within or at the open end of the cage to ensure that the earth is evenly compacted and to insert the horizontal wire ties as the filling proceeds.

The open top of the cage is not turfed, but filled proud of the cage lip with better topsoil into which the young hedge will eventually be planted. The cage is overfilled a little to allow for any settlement of the core earth filling.

The new hedge-bank is left to consolidate, and so the turf sides root well into the bank filling before the hedge is planted into the top a year or two later. If good quality meadow turf is used, within one year the bank will have become naturalized and the mesh will be overgrown and fully concealed. Any settlement of the filling may require further topping up with topsoil before the hedge plants are lined out at the rate of eight to ten per metre run, at staggered centres.

Grants are often available from DEFRA or the local authority for the restoration of damaged or overgrown hedge-banks, and for the construction of new banks in places visible to the passing public, such as beside public roads, footpaths or bridleways.

THE PEMBROKE HEDGE-BANK

Stone-faced or Pembroke hedge-banks are as common as turf hedge-banks in parts of Cornwall and South Wales. In many cases these wall banks do not have hedges on the top.

In South Wales, Dyfed County Council continues to use the Pembroke hedge-bank where road widening and road improvements require the reinstatement of an existing wall-bank, especially where

A Pembrokeshire stone-faced hedge-bank. A cross-section of its construction shows the large base stones with turf infill between them, prior to filling the core with good topsoil. The stones reduce in size as the wall rises. The whole construction relies on the angled sides being supported as each layer is built upon the lower, wider stone course, with the turfs acting as 'cement' to cushion each course and keep the earth infill in place.

The completed Pembroke stone and turf hedge-bank. Note the grassy turfs protruding out between the stones; they will soon grow to seal the wall sides from potential erosion. A hedge will be planted on the top of the wall in a couple of years to add height, and to enable its roots to add to the strength of the whole bank.

suitable stone can be found locally at a reasonable cost. A wall-bank takes longer to construct, and it requires extra skills to achieve the necessary quality.

The only preparation required for the foundations is to strip off the topsoil to a depth of 10cm (4in), so that the large base stones can be set into a firm and level ground footing, and to prevent them slipping outwards with the weight of the subsequent stone courses above. No other footings are necessary.

The Pembroke stone bank has a wider base than the Devonwade hedge-bank, starting at 1.50m (5ft) width and tapering to 0.60m (2ft) at the top. The height of the wall is the same as the turf bank, at 1.20m (4ft). In many cases a further 20–30cm (8–12in) of earth is heaped on top to form a domed cap, to allow for settlement in the months following completion as the earth core compacts.

Once the first course of large stones has been laid, good clay-loam subsoil is placed into the base centre. Thick turfs

A mature stone hedge-bank, now well overgrown from the original turf bedding between the courses of stone. The hawthorn hedge on the top is well established and growing vigorously; its roots will be playing their part in securing the wall from within.

(60mm/2.4in thick) are laid on top of the first course of stones, with the edge of the turf sticking out slightly proud of the stone face, to act as a bedding 'mortar' to accept the next layer of stones, which will be slightly smaller than the base stones. Again, the centre is filled with subsoil before another turf bedding is placed on top of the stone layer, and so the wall building proceeds upwards to a final height of four stone courses.

The two stone faces of the wall should be between 30 and 45cm (1 and 1.5ft) thick, and angled inwards at 45 degrees to the vertical. This, combined with the turf bedding layers between the stone courses and the soil core, forms a strong and durable wall. Within a year the turfs will have sprouted to partly grass cover the stone face, and their rooting into the core soil helps to bind the whole wall together.

A year after building the wall it is possible to plant a closely spaced double line of hawthorn transplants into the better quality topsoil used for the cap.

Dyfed County Council requests the wall builders to re-use the soil salvaged from the former old wall where the new wall is a reinstatement. This ensures that as much as possible of the insect population from the old wall is put back into the new wall.

Within two to three years the new wall will have become overgrown, blending into its surroundings as if it had been there for decades. It is reassuring that local councils in these regions take such care to retain traditional hedge- and wall-banks.

A HEDGE WITH TWO FACES

A stock farmer or anyone wishing to mix conservation with traditional hedge management could consider planting a double line hedge with a difference. The inner plant line of the hedge, facing a field regularly used for grazing stock, should be planted with hawthorn only, the small plants at 25/30cm (10 to 12in) spacings, to provide a thick stock-proof hedge that can be trimmed as required to keep it growing tight.

The outer (second) plant line of the hedge is put in about a metre (3ft) away with a variety of other conservation species, such as field maple, common dogwood, hazel, purging buckthorn, dog rose, guelder rose and wayfaring tree; the choice of species should be related to the local soil type and to personal preference. This plant line should be allowed to grow up with infrequent trimming to provide a better habitat for wildlife.

A 'hedge with two faces': the outer half, or field side, is planted with closely spaced hawthorn and trimmed to provide an intruder or stock-proof barrier, whilst the inner half is planted with a wide selection of more interesting and attractive species to provide either a taller screen at the end of a garden or as a feature for the benefit of passers-by, depending on its position.

This 'hedge with two faces' is ideal for a stock field beside a road, a lane, or on a boundary that is not bordered by another stock field. It will provide the farmer with a good stock-proof hedge to ensure that his animals are kept safe in their field, yet it will offer a good sanctuary for birds and other small mammals in the bushy, more diverse half. This diversity of species in the outer half of the hedge will also enhance the beauty of the countryside for the pleasure of others.

OSIER WILLOW HEDGES

The pollarded willows that line so many miles of our rivers and streams are a familiar sight throughout the country, but other traditional uses for willow are now rarely seen. The reduction in demand for basket-making material has led to a decline in the need for osiers – the long thin shoots, or 'wands', that the stools of *Salix Triandra* (the almond-leaved willow), *Salix Purpurea* (the purple willow) and *Salix Viminalis* (the common osier) produce in a one-to-two year cycle of cutting.

Willow is one of the fastest growing plants with a potential for hedging use. The very vigorous growth of a wide range of willow species make them suitable for planting as a windbreak hedge in moist and loamy soils. They will not grow so fast in dry, sandy soils but will still provide a respectable hedge within three to four years, as long as the new hedge line is kept weed-free.

The open landscape of East Anglia and the Fens could benefit from the wider use of hedges in general, and willow is an option to consider. The willow, with its many different coloured stem species, would break the monotony of the flat fenland fields, providing both protection to adjacent crops and a variety of useful by-products from a biennial cutting. There is the added benefit from planting the coloured stem species to provide superb winter colour.

A year's growth on an annually cut willow stool-bed shows the potential for a renewable hedge. If the line of willows is kept weed free in the early years of establishment, similar vigorous growth can be expected. A wide range of varieties and different colours are available to suit the purpose for such a hedge.

A tray of prepared willow cuttings, each about 30cm (1ft) long, ready to plant a hedge line similar to that shown in the above illustration. The base of each cutting has been dipped in hormone rooting powder to ensure that they all grow well.

Willow 'sets' consist of vigorous one-year shoots cut into 30cm (12in) lengths and simply pushed or planted into the ground in late winter (February to March) to a depth of 15cm (6in). An overall herbicide spray of 2.50kg Propyzamide (Kerb) per hectare after planting will control weed germination during the spring. A further top-up application of Kerb can be made as an overall spray, six to eight weeks later, in early summer, to retain the weed suppression throughout the growing season. The same weed control recommendation can be repeated the following year to keep the hedge line clean until the willows are well established.

The willow sets should be planted at 50cm (2ft) intervals as two staggered lines planted 1m (3ft) apart. This allows adequate spacing for each plant to produce a good growth of shoots, and the space between the two rows will allow the owner room to cut down one row each year in rotation, thus retaining good wind protection and the visual appearance of a thick hedge. The cutting down of alternate rows each winter will maintain the willow's vigorous growth habit and control the overall height and size of the hedge.

Short Rotation Coppice Production

Recent government initiatives for the production of energy from renewable resources has led to increasing interest in the growing of willow on a field scale to meet the potential demand from local power stations, who are being encouraged to source such supplies to replace a percentage of their fossil fuel usage. The planting of willow hedges to provide crop protection around exposed fields and for the reduction of wind erosion on light soils could be combined to provide a small income from the biennial coppicing of willow wind-break hedges to produce dry matter biomass for power-station fuelling.

If such a hedge is to be planted, it may be wise to select willow species that are more vigorous than the traditional species *Salix alba*, *trianda* or *viminalis*. New, more vigorous clones are continually being developed, with *Salix tora* among a wide range being trialled for growth rates and disease resistance, the latter being of great importance if the plantation or hedge is to remain healthy and vigorous over a productive lifespan, up to twenty years.

The use of willow for new hedges may not attract grant aid for planting in some areas of the country, but willow should still be given serious consideration in view of the new options open for a windbreak hedge that would pay for its maintenance.

Coloured Willows

If a willow hedge is to be planted for both its appearance as well as screening, choose species with attractive winter bark colours, such as *Salix britzensis* (a rich orange-scarlet), *Salix chermasina* (bright orange to red) or *Salix vitellina* (a striking golden- yellow).

Where wind protection is the main requirement, plant the taller and more vigorous cultivars *Salix alba* ('white willow', with a brown bark) and *Salix viminallis* ('common osier', with a green/yellow bark). Use at least two cultivars in the hedge, as this will reduce the risk from the spread of willow diseases, such as leaf rust and scab. It may be preferable to leave the rows uncut and maintain a dense and taller hedge for a few years; but the natural vigorous growth of willow will require controlling sooner rather than later.

In a garden situation, willow is being used to form woven hedges, arches and a variety of shaped structures and children's play 'dens'. Rooted willows, or simply long willow sets, are planted at 30cm (12in) intervals to form the hedge line or base foundation for the structure desired. The long wands are then woven to form a lattice as a hedge or to the shape of the arch, arbour, tunnel or other enclosure desired. In subsequent years the woven lattice must be close pruned to keep the vigorous growth under control and to ensure that young growth is maintained close to the original woven framework. It is likely that the vigorous growth habit of many willow cultivars will, in the end, become a problem, making it increasingly difficult to maintain the original desired shape of the structure.

HOLLY HEDGES

The principal advantages of using holly for hedging are that it is evergreen and produces an attractive, dense growth when trimmed annually. The drawbacks are that it is slow growing and will need protecting from deer, hares and rabbits during its formative years; but if you are prepared to wait for holly to grow, it will reward you with a superb final result. In its early years it will need to be watered during dry weather, as well as protecting from vermin.

The case for growing holly hedges in the countryside rests on their value as a source of cut foliage for the Christmas decoration and wreath trade. Holly grows naturally in the shade and shelter of moist woodland soils; a lot of the Christmas holly sold is cut from woodland or wayside trees. However, there are a few holly growers in the country who have planted 'orchards' for the commercial production of cut foliage. These are grown as individual trees or thick hedges that will get an annual pruning just like any other orchard tree or hedge to provide the 'crop' and to maintain the vigour of the bush. So, there is the option to plant holly for its attractive appearance, its screening value, and for the sale of cut foliage to provide some income to cover its maintenance.

A garden holly hedge should be trimmed once a year to produce dense bushy growth. Trim lightly when the new growth is between 10 to 15cm (4 to 6in)

Holly hedges: a formal garden hedge using both green and variegated varieties to good effect. Selected plants have been allowed to grow up above the trimmed level to form small, clipped tree forms, adding to the attractiveness and visual interest. The hedge is trimmed twice a year during the growing season to keep it tidy and to ensure that the growth remains tight to maintain a compact hedge.

long, usually during early July. As with many other garden hedge forms, it is better to trim 'little and often'; this results in less overall work, with less bulky prunings for disposal. The soft trimmings will wither quickly and not have spiky edges. Trimming holly later, in August and September, results in no re-growth, so risking the appearance of bare patches around the pruning stubs, which would be camouflaged with new re-growth if trimmed earlier, as mentioned above.

Most holly cultivars are either male or female. Only the female cultivars will bear a berry crop, so the ratio of male to female plants should be one to ten to ensure adequate pollination for regular crops of berries. It is possible to graft or bud scions from male cultivars on to branches of female bushes, thus removing the need for having any non-berried male trees in the hedge or plantation.

In addition to the native green-leaved holly, there are numerous variegated cultivars available to provide plenty of colour in the absence of berries due to the vagaries of the season or the attention of birds. The variegated cultivars have white to cream-coloured margins, and are so attractive that their presence can overshadow the impact and necessity for the blood-red berries.

If a selection of both green and variegated cultivars is planted to form a garden hedge, space the individual bushes at half-metre (20in) intervals, and allow for a ratio of one male plant to eight in the line. For a holly orchard, line out the plants at up to 5m (16.5ft) spacings in the row, with a wider access path between rows. In the early years this spacing will seem large, but given good growing conditions, each plant will have space to grow to form a large bush with a little room around each for access and pruning.

Choice of Varieties

There are numerous cultivars to choose from; those listed below are a small selection of favourites that have a proven record in a range of soils; and all have foliage and bear berries that are in demand for wreath-making.

Female Cultivars

Aquafolium: 'Common holly' is found in the wild in both female and male forms. Plants can be raised by collecting mature seed from healthy, vigorous bushes in the early autumn. The seed will take two to three years to germinate if sown direct into the ground after collection and is kept free from both bird and vermin depredation. Propagation is from semi-ripe, nodal cuttings taken during the period October to December; although these are difficult to root, they will ensure that one retains the same sex as selected.

The leaves are dark green with a glossy surface, and an undulating and spiny margin.

***Aquafolium* 'Golden King':** This *is* a female cultivar with a male name (the direct opposite to the male cultivar below with the female name!). The leaves are broad, green and almost free of spines, with a cream to golden margin. Another favourite of the wreath-making trade.

Argenta marginata: A vigorous growing, compact, pyramid shape. The leaves are broad and ovate, green, with an irregular, narrow, silvery to white margin, and an undulating, spiny edge. One of the best silver-variegated varieties.

Camellifolia: A vigorous, bushy, pyramid form. The leaves are oblong, very glossy, and dark olive green, with a smooth, flat and spineless margin, except for a sharp pointed tip to the leaf. A handsome form bearing bright red berries.

Madame Briot: A compact and vigorous, pyramid form. The leaves are broad, oblong to ovate, and dark green. The margin is cream to yellow, undulating, and with pronounced long spines. It has an attractive leaf.

Pyramidalis: A compact, conical and vigorous shape, becoming broader with maturity. The leaves are long, narrow, and glossy green. The margin is flat, smooth and spineless, except for an occasional spine close to the tip.

J. C. van Tol: Highly recommended for its heavy crop of red berries. The leaves are dark green, glossy and smooth, and the margin is spineless and somewhat convex. It is excellent for the Christmas wreath-making trade.

Male Cultivars

These are necessary for pollination.

***Argentea regina* 'Silver Queen':** This cultivar is male but has a female name! It has an attractive compact, pyramid shape. The leaves dark green, broad and lance shape. The margin is pale cream to white, with gentle undulations and irregular short spines.

***Argentea mediopicta* 'Silver Milkboy':** This has bright, dark green leaves with an irregular central cream blotch; the margin is undulating and spiny. A respected holly grower has observed that yellow-leaved varieties tend to be less winter hardy that silver-leaved ones. This is only an observation, but may be worth bearing in mind if you are planning to plant hollies in a low-lying area liable to frost damage.

THE HOLM OAK (OR EVERGREEN OAK)

The holm oak (*Quercus ilex*), sometimes referred to as either the evergreen or holly oak, is a native of southern France, Italy and Spain. It was introduced to Britain during the sixteenth century, and is planted as a parkland tree or in a large garden setting, where it will grow to become a well filled, bushy tree of character. It is noted for its dense foliage and handsome, balanced crown. Boucher, writing in his *Treatise on Raising Forest Trees (1775)*, noted that the tree will make 'warm and lofty hedges, 40 to 50 feet high, in a short time'.

The holm oak has a mass of dark green, shiny leaves that are whitish and downy on the underside; they are variable in size, and many are holly-like with spiny tipped edges, but others can be quite plain and untoothed. They

Leaves of the Holm Oak.

Holm oak growing within a hawthorn hedge and trimmed annually to add to the beauty of the hedge. Note that it has produced a good tight growth, similar to a well trimmed beech hedge, for which it is an excellent possible alternative.

remain on the tree all year, and do not fall until the arrival of fresh young leaves in the spring.

The holm oak grows better on deeper calcareous or sandy loams, rather than heavy or clay soils. It can suffer from frost damage in severe winters, but the scorched leaves fall to be replaced with a fresh crop of young leaves by the following summer.

The author has a few trees that were planted at random into a gappy hawthorn farm hedge. They have since been treated as part of the hedge, receiving an annual trim with a flail hedge cutter. The plants have grown well to form an excellent example of a close, well trimmed and tidy hedge that would make a fine garden screen, their glossy leaf surfaces contrasting well with their silvery and downy underside. The holm oak would make a good alternative to holly or yew, and would provide as good a hedge in a shorter time.

Gardening books list numerous shrub and tree species that can be grown to form excellent garden hedges. This book is primarily concerned with native plants found in the 'wild' (open countryside). I have strayed a little from this brief with the above descriptions and the uses of both willow and holly cultivars, simply because the use of these species crosses the 'borderline' through their commercial value to farmers and growers.

THE 'HEDGEROW HARVEST': FIREWOOD AND FRUITS

A hedge can do more than simply offer protection and screening: why not select species that will provide a 'hedgerow harvest' in the autumn, as well as carrying out their usual roles in the garden or on the farm?

Firewood

Traditionally, when a hedge needed trimming or laying, the 'salvage' of wood for a variety of purposes was a valued farm by-product that could be used for the benefit of all the farm staff, or sold to add to the farm's annual income.

If a mature hedge was to be cut back, rather than laid, the brushwood would be bundled to form 'faggots' that were stacked to dry and then used for fire

Collecting bundles of faggots, 1937. The caption with this picture from the Farmer's Weekly *magazine read: 'as time goes on, more and more hedgerows will disappear from England's rural scene'. The picture has been selected to show that there was a use and value to the by-product from trimming hedges, which was not wasted by burning in the field. (The Museum of English Rural Life, The University of Reading)*

lighting. The local baker would have bought such bundles of faggots to fire his bread ovens, and would have been a valuable customer to a local farmer because he needed firewood every working day of the year. The same could be said of those who worked on the land: there would have been a fire gently glowing in most grates to boil water for washing, cooking and cleaning. Another use for small bundles of faggots was to place in the bottom of drainage trenches where clay tiles could not be bought or afforded to drain fields.

Hazel rods would be selected and saved for bean poles or other plant supports, unless they were too thin and whippy, in which case they would be saved as binders for hedge laying elsewhere on the farm. If the hedger came upon any unusual stem shapes, or straight blackthorn rods with horizontal roots, they could be suitable for making walking sticks, or the 'hooks' used by the men when cutting grass or corn with a sickle.

Where willow was to be found in the hedgerow it was often cut by gypsies to make clothes pegs. Sometimes passing gypsy families would undertake hedge trimming for the farmer in exchange for the right to cut the willow for peg making. The varieties commonly used were common sallow (*Salix cinerea*) and goat willow (*Salix caprea*).

Most of the above by-product uses are no longer relevant to today's society, but we should be aware of what is available to us should the need arise, or for those wishing to revive a self-sufficient life-style, utilizing all that a hedge can offer as a by-product of its routine maintenance.

Fruiting Hedges

For a hedge to provide a source of fruits, it will have to be left largely untrimmed so that the individual species can bear their fruit, which they will not do if they are trimmed regularly, because this pruning removes the older branch growth upon which the fruit will be borne. All of us have picked blackberries from a hedge at some time in our lives: this is one of several fruits that can be gleaned from the hedgerow to make jams, jellies and syrups.

In 1945 the Ministry of Food produced a very attractive small leaflet, entitled *Hedgerow Harvest*, which listed a number of fruits that could be picked to make home-made preserves. To quote from the cover of the leaflet:

> There is a wealth of wild foods in our hedgerows and fields for those who are within reach of the countryside. None of this harvest should be wasted, but be exceedingly careful how you gather it in. There must be no broken hedges, no gates left open for cattle to stray through, no trampling of growing crops. When you go berrying, don't injure the bushes or trees. When you pick mushrooms, cut the stalks neatly with a knife, leaving the roots in the ground.

Here is one of those recipe options for using the fruits of the hedgerow. These fruits will provide the pleasure and rewards that are available to those who wish to spend a little time and effort collecting and preparing their own preserves:

> In the case of jams and jellies, it is important to remember that if they are required for keeping, the yield should not be more than 5lb (2.27kg.) of preserve for each 3lb (1.36kg) of sugar used.

The range of preserves listed included:

- blackberry and elderberry jam
- elderberry and apple jam
- rosehip syrup
- sloe and apple jelly
- crab-apple jelly

Sloe gin was not mentioned, probably because it was not possible to get gin during wartime, and it would not have been regarded as a healthy food!)

The leaflet also covered the gathering of hazelnuts, beechnuts and walnuts; they should be gathered when ripe and dry. Recommended storage conditions were given for each of the nuts. Today it is a race to collect the nuts before the squirrels get them, which would not have been such a problem in the days of more extensive game-keeping.

The period photograph shows children looking for blackberries. This activity gave them an insight to the countryside, and an understanding of the bounty from the hedgerow. Today's increasingly urban population could gain both pleasure and recreation from a similar involvement with their rural roots. Conservation and education groups should consider planting new hedges with a view to their fruiting potential, by adding in the species that have been discussed.

Hedgerow species with the potential for coppice, firewood and fruiting by-products include:

- hazel, for bean poles and plant supports, and also hazel nuts;
- willow, for basketwork and traditional clothes pegs;
- wild roses, for rosehip syrup;
- wild crab, for crab-apple jelly;
- blackthorn, for sloe gin;
- blackberry, for blackberry jam and cordial;
- elderberry, for wine and jam/ jelly.

CHAPTER 7

The Use of Trees in Hedgerows

During the early 1970s Dutch elm disease devastated the hedgerow elm population. Until that time we had regarded the presence of trees within the hedgerow as being a traditional part of the landscape of lowland Britain.

Elm suckers continue to emerge years after the original mature elm was killed by Dutch elm disease. In this case the farmer has cleared an area of suckers to plant a horse chestnut, a vigorous and fast-growing species that is capable of competing with the elm sucker growth to grow into a fine tree. The suckers are destined to grow for a few more years before they will be large enough to be affected once more by the beetle infestation and die back

The disease had been first recorded in Britain in 1927 as causing the widespread death of elms in some parts of southern England, but the epidemic declined after 1937, thereafter causing only local outbreaks. During the late 1960s a number of outbreaks of a much more virulent form quickly spread across the whole of southern Britain, and by the mid-1970s the elm population had been all but wiped out, leaving the hedgerow landscape changed for ever.

The loss of the mature hedgerow elm tree has now been replaced by vigorous elm sucker re-growth that appears to survive until the young trees reach a height of about 6m (20ft), when the disease returns to kill them once more. The disease is caused by a fungus, *Ceratocystis ulmi*, which infects elms but in itself is not fatal to the tree: the fungus produces a toxin that not only poisons the affected branch, but also stimulates the conductive vessel walls of the branch to produce a substance that blocks the vessels, preventing the conduction of water, so leading to death from lack of water. Two species of elm bark beetle then feed and breed under the dying bark, and it is the actions and life cycle of these beetles that exacerbate the effects of the fungus, causing the death of infected trees and spreading the fungus to adjacent trees. Until this cycle is broken no nurseryman will produce elms for sale, thus leaving us to consider what other trees could, and should, be planted into both existing and new hedgerows across the country.

The loss of such a fine landscape feature as mature elms on a winter's day is one that will not be restored in the near future. With time the sucker growth from old tree sites may develop resistance to continuing infestations of Dutch elm disease.

Unfortunately Dutch elm disease is not the only disease causing problems to foresters and land owners at the present time. In the mid-1990s alders were found to be suffering from a fungus of the *Phytophthora* genus. The disease has spread to infect some river and stream-side trees, although it has not become as devastating as Dutch elm disease. As we move into the early 2000s the concern for tree diseases is now focused on the appearance of a potentially damaging fungal disease affecting oaks. A new strain of *Phytophthora ramorum*, which is causing severe damage to oaks in the United States, has been found in Britain. Rhododendrons have been identified as the main host and source of infection, succumbing to the disease in a matter of weeks. The disease can spread quickly in a moist climate and is causing concern in the South West. There have also been localized problems from ash 'dieback'; a number of causes have been identified, but the main ones appear to be the action of the ash bud moth affecting trees that have suffered root damage from close ploughing.

Until recently farmers have not been enthusiastic about replanting hedges, and even less keen to replant hedgerow trees, because of their memories of the area of crops lost within the shade and root influence of large hedgerow trees. William Pontey, writing in 1805, was not in favour of trees within a hedgerow. He offered reasons that are as valid now as when he set out his views in his treatise *The Forest Pruner*:

> ...in hedgerows, dividing fields, where grain etc. is cultivated, the matter is of still worse consequence; as there is the shade alone, beyond the limits of the drip (of rain), frequently does more harm than the drip itself. Shade prevents the grain filling and ripening sufficiently, and also, has a direct tendency to promote the mildew; an evil, under which this country, at this moment (1805) is suffering severely....

Many of us have fond memories of the majesty of a fine elm on a frosty morning; its familiar spreading canopy covered in hoar frost against a clear blue sky was a sight to gladden many hearts. To the farmer, such a tree represented a large area of lost cropping and a constant source of extra work, clearing up fallen branches after each storm; but we must remember the beauty and value of timber trees in the landscape and make every effort to replace lost trees.

Some hedgerow trees were regarded as a good source of potential income, especially where they had been pruned and trimmed to ensure a good straight trunk for planking; or a tree whose branches arched in a particular way would have been selected to provide ready-shaped roofing timbers, or for making curved parts of farm wagons, such as the side rails or wheel rims. With the demise of wooden farm wagons and the importation of straight softwoods for modern lightweight roof trusses, the hedgerow tree lost its value to the landowner. It became a nuisance, and many farmers gladly removed it with the aid of hedgerow grubbing grants that remained available right up to the early 1990s, when the dramatic losses to our hedgerow heritage at last made an impact upon a government no longer wishing to encourage farmers to produce more food.

Today, farmers are being provided with increasing inducements, and requirements, both to replant hedges and to manage existing hedges for the benefit of wildlife and the appearance of the countryside. The climate is now right for the return of the hedgerow tree.

William Pontey (1805) readily accepted that some trees along a hedge are an attractive addition to the scenery, and they do provide shade or shelter for stock on a hot summer's day or during cold winter weather. There is also now an awareness of the needs of other animals in the countryside. Trees provide songposts for some birds, nest and vantage points for others. Rodents live and forage within their shade; all are part of nature's life cycle in the fields.

A mixed habitat of hedges, trees and adjacent field margins will ensure that a rich diversity of wildlife can live and thrive around every cropping field with minimal detrimental effect upon those crops.

The Forestry Commission Research Information Note 195 *The Establishment of Trees in Hedgerows* sets out the problems faced in planting trees into existing hedges, and how to overcome them; it also covers planting into new hedges. Planting trees at the same time as a new hedge will make the establishment of both a much easier task, as they will compete and grow on equal terms.

SUITABLE TREES FOR PLANTING IN HEDGES

The species most commonly found growing in existing hedges today are ash, oak, sycamore and beech. To a lesser extent one will find common alder, horse chestnut, aspen and a variety of willows, most of these latter being little more than large bushes. Ash and oak will be among the first to be chosen, but there are other species worth considering.

A mature field maple (Acer campestre) *growing in an old hedge. It does not grow into a large tree, remaining relatively small with an uneven, almost ragged, shape; but it is nonetheless an attractive tree that can be long-lived. It is the only maple species that is native to Britain.*

Slender branches and a rather untidy shape render the hornbeam (Carpinus betulus) *a somewhat ordinary hedgerow tree that is not commonly found. It is slow growing, and thus will not become a problem regarding trimming and maintenance.*

Old wild crab trees in full bloom along a parish boundary hedge. The crab (Malus silvestris) *grows into a spreading, untidy small tree, but is a great asset to a hedgerow for its superb display of spring blossom, which is followed by an abundant crop of small crab apples in the autumn. The fruits are very popular with many species of bird that will eat the apples both for the flesh and the seeds in the core.*

Small Trees

Field maple (*Acer campestre*)**:** A native of Britain that is common as a hedgerow shrub. It will grow into a small, slightly domed tree; it can grow up to 15—20m (50—65ft) tall. It is attractive for its ribbed bark and its pale green foliage, which turns golden yellow to flame red in the autumn.

The field maple will grow on most soils and is drought tolerant, so can survive on poor, or made-up soil sites.

Hornbeam (*Carpinus betulus*)**:** Another hedge plant that will grow to form a broad-headed tree. It is slow growing, does not attain great age (100—150 years), and rarely reaches more than 18m (36ft) in height. It is often mistaken for beech, having similar bright green foliage and smooth bark when young. This is a pleasant-looking tree, which produces winged seed that hangs in a cluster like a Chinese lantern. Its leaves turn bright yellow in the autumn. The hornbeam prefers moisture-retentive loam soils.

Wild crab (*Malus silvestris*)**:** This is a native to Britain, and commonly found in older hedgerows. It will grow up to form a small, bushy, spreading tree no more than 8—9m (26—29ft) tall. It produces a profusion of pink-white flowers in May to yield abundant small crab apples in late summer. The crab apples are an excellent food source for birds in the autumn, and can be collected to make delicious crab-apple jelly.

The distinctive columnar shape of the wild pear (Pyrus communis) *in full flower; a somewhat rare tree that could be planted more often as a hedgerow tree. Its upright shape, spring blossom and autumn fruits make it a real asset to the countryside. The fruits are very hard when they fall, but as they ripen on the ground they soon attract birds and other hedgerow mammals searching for a good source of food.*

The leaves and fruit of the wild pear.

The wild crab will tolerate a wide range of soil types, but will be more susceptible to mildew if it has to endure drought conditions in the summer.

Wild pear (*Pyrus Communis*)**:** A native, but rare tree that is worthy of further planting. Its compact, upright form and distinctive fissured bark with shiny green foliage are features that make it an attractive and interesting tree, ideal for hedgerow use. Its profusion of white spring blossom can be transformed into a heavy crop of small, hard pear fruits, many of which do not contain viable seed due to the absence of a suitable local source of pollen from other pear trees.

The wild pear will grow steadily on a wide range of soils to reach a height of about 12m (40ft).

Mountain ash (*Sorbus aucuparia*)**:** A small, slow-growing native tree with a compact upright habit. It rarely grows higher than 15m (50ft), and often much less than this if on an exposed site.

It will grow on a wide range of soil types, but does not like thin chalk soils.

Its upright habit makes it ideal for planting in a hedge, and its crop of bright red berries are very popular with blackbirds and thrushes.

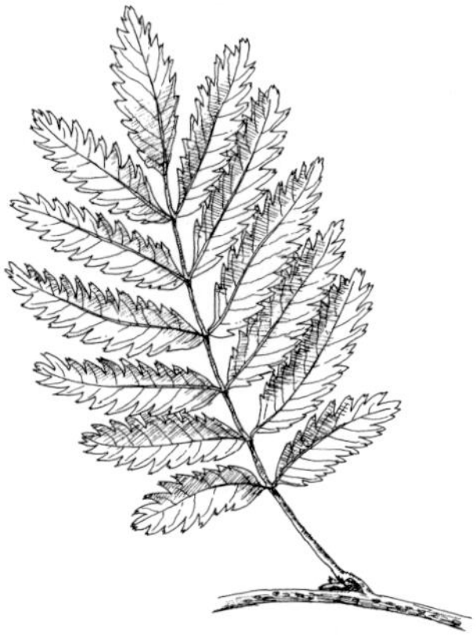

The leaves of the mountain ash.

Common dogwood fruits.

Field maple winged seed (keys).

Common dogwood flowers.

Field maple flowers.

Hazel catkins.

Hazel fruits (nuts).

Hawthorn ('May') flowers.

Hawthorn berries.

Spindle flowers.

Spindle berries.

Wild privet fruits.

Wild privet flowers.

Wild crab fruits.

Wild plum fruits.

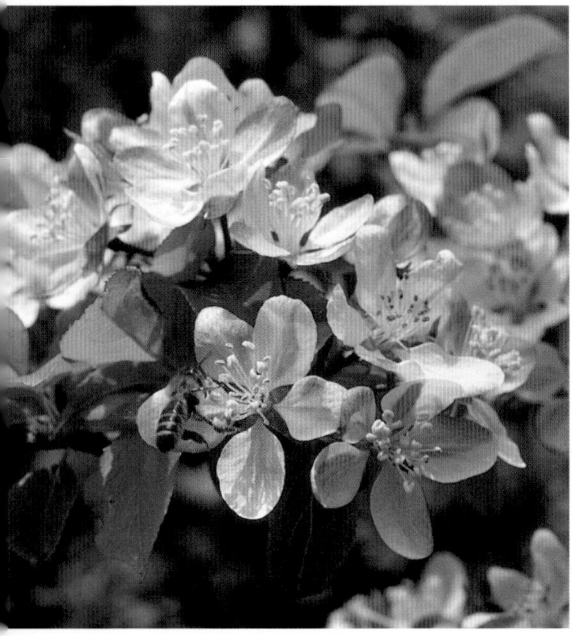

Wild crab blossom.

Wild plum flowers.

Blackthorn flowers.

Blackthorn berries (sloes).

Purging buckthorn flowers.

Purging buckthorn berries.

Dog rose fruits (hips).

Dog rose flowers.

Guelder rose fruits.

Wayfaring tree flowers.

Guelder rose flowers.

Wayfaring tree fruits.

Taller Trees

Sycamore (*Acer psuedoplatanus*)**:** A fast-growing tree that will develop a fine domed canopy in maturity. It will grow to a height of 30m (100ft) with a good upright trunk to keep it well clear of hedges. The sycamore carries nectar-rich flowers on pendulous spikes, which become the familiar winged seed by autumn. The broad and bright green leaves with three to five pointed lobes have distinctive pink to red stems.

It is currently out of fashion with foresters because of its ability to regularly produce large quantities of seed, which germinate readily under most conditions to produce a mass of young saplings. In a woodland setting these saplings need to be controlled to prevent their swamping other, more desirable tree species. Sycamore are at present a target for grey squirrels, who strip off the bark at the top of young trees to get at the sweet and tender sap wood, leaving the tree with a dead crown — a further problem for foresters.

Conservationists shun the sycamore because it is not a native species, having been introduced into the country some time between the end of the Roman occupation and the Middle Ages. But the reality is that the sycamore produces fine, hard, close-grained timber that has many and varied uses. The tree also supports a large number of aphids through the growing season, and it will be buzzing with bees in spring as they gather its abundant nectar.

With the growing implications of climate change and disease problems in some of our native species, it is time to become a little more realistic in the seletion of hardwood tree species. The sycamore is an ideal candidate for planting in a hedgerow where its seed productivity would not be a problem, and its ability to feed a large aphid population would be of great benefit to birds and other hedgerow inhabitants. Furthermore,

A mature sycamore (Acer pseudoplatanus) *growing in a roadside hedgerow. This tree is grossly undervalued by both conservationists and tree planters alike. It carries numerous aphids that are a valuable food source for many birds. Its flowers are rich in nectar, attracting bees from afar, and it also attracts many small mammals to forage under its canopy. It is better suited to planting on poorer soil sites because of its vigorous growth. It will also tolerate wind exposure and industrial pollution.*

The leaf of the sycamore.

Young and older ash trees growing on either side of a country lane. The ash is a hardy tree of vigorous growth, and is now one of the most common hedgerow trees. It has an untidy shape and can drop branches as it matures, but the quality of its timber and its ability to grow on a wide range of soils make it an excellent all-round tree.

in addition to the benefits it bestows on man and wildlife, the sycamore is a very attractive tree in the landscape.

Common ash (*Fraxinus excelsior*)**:** The demise of the elm has focused our attention on the ash, as it has now become the most common hedgerow tree. Many examples growing in hedges are subject to savage annual flailing, which results in numerous stunted 'mini pollards' that produce vigorous shoot growth out of the hedge top each season. A much greater effort should be made to tag these trees to allow them to grow up into hedgerow trees, thus escaping their annual 'shearing'.

The ash will grow quickly on a wide range of soil types to form an upright, open canopied tree. In poor growing conditions it will grow more slowly to produce an untidy, uneven shape with sparse branching. It is one of the last deciduous trees to come into leaf in the spring, and one of the first to lose its leaves in the autumn.

If planted into a hedgerow and kept free from the dangers of the hedge trimmer, ash can become a valuable timber source, with a little formation pruning in its early life to ensure a straight trunk. It produces a light, smooth-grained, hard-wearing, strong timber that is highly valued for the manufacture of coachwork, furniture, implement handles and for interior uses in house building. The best timber will be produced from trees grown on deep loam soils.

The leaves of the ash.

When a mature hedgerow ash has been felled, a number of new shoots will arise from the stump; one or more of these can be selected to grow on to be coppiced at a later date for firewood or for tool handles.

English oak (*Quercus robur*)**:** A majestic native tree that is synonymous with everything that is traditional in the English landscape. A stout trunk supports a broad, spreading crown. It produces valuable timber when felled in its prime, but if allowed to grow on it will become a tree of great age, with examples that are over 800 years old.

Whilst it grows quickly to produce a broad crown, it does not prevent a hedge from growing properly within its shade. In its early life it will not rob the adjacent ground of moisture and nutrients because of its tendency to produce deep tap roots to aid growth and stability. Later it puts out an extensive root plate with smaller tap roots; these combine to give the tree excellent drought tolerance.

The common oak will thrive on a wide range of soil types and can colonize quite poor soils if the seed is able to germinate and grow unhindered by grazing deer or other vermin. It earns high marks for its conservation values, supporting as many as 284 species of invertebrates living or feeding on a mature tree. Birds, squirrels, mice and other rodents are attracted by a good crop of acorns, which in turn attracts owls hunting for such prey at night. The oak supports more wildlife than any other tree species in Britain.

The **sessile oak** (*quercus Petrea*) is found in northern counties and Scotland, preferring higher rainfall areas and deeper loam soils. Like the English oak, it will tolerate poorer soils if able to establish itself, especially in older, natural woodlands. Where the two species grow alongside each other, hybrids will be found growing more commonly than the 'parents', making identification difficult.

The leaves of the English oak.

Fine, mature English oaks (Quercus robur) *growing in a roadside hedge. The oak is an excellent tree for both hedgerow and woodland planting for its visual appeal, timber value and its ability to support the greatest diversity of wildlife within its canopy. The richness of insect and small animal life supported by a mature oak is far greater than that of any other native tree.*

A line of mature common alder forming a field margin on low-lying land. The alder (Alnus glutinosa) *becomes somewhat bare stemmed and sparsely topped with age, but is an ideal tree to plant in wet sites or as a hedgerow tree because of its ability to fix its own nitrogen needs, thus making little demand on adjacent plants. It carries a regular crop of seed cones that attract flocks of finches in the winter months.*

Trees for Wet Sites

Common alder (*Alnus Glutinosa*)**:** A true native tree. It is found growing alongside ditches, streams, river banks and other damp sites. The alder is capable of growing in areas too wet for poplars and willows.

The alder will grow on a wide range of soil types where there is adequate moisture to form a small, short-stemmed tree (15m/50ft high at the most) with an untidy crown. It does not live to a great age, and its timber has little use beyond firewood.

Alders bear attractive catkins in the spring, and seed cones in the autumn. Its roots have the ability to fix nitrogen in the soil, so it will not rob adjacent crops of nutrients. The alder's nitrogen-fixing ability is one factor in the choice of Italian alder (*Alnus cordata*) as a windbreak hedge tree for protecting orchards and other valuable cash crops.

The catkins and leaves of the common alder.

Trees to Avoid in Hedgerow Planting

Common white birch: An attractive, small native tree with pendulous branches. It produces male and female catkins in the spring, the latter lasting until the autumn. The bark is white with horizontal lines and large fissured cracks on older trees. It is not a long-lived tree, but is a valuable source of aphids in the spring for tits and warblers to feed their young. Its relatively short life renders it unsuitable for hedgerow planting, where more majestic timber trees are to be preferred.

Beech and sweet chestnut: Both are large trees that spread widely from low down on the main trunk, ideal for providing shade to cattle grazing in a parkland setting, where competition with adjacent crops is not a problem. This feature is not ideal, however, for trees growing in a hedge beside field-grown crops.

Aspen and broad leaf lime: These trees are liable to sucker from the trunk base, and the latter is capable of growing to a great height, both of which features are not suited to hedgerow trees growing adjacent to farm crops.

Wild cherry: It is used in small numbers for mixed woodland planting but is not suitable for hedgerow use because of its spreading form and its inherent tendency to suffer from bacterial canker: this can appear when the tree is quite young, so reducing its useful life to little more than thirty years – or less in some cases. New clones selected for resistance to bacterial canker are available, but be sure that you choose a clone that has a proven record of being free from the disease; many have been found to be little better that the common wild cherry.

PLANTING

The establishment of trees in a new hedge is relatively easy because all the plants are growing away together from an equal start. Each tree will benefit from an individual mulch mat, and will require a tubular tree shelter and stake to encourage stem growth and protect it from deer damage, so ensuring that it gets a good start ahead of the adjacent hedge plants. These measures should also ensure that the tree does not suffer damage from mechanical hedge trimming.

Where 45-60cm (18—24in) transplants are used for the hedge planting, it is recommended that a larger 60—90cm (24—36in) transplant, or a 90–120cm (36—48in) 'whip' is used, to give the tree a head start. This will help to ensure that it is noticed, should the hedge be mechanically trimmed early in its life.

The young tree must be planted into a larger hole than those dug for the hedge plants, many of which may only be notch planted. Dig the hole at least 30cm (1ft) square and to the depth of the spade's blade, loosening the soil in the bottom of the hole to aid penetration of new root growth. Spread out the tree's roots evenly and replace the soil, ensuring that it is well mixed within the root mass by shaking the tree stem when the friable soil has been partly replaced. Firm up carefully with the feet on completion.

If the soil dug from the hole is impoverished, weed-infested, or of poor quality, it is often possible to dig up some clean, nutrient-rich soil from an adjacent cultivated field to place immediately around the roots. You may be fortunate to find some fresh molehill earth handy, which will be very friable.

Once planted, stake or cane the tree and enclose it with a plastic spiral guard or a tubular tree shelter for protection;

A tree shelter within a newly planted hedge line. The shelter will both protect the young tree and provide a 'greenhouse' environment to encourage growth. The physical presence of the guard should protect it from any early mechanical trimming, acting as a visible marker to alert the operator to avoid the tree.

the latter will have the added advantage of stimulating growth. Tubular tree shelters provide the young tree with its own microclimate – a 'greenhouse' effect, encouraging early and vigorous growth, free from cold and desiccating wind as well as preventing damage from deer and other rodents. Ensure that the tube is pushed firmly into the soil to prevent rodents from getting inside the tube to nest in the warm, sheltered conditions. Mice and voles that get inside the tubes will often eat the bark at the base of the tree, killing it quickly.

If the young tree is being planted into a mature hedge, it is important to tag each tree to prevent it being damaged by the hedge trimmer. It will be necessary to clear an adequate space in the hedge to accommodate the new tree. Dig a hole big enough to ensure the young tree has a good start, adding some fresh soil or a soil-based compost to give the roots a chance to establish and be able to compete with the adjacent hedge plants in dry conditions.

The position of trees in a hedge should be related to personal choice and to the eventual size of the mature tree. A spacing of 30—40m (100—130ft) apart is a

A young oak tree in a guard that protected it until a careless hedge-trimming operator could not be bothered to raise the cutter arm, cutting the top out of the tree and tearing open the guard – an all-too-common sight.

A diagram that shows how a mature tree plays an invaluable role in so many ways, removing carbon dioxide from the atmosphere and converting it to oxygen, operating its own recycling operation to enrich the soil, providing shade, shelter and food for both man and wildlife as well as adding to the beauty of our landscape.

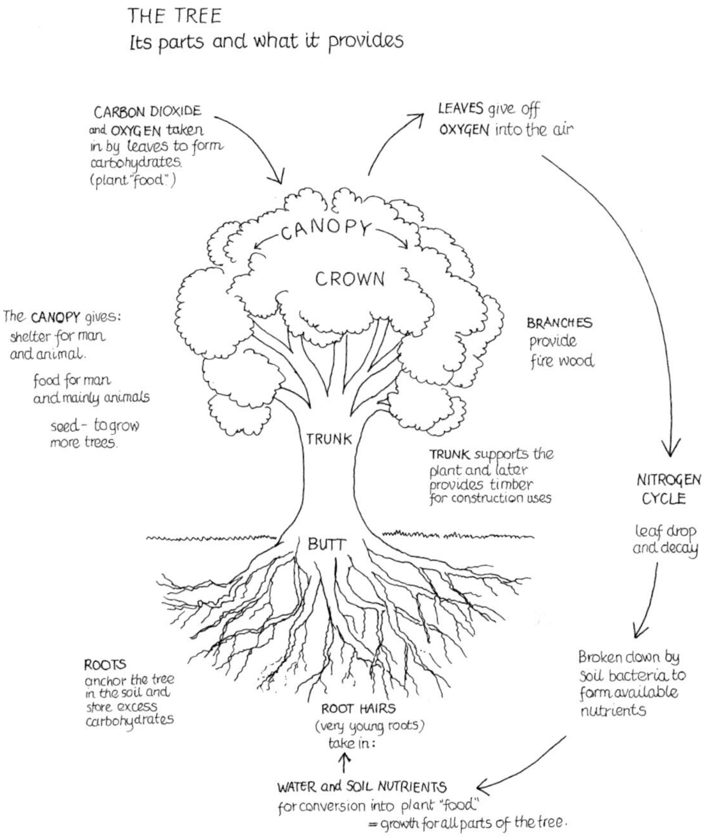
THE TREE
Its parts and what it provides
CARBON DIOXIDE and OXYGEN taken in by leaves to form carbohydrates. (plant "food")
LEAVES give off OXYGEN into the air
CANOPY
CROWN
The CANOPY gives: shelter for man and animal.
food for man and mainly animals
seed - to grow more trees.
BRANCHES provide fire wood
TRUNK
TRUNK supports the plant and later provides timber for construction uses
NITROGEN CYCLE
leaf drop and decay
BUTT
Broken down by soil bacteria to form available nutrients
ROOTS anchor the tree in the soil and store excess carbohydrates
ROOT HAIRS (very young roots) take in:
WATER and SOIL NUTRIENTS for conversion into plant "food" = growth for all parts of the tree.

good rule of thumb. However, it is better to space the trees at random to give a natural appearance, to blend into the surrounding landscape; if the trees are spaced at even intervals, it gives the impression of an estate avenue – though this is fine if it is the effect desired.

Physical or natural features may dictate the positioning of trees to give a desired effect – there are no rules that have to be followed, unless it is that they must not be planted too close to one another so they eventually crowd each other and stunt the growth of the hedge beneath their spreading canopy.

Beware of overhead or nearby electricity or telephone lines, or even pylons. Keep clear of buildings, walls and roadways. Try to envisage the area that the tree could occupy once it has grown to its full, mature size; hopefully this will overcome later problems of maintenance.

The full benefit and enjoyment from a new hedge can be realized within eight to ten years, but trees take longer to reach a size where they can be appreciated. We are now enjoying the beauty of mature trees planted in the Victorian era, so it is fitting that each succeeding generation should plant hedges and trees to maintain the continuity for the pleasure and benefit of future generations.

The simplified drawing shows how a mature tree and its constituent parts work together to create a life cycle of benefits that it bestows upon man and wildlife alike.

CHAPTER 8

The Value of Field Margins

Field margins are set to become one of the cornerstones of the government's future policy for the management of farmland, to improve the balance of nature in a countryside that has suffered as a result of the post-World War II drive to modernize agriculture. No longer is the need to feed ourselves the driving force. The new 'force' is the voice for the conservation of our rich landscape heritage.

The value of most arable crops continues to decline at a time of excess production across much of Western Europe, so it is logical the government should redirect efforts to restore the countryside to some of its former glory. It is not trying to turn the clock back to a romantic image of the Victorian era: it is the need to redress a severe imbalance within the fabric of the countryside.

The post-war boom in the discovery and use of an amazing array of herbicides, pesticides and fungicides has transformed crop production from being the skill of crop management using good rotations and husbandry techniques honed by generations of experience, to one of specialist crop advisers offering instant pesticide solutions to the problems arising from increased mono-cropping.

A wide field margin established to offer added benefit to any wildlife seeking shelter, and a food source adjacent to the hedge. The hedge should be allowed to grow up considerably and thicken out in order to provide a better habitat for both birds and mammals.

The drive to increase crop output encouraged farmers to cultivate as much of every field as possible, including field margins. The practice of spraying or rotavating a one-metre strip between the crop and the field edge to prevent the spread of sterile broom, cleavers and other unwanted weeds indicates that farmers are prepared to sacrifice some land to ensure a cleaner crop and higher yield within the rest of the field. Encouraging farmers to treat this 'hygiene' strip as a wildlife corridor and habitat should be only one painless step sideways.

Farmers will point out that to leave an unsprayed strip could lead to an influx of noxious weeds from the hedgerow. However, many of the problem weeds emanating from the hedgerow thrive on fertilizer inadvertently spun into the hedge bottom or because this strip has been sprayed or disturbed by cultivations. Where field margins are uncultivated and kept free of fertilizer and herbicides, it does not take long to restore a balance of vegetation in favour of a broader selection of grasses and perennial plants.

The provision of a sown two-metre margin around the field crop will minimize the intrusion of unwelcome weeds and provide a habitat for host insects, many of which – for example, hoverflies – will predate upon the pests in the field crops. FWAG has produced a number of leaflets on the creation and benefits of field margins.

CREATING A FIELD MARGIN

Crops growing close to a hedge will yield 10–15 per cent less than the rest of the field; thus if a margin is provided around the field edge, there is less to lose, as well as the saving on growing costs. The width of the field margin is partly a matter of choice. The government's new single farm payment regulations require the formation of field margins, but the land owner is free to extend their width if there are other management benefits to be considered, such as ease of maintenance of the strip, or to improve its value for game conservation.

The area for the margin can be marked out easily when ploughing or cultivating the field prior to cropping. The uncultivated strip should be mown to control any aggressive or noxious weed species, and to help convert the range of plant species to a better balance of flowering plants and grasses; these will re-establish themselves as the fertility of the soil along the margin declines with the absence of fertilizers and spraying. Natural regeneration is more likely to give better results on light than on heavy soils. Furthermore, a natural sward can only result if there is an adequate reserve of dormant seed in the soil itself, in the adjacent hedge bottom or on a near-by ditch bank.

The changes in the composition of the sward will be most rapid in the first two years; thereafter the rate of change declines. The dominance of annual plants is most noticeable in the first season; perennials will then begin to establish a dense sward and exclude the annuals. The dominant perennials will be those best able to draw upon the declining nutrient levels remaining in the soil.

For those wishing to ensure or to speed up the transformation to a diverse plant mix of wild flowers and grasses, it is possible to sow a chosen wild-flower seed mix to suit the soil type, or a mix for those keen to enhance the retention of game for the shooting season. The sowing of a wild grass or farm ley mix will help control weeds where natural regeneration chances are poor. Sowing is also a good way to establish an attractive plant mix that will enhance the margin. ADAS, FWAG and other local conservation groups will be pleased to help choose

Field margin trials undertaken at the University Farm at Wytham, near Oxford, in 1991 to establish which grass and wild-flower mixes could enhance the biodiversity of the hedgerow and field margin. Different seed mixes were sown and then subjected to different mowing regimes to find the optimum habitat for both birds and insects alike. The pale-coloured grass in the foreground is a section of cocksfoot between other trial sections.

a suitable mix according to the locality and soil type.

Land preparations for sowing margins with grass or wild flower mixes need to be as thorough as those undertaken for other farm crops.

SWARD MAINTENANCE

Comprehensive trials were undertaken on a clay loam soil at the University Farm, Wytham, near Oxford from 1987, to investigate the frequency, timing and effects of mowing on the establishment and development of both natural regeneration and sown field-margin swards.

Changes on experimental fallowed crop margins followed a similar pattern to that recorded on abandoned arable fields in North America during times of farming depression. A large number of plant species colonized at the outset, with both annuals and perennials establishing together. But by the end of the second season, a dense cover of perennial plants had effectively excluded the further establishment of annuals. Perennials were more adept at colonizing any remaining gaps in the sward.

The use of sown grass ley mixes proved advantageous over natural regeneration. For both regenerated and sown swards, mowing at specific dates was necessaryto prevent the spread of noxious and rhizometous perennial weeds. The inclusion of oxeye daisy in seed mixes gave an instant and dramatic visual impact, but it became less dominant if subject to spring mowing. All grasses included in the seed mixes established well, but crested dog's tail declined quickly if the margins were left uncut. Scabious and knapweed established readily. Cowslip required three years of growth before flowering – they germinated when freshly sown in summer or following a cold winter.

Problem weeds, such as sterile brome, blackgrass and wild oats, which flower in that order, required cutting at specific times to control their spread. Brome had to be cut early in its growth, before it bolted. The growth of blackgrass and wild oats was reduced by a summer cut prior to flowering, and declined within two years. Couch was similarly weakened by summer cutting. ADAS or FWAG advis-

The Salt Way, an ancient trade route and drove road running through Gloucestershire. The wide margins bordered by old mixed-species hedges provide an excellent undisturbed habitat for all forms of wildlife. Grasses, wild flowers and the hedgerow plants combine to offer both food and shelter in abundance, and so enrich diversity throughout the seasons.

ers will provide precise details of optimum cutting times related to the mix of flowering plants and grasses in your field margins; poorly timed cuts can be ineffective, costly, and may be detrimental to achieving the desired effect.

The encouragement to establish field margins is linked to improving the habitat for wildlife, and butterflies in particular. Many butterfly species do not move far from their established habitat, so you can influence the survival and spread of a particular species present in your margins by taking note of its habitat requirements and ensuring the necessary plants are present, and in flower, at the correct times for its life cycle. Many butterflies remain within one field area for their whole life cycle, and hedgerows offer an invaluable shelter to them. The combination of a hedgerow and its adjacent grass and wild-flower margin will provide the butterfly, as well as many other insects and mammals, with all the necessary 'ingredients' for a good habitat.

It is important to be aware that butterflies require different food sources for their larval and adult stages. In addition, different butterflies feed on different plants – small tortoiseshell live and feed on short nettles, such as the re-growth following summer mowing. Peacocks feed on tall nettles in south-facing, sunny locations. Meadow browns gather on oxeye daisy for its rich source of nectar. Their requirements are numerous and varied, a reality that will apply to all the potential inhabitants of a field margin and its related hedge. A good mixed-species hedge, allied to a margin with a rich flora, will go a long way towards redressing the plight of wildlife in the countryside.

The exclusion of fertilizers and pesticides from hedge bottoms and field margins is crucial if improvements in the diversity of animal and plant life are to be achieved. Fertilizer applicators should be fitted with a blanking plate to prevent the spread on to the field margin for the first bout round each field. Similarly the end nozzle of the sprayer boom should be fitted with a stop tap or a blanking cap to prevent chemical drift on to the field margin. Both control measures must become routine practice around the edges of all crops in order to prevent damage to wildlife, as well as helping to reduce variable farm costs.

CHAPTER 9

Weed Control

Good control of the competition between weeds and the young hedgerow plants is essential to obtain vigorous growth in the early life of the hedge. Once the hedge is established it will be able to compete with weed growth on equal terms.

Nurserymen successfully use a range of herbicides for the control of weeds in the production of strong transplants for hedgerow planting. These same chemicals are available to those planting hedges, and their use will greatly enhance survival and growth rates in the early years after planting. Grass and broadleaved weeds allowed to grow around a newly planted hedge will compete with it for moisture and nutrients, and may also harbour pests such as mice and voles, which can eat away at the tender bark at the base of the plants, protected by the weed cover. The large number of closely spaced plants in a new hedge favours the use of herbicides in preference to other weed control measures adopted for wide-spaced individual trees in woodland planting, such as the use of plastic or felt mats around each tree, which would be uneconomic for hedges.

The complete control of weeds in a tree nursery shows the strong and vigorous growth that is possible in the absence of weeds and with adequate watering supplied. The wild cherry plants have grown from 30cm (12in) seedlings into fine, saleable 90–120cm (3–4ft) transplants in one growing season.

ORGANIC MULCHES

The use of bark chips, compost, straw or other organic mulch material can be costly and time-consuming to spread. It is important not to spread the mulch too close to the stems of the plants to prevent mice and voles using the cover of the mulch to gnaw at the stems in adverse or dry weather conditions. They may also use the mulch as a place to hibernate.

If rotted straw or manure is available on the farm or from a local supplier, this can be a cheap mulch that will provide somenutrient value as well as an effective weed suppressant. Bark chippings or other shredded waste, such as tree prunings, will provide a better structured mulch with a longer life that is probably not quite so attractive to rodent 'squatters'. The use of this type of waste will benefit from the application of a little nitrogen fertilizer to help its decomposition, as well as giving the young hedge extra nutrients. The application of an approved residual (soil-acting) herbicide to the ground before laying an organic mulch can reduce the risk of weeds penetrating the mulch cover.

The Forestry Commission undertook trials to assess the effectiveness and longevity of a black polythene mulch versus herbicides: in fact both of these methods greatly enhanced the survival rate and subsequent growth of trees.

POLYTHENE SHEET MULCHES

In the trials, poor quality trees survived and grew away when protected with a polythene mulch, but died when planted into adjacent ground without a mulch. The trial highlighted the need for the polythene mulch to cover an area of 1.25sq m (14sq ft) around each plant. Applying this principle to hedges means that the mulch should be a continuous sheet with the plants planted through holes in the sheet – not an easy task.

The benefits from using a polythene sheet mulch are as follows:

- The complete suppression of weeds.
- Reduction of moisture loss from the soil surface by evaporation.
- Retention of nutrients, and moisture, in the topsoil.
- It makes the nutrients readily available to the young surface roots.
- The soil warms up earlier in the spring, encouraging early growth.

There is one possible problem, in that the polythene mulch can cause shallow rooting in some adverse soil conditions, which could render the young plants vulnerable to moisture stress should the cover be removed by accident, or before the plants have established themselves fully. For optimum benefit the polythene should remain in place for at least three years.

Hedges have been established by planting through a continuous polythene sheet that has been laid mechanically, with its edges buried by the laying machine. However, use of a sheet-laying machine requires cultivated ground along the length of the proposed hedge line, and this may not always be possible if the new hedge is to be planted close to a road, fence or wall.

For those who are keen to use a polythene sheet mulch, it is possible to plant the young hedge and then cut all the plants back to a height of no more than 10cm (4in), with a clean sloping cut to each plant. Lay the polythene sheet over the top of the cut-back plant lines, dig in the sheet edges, and finally press the sheet down around each plant to poke each one through the sheet. It

A polythene sheet mulch was laid when this hedge was planted, to reduce weed growth and conserve moisture. It will continue to control weed growth even after this hedge has been laid. Hopefully it will begin to degrade soon to allow the establishment of plants in the hedge bottom.

will take courage to cut back the plants in this manner, especially having paid for the height that you have cut off! But the reality is that young plants cut back and planted in this manner will grow away very vigorously, and will have an excellent chance of being taller than untrimmed plants at the end of the *first* growing season.

THE USE OF HERBICIDES

The most common and effective way to control grass and weed growth is by the use of approved herbicides (the collective term used to describe chemicals developed to control/ kill weeds).

In recent years there has been increasing legislation governing the scope and use of all herbicides. Pressure from conservation groups, and public concern at the long-term effects of chemical usage on the land, which is now affecting the quality of groundwater supplies, has led to increasing restrictions on the scope and use of such chemicals.

Since the end of World War II, the chemical control of pests and weeds has progressed at an amazing rate, allowing farmers to increase crop yields dramatically, and reduce manpower on the land. Gone are the gangs of workers singling and weeding sugar beet and vegetables across southern and eastern England, and the pressure to produce crops at lower prices forced the pace and development of a very wide range of specific crop chemicals. But many of these are now being steadily withdrawn, thus limiting the farmers' 'arsenal' of control options; this is because many of these chemicals have been found to produce problems of soil residues. The appearance of plant strains resistant to specific chemicals, and the longer-term pollution of groundwater supplies, have combined to restrict their usage.

The Food and Environment Protection Act (FEPA) 1985, and the Control of Substances Hazardous to Health Regulations (COSHH) 1989, came into force to regulate the use of all pesticides. It is important that anyone contemplating the use of pesticides for the control of weeds, pests and diseases on new hedges must be fully conversant with all regulations governing their use. The complex and ever-changing regulations governing pesticide use are so extensive that this book cannot cover the subject or keep pace with changes, so it will not attempt to do so.

The herbicides listed for the control of grasses and weeds in new hedges have obtained either full or 'off label' recommendations *unless otherwise stated.*

There are anomalies with the interpretation of all legislation. Chemicals cleared for use with hedges and in woodland appear under the heading of 'forestry' or 'woodland on farms', but the *production* of trees and shrubs is classified under 'ornamentals – nursery stock' or 'ornamentals – trees and shrubs'. A limited range of chemicals are cleared for 'forest' use, yet if the same plants are grown in an 'ornamental' setting, there is a much wider selection of options available.

Official approval of chemicals for specified crop uses does not cover the optimum application rates, water volume, addition of wetting agents, or their compatibility with other chemicals. These factors will vary according to soil type, weather conditions, crop-growth stage, and the individual plant species. Farmers, growers and contractors will have access to the information, or employ advisers, to be able to make the right decision.

Those wishing to carry out chemical weed control along a new hedge must be certified to do the work. If you do not have the required experience or certification to apply herbicides, you must contact a certified contractor, or ADAS, to seek advice. Your local National Farmers Union branch or local training group will be able to advise you on the best course of action. Agricultural chemical suppliers employ their own agronomists to advise customers, and will be able to help find a suitable contractor. All these bodies are either conversant with the pesticide regulations, or can advise you where to seek the necessary information.

The following descriptions are a basis for selecting the most suitable herbicide. It is imperative that the manufacturer's product label is read carefully before applying any chemical.

Herbicides fall into four 'mode of action' categories. The first three categories have both advantages and limitations in their abilities, but the choice of chemicals within each category offers the user a selection for use in connection with young trees and shrubs according to the range of weeds present, their size and severity.

Contact Herbicides

The herbicide kills weed plants by contact with its leaves. It will only desiccate existing foliage, so plants with large roots, for example perennials, can soon regrow after treatment. Contact herbicides are best suited for the control of seedling and small weeds, which do not have an adequately developed root system to recover.

Translocated (Systemic) Herbicides

The herbicide is absorbed through the plant's leaves into its translocation system. Translocated herbicides kill plants in different ways, according to the chemical's mode of action; some stimulate the treated plant to grow at an excessive and fatal rate, whilst others destroy certain plant tissues or damage the metabolic systems within the plant.

Residual Herbicides

The herbicide is sprayed on to the surface of the soil and acts upon the developing hypocotyls or the young root, sometimes killing those present, or killing them as they germinate. The sprayed chemical binds on to the soil particles, and remains active in the top few inches of the soil surface for weeks or months. It can be compared to the effect of paint in preserving the surface of metal from rusting – so long as the paint cover remains intact no 'rust' can form; disturb the surface-covering layer, and the 'rust' will flourish on exposed areas. In the case of plants, they will be able to germinate once the covering layer is broken or when the active life of the chemical is exhausted; the latter usually occurs because the chemical is slowly broken down by the action of rain or by prolonged exposure to sunlight.

Selective Herbicides

The herbicide's action is selective, in that it can eradicate a particular plant type within a crop of closely related species. For example, 'chlorotoluron', a contact and residual urea-based herbicide, will kill wild oats in most cereal crops, except oats. In this latter group the mode of action will be that of one of the three preceding groups – contact, translocated or residual – or a combination of some of them.

WEED CONTROL PRIOR TO PLANTING

It is advisable to plant a new hedge into weed-free ground. The ground may be cultivated to remove weeds present, and to prepare the soil into an open texture for ease of planting. If the land cannot be cultivated in advance of planting, the only option for clearing weed is to use one of the following herbicides.

Glufosinate Ammonium

A non-selective, non-residual contact herbicide that will desiccate the green leaf tissue parts of grasses and broad-leaved annual weeds; however, some grasses – for example, annual meadow grass – and deep-rooted perennial weeds may recover.

Glufosinate Ammonium is used as a guarded spray around plants in the growing season to reduce weed competition. Great care must be taken to avoid spray drift into the bark or leaves of the young plants. Every precaution must be taken to read and follow the instructions for use with the greatest care. *It is only available to farmers, growers and contractors who have the appropriate qualifications to apply such herbicides.*

To achieve the best results, spray the weeds when they are growing actively in spring and early summer, during warm, moist conditions to ensure a good uptake into the weed leaf. Do *not* spray in very cold or hot weather, or when rain is imminent, as these conditions will reduce the effective uptake of the chemical, resulting in only a partial kill.

The chemical is degraded after contact with the soil, allowing planting to be carried out soon after spraying.

Glyphosate

A translocated, non-residual herbicide that will kill the aerial and root parts of most weeds. Grasses such as couch must have an adequate area of leaf that is growing actively to ensure a good uptake of the chemical, which in turn will ensure a good kill of all roots present; the same requirements apply to persistent perennial weeds such as docks and thistles, which are best sprayed just before they come into flower.

Glyphosate takes longer to achieve a complete control of weed growth than desiccants, so is best applied in spring or early autumn. To obtain best results do not spray in dry, hot weather or when frost or rain are predicted.

The chemical is rapidly deactivated upon contact with the soil. Allow at least fourteen days before cultivating the sprayed weeds to ensure full uptake and activity within the plant tissue.

Although Glyphosate is not subject to the poison rules, every care must be taken with its handling and application, as set out above for the use of Diquat/Paraquat. Even greater care must be taken to prevent damage from spray drift because of the greater activity of the chemical within the affected plants.

WEED CONTROL AFTER PLANTING

Isoxaben

A soil-acting residual herbicide for use on a wide range of fruit and horticultural crops, including hedge plants. It is excellent at maintaining weed-free conditions on a clean planting site. Weed control may be reduced if applied under dry conditions. The chemical will not control emerged seedling weeds.

Isoxaben can be sprayed at the appropriate time over the top of the planted hedge, prior to bud burst. It is safe to spray over the hedge during the growing season. A maximum individual dose of 2.0 litres may be applied only twice in a year.

Best results are achieved by spraying onto clean, clod-free, moist soil in late winter after planting. Soils with a high organic content will reduce the activity of the chemical more readily than do lighter sandy soils. A second application may be made in weed-free, moist soil conditions later in the summer to maintain weed control.

It is a relatively safe chemical to use, but follow the manufacturer's instructions with the usual due care at all times.

Oxadiazon

A very effective contact and residual herbicide for fruit and woody ornamentals. The dictionary definition of 'ornamental' is 'a plant grown for its beauty'. Thus, if the hedge is planted for commercial or farm use, this herbicide may *not* be used. If the hedge is to be planted for its ornamental value (beauty), then Oxadiazon may be used for the control of weeds around the hedge bottom.

The chemical should be applied as an overall spray, at the recommended rate, after planting in late winter/ early spring, before weeds have begun to emerge. It must be applied *before* buds have begun to break on any of the species planted, to prevent scorch damage to the emerging leaves. Once the leaves have broken bud, it will only be possible to use this herbicide as a directed spray on to the soil around each plant.

Oxadiazon must *not* be used over a growing crop. It will control a wide range of seedling weeds, including groundsel and willowherb. The control of perennial weeds (for example, bindweed) will be enhanced by applying the chemical as they are emerging as small seedlings; however, chickweed and volunteer cereals become resistant after emergence, and mixing the oxadiazon with propyzamide will help to control them. Consult your ADAS adviser, agronomist or local chemical supplier for details of such mixes, and follow the manufacturer's instructions closely at all times.

Pendimethalin

A residual, soil-acting, dinitroaniline herbicide for the pre-emergent control of problem weeds such as annual meadow grass, black nightshade, cleavers and knot grass, among others. It must be applied to the weed-free crop when it is dormant, immediately after planting. As with most residual herbicides, it will require moist soil conditions after application to be active in the control of germinating weeds. It has an 'Off Label' approval for farm forestry use, which would cover hedge and tree planting in a farmland situation.

It is important to follow the manufacturer's instructions with care, and apply as instructed on to fine, firm, moist soil conditions. Rainfall after application will greatly enhance the herbicide's activity in the soil. Conversely, dry conditions after application will reduce its effectiveness.

Napropamide

A soil-acting, residual herbicide for use on a range of fruit, woody ornamental and some vegetable crops. It is best applied to weed-free soils after planting in the winter months, before bud burst, whilst the hedge is still dormant. Do not use on very sandy or high organic soils. Apply to moist, weed-free soil; only one application per year is approved.

Napropamide may be tank-mixed with certain specified contact herbicides to give control of germinated weeds; but the approved mixes must not be applied over the planted hedge. Such mixes must be applied by a shielded sprayer around the base of the hedge plants, avoiding any contact with the stem or aerial parts of the plants.

Follow the manufacturer's instructions carefully at all times to get the best results without damage to the plants.

Propaquizafop

A foliar-acting grass herbicide that can be applied over the growing crop to give an excellent suppression of couch and other grass weeds. The chemical should be applied to the grass when it is growing actively in the spring. A further application may be made later in the summer if the grasses recover; again, apply when the grass has produced new young shoots.

Propaquizafop should be applied to dry foliage in warm conditions, but preferably not during prolonged hot weather, to ensure a steady uptake of the chemical to obtain the best, long-term suppression.

The chemical is relatively safe to use, but follow the manufacturer's instructions with all due care to obtain the optimum results.

CHECKS TO MAKE WHEN USING HERBICIDES

Herbicides can do a very good job at controlling weeds when the right chemical has been selected and it has been applied correctly. Herbicides and pesticides may only be applied by persons with the required certification, or who have qualified for age exemption to apply such chemicals. The following notes are to assist that goal:

- Select the correct herbicide in relation to the weed spectrum present.
- Read the manufacturer's instructions carefully.
- Wear the correct protective clothing for the application of the chosen chemical.
- Use a spraying machine that is correctly calibrated and is in sound working order.
- Check for the correct chemical dilution rate to achieve optimum results.
- Check for the correct nozzle, spray pressure and application ground speed.
- Ensure the weather is suitable for spraying, and that it will remain so for the length of time required for the herbicide to do its work as specified.
- Clean the sprayer after use to avoid contamination for future use.
- Record all details of the herbicide application operation, including the weather at the time of application.
- Dispose of the chemical container according to current regulations.
- All chemicals and empty containers must be stored in an approved storage building or bonded cabinet.

CHAPTER 10

Disease and Pest Control

Nurserymen have to protect their valuable crop of young tree and hedge plants from damage by both diseases and pests if they are to produce quality plants to sell to their customers. They are also concerned that their plants leave the nursery in clean health to be able to grow well in the following years. It is therefore equally important that the end user of these plants also maintains the health and vigour of the plants he has bought to ensure that they grow strongly to form a good hedge as soon as possible.

The nurseryman and the end user are both strictly regulated by the range and application of pesticides that they can select to maintain healthy and vigorous growth.

DISEASES

The two most important diseases of the hawthorn hedgerow are fireblight and mildew.

Fireblight

This disease was first discovered in 1780 on apple and pear trees in the Hudson valley, United States. By 1900 it had reached the Pacific coast, and it was first reported outside the United States in New Zealand orchards in 1919. The disease spread to England in 1957, when it was identified in a Kent pear orchard. It has since been recorded throughout northern Europe, and has spread into most counties of central and southern England.

The disease is of particular concern to apple and pear growers, because an infection can cause severe dieback of fruiting branches, leading to the death of trees that are not treated in adequate time.

Fireblight is caused by the bacterium *Erwinia amylovora*, which affects other members of the sub-family *Pomoideae*. It will attack other ornamental species, particularily *Crataegus* (hawthorn), as well as *Cotoneaster* and *Sorbus*. *Prunus* and *Rosa* are not affected.

The bacterium lies dormant over winter to spread rapidly during moist, warm weather in summer (18°C/64°F). It can be spread by rain and wind as well as by pruning and saw cuts. Blossoms are susceptible to infection, and the disease spreads through cuts and other wounds to the bark, such as hedge cutting in late spring. The bacterial spores are capable of spreading over a distance of 200m (650ft), but are more likely to be transferred over short distances from an infected tree to its immediate neighbours.

The first symptoms will be seen when clusters of blossom wilt and die prematurely. Later infections often start with young shoots becoming limp, wilting, and hanging over like a shepherd's 'crook'. The leaves then turn dark brown, though do not readily fall off. Scraping the bark of an infected branch or shoot will reveal reddish-brown stained tissue underneath. It can turn a dark green to brown colour as the infection spreads. Sometimes the infected wood produces a watery ooze. It is often necessary to scrape the bark back a substantial distance from the infected area to reach fresh, uninfected tissue.

Once fireblight has been identified it is important to cut off all infected branches. Cutting down complete bushes or trees may be necessary to ensure that all infected wood is removed. Immediately burn all the prunings and timber to prevent the spread of infection.

If the disease breaks out in a nursery or in a young hedge, dig up all the infected plants and burn them immediately. Carry out regular inspections of the crop/hedge twice a week until there are no more symptoms of the disease spreading to adjacent plants in the same area. Unfortunately the disease can 'jump about' in the area, and may 'jump' from an outbreak in one small patch, to reappear some distance away from the initial source of the infection. Examine the whole area carefully at each inspection, and take every precaution to avoid damaging any of the nearby plants in any way, which may provide the disease with an easy point of access to spread.

Where orchards, or plant nurseries, are surrounded by hawthorn hedges, do not trim the hedges until late autumn, and keep them trimmed tight each season to reduce the amount of flower bud formation, thus reducing the risk of spring blossom infection. For this reason many orchards and nurseries now use Italian alder as a safer alternative to hawthorn for windbreak screens.

There is no chemical control for the disease. It can only be prevented from spreading by adopting the strict procedure outlined above, and by the disposal of all infected wood by immediate burning. It is strongly recommended that saws and secateurs are cleaned in a disinfectant liquid after each cut.

Fireblight is a notifiable disease, and any outbreak should be reported to your local branch of ADAS, or to the Plant Health and Seeds Inspectorate branch of DEFRA.

All reputable growers of hawthorn and other related species will pay for annual DEFRA inspections to obtain a 'plant passport', which states that the nursery is free from fireblight and so certified to supply disease-free plants to other regions or countries. When purchasing any plant material that is susceptible to fireblight, you should enquire if the nursery has been issued with a 'plant passport', to ensure that you are buying healthy plants.

Mildews

Hawthorn, the backbone of the English hedgerow, is the species that is most susceptible to mildew infection. The powdery mildew of hawthorn is caused by the fungus *podosphaera clandestine*, that infects the leaves and young shoots, covering them with a white down of fungal mycelium. Severe leaf infections cause a purplish discoloration, leading to curling and shrivelling before the leaves fall. Plant growth can be severely stunted if no remedial action is taken quickly.

Dry, sunny, warm days in spring and summer with dewy nights favour the development of the white mycelium, which produces abundant powdery spores. The spores are carried on summer breezes to spread the infection to adjacent plants along the hedge.

The disease will over-winter as a mycelium on bark, young shoots and in the buds. It can be easily introduced into a new hedge via infected young planting stock.

Field maple, blackthorn, wild plum, wild crab, dog rose and other wild rose species are all susceptible to infection from various strains of mildew. Wild crab can be severely affected and its young growth stunted as a result, which is serious if the crab is being encouraged to grow up as a hedgerow tree, rather than as a shrub within the hedge.

Currently, no fungicides have been specifically approved for hedgerow or woodland use because of limited potential demand. However, commercial growers raising plants for sale to the public are fortunate in having a range of chemicals that can be used without the clearance approval required for edible crops. The following fungicides are used, in rotation, for their proven ability to offer good eradicant and/or protective control of both mildews and black spot diseases.

Myclobutanil A systemic, protectant and curative triazole fungicide giving good control of mildew on a wide range of fruit and ornamental crops, including hedge plants. The chemical is harmful to fish and other aquatic life, so do not use near ditches, ponds or watercourses. Follow the manufacturer's instructions carefully for correct use.

Carbendazim: A systemic benzimidazole fungicide with curative and protectant action. It is approved for use on a range of flower, fruit, vegetable and ornamental crops. Do not apply in drought conditions or to any crop under stress from other physical stress problems. The chemical is harmful to fish and other aquatic life, so avoid use as previously mentioned. Follow the instructions for use fully, and apply with care.

Fenpropimorph: A contact and systemic morpholine fungicide giving good mildew control on a range of cereal, vegetable and soft fruit crops. On soft fruit crops only three sprays may be applied in one growing season. Do not apply during hot weather conditions, which can cause leaf scorch. The chemical is harmful to fish and other aquatic life, so do not use in situations as outlined above. Follow the instructions provided with care.

Two years' growth of a mixed species hedge beside an arable field. The line of plants closest to the field has grown more vigorously due to less localized weed competition, and the benefit from fertilizer and disease-control sprays applied to the cereal crop.

Sulphur (Sulphur, various brands): A broad spectrum, inorganic protectant fungicide with added foliar feed and acaricide properties. It is cleared for use on a very wide range of edible fruit and vegetable crops. Because it only has the ability to protect the crop, it must be applied before the disease first appears, and it will require repeated spray applications during the summer months to keep the plants free of mildew. A maximum of four sprays only may be used on apples during one season. Sulphur acts as a foliar feed, and will also control red spider and other mites on a range of susceptible crops. Do not use on plants when the leaves are young, under stress, or in frosty conditions, as leaf scorch is likely to occur. Follow the instructions provided with great care, especially as there are several formulations of the chemical that have differing application requirements.

Potassium bicarbonate (Food grade bicarbonate): A very new approach to the control of mildews, using a simple and safe food product that has recently been found to give good contact control of mildew. It has no lasting or systemic properties. A maximum individual dose of 20g (0.7oz) potassium bicarbonate per litre of water is advised, with a maximum of 60kg (132lb) of the product allowed per hectare/annum. Follow the application instructions fully and with due care.

Note: Under the 1986 Control of Pesticides Regulations, it is illegal to use any pesticide (chemical) except those approved for specific uses. The *UK Pesticide Guide*, published annually, covers all products approved for UK crop use by the Pesticides Safety Directorate and the Health and Safety Executive.

Check with your agronomist or a crops adviser prior to carrying out any intended pest or diseases control measure. Always read the pesticide product label with great care to ensure that the product is applied to achieve its optimum potential without damage to the plants, adjacent crops, or the environment in general.

The *UK Pesticide Guide* is available from CABI Publishing, CAB International, Wallingford, Oxon OX10 8DE.

Diseases Caused by Viruses

Viruses are minute, single-cell organisms (smaller than bacteria) that exist in the living cells of animal and plant tissue. They are transmitted from one host to another by vectors (carriers) such as insects (for example, aphids). Some are carried by pollen, others in seed, and some are transmitted by vegetative propagation, particularly in the case of woody ornamental plants. They are able to spread across the union of a graft, allowing a diseased rootstock to infect a healthy scion, and vice versa.

The damaging effect of a virus is often so small as to go undetected, only showing up for a short period during the growing season. This makes it very difficult to avoid and isolate when selecting scion wood for grafting.

Seed collectors are attracted to trees that carry a regular, heavy crop of seed; yet this may be the direct result of a virus infection affecting the tree's growth.

It is important to check on the subsequent growth and vigour of young plants raised from seed to eliminate any seed source that results in the spread of a specific virus.

Unfortunately, healthy and vigorous seed trees often produce the least seed.

Nematodes (microscopic parasitic worms) in the soil can transmit viruses from a diseased crop to subsequent healthy crops, even when the susceptible crop is only one in a long rotation that is designed to minimize this very problem!

Soil Sterilization

Soil-borne viruses and nematodes can be controlled by soil sterilization. The sterilization of soils carrying high value crops has been commonplace in the glasshouse industry for many years. Steam sterilization remains the safest way to cleanse soils for intensive crop production. On a field scale, the incorporation of a chemical sterilant is the most cost-effective way of cleansing infected soils.

Sterilization has the disadvantage that the chemical is not selective: it will control the damaging soil nematodes, but it will also kill other soil organisms, many of which can be beneficial to crop growth. The decision to use chemical sterilization must therefore only be taken when there are no other options available.

The most widely used soil sterilant for field-grown vegetable and tree seedling crops is Dazomet (Basamid), a granular soil fumigant for the control of soil-borne diseases, nematodes, soil insects and weed seed germination. It can be purchased and applied by any competent person without specific qualifications, although the manufacturer's label instructions must be followed carefully to ensure correct and safe application. For small-scale use the finely ground granules can be applied using a small, hand-pushed, lawn sand and fertilizer distributor. For larger, field-scale applications, it is recommended that an approved contractor be employed, or the correct machine can be hired to do the work efficiently.

The ground to be treated should be prepared to a fine tilth prior to the application of the granules, which must be incorporated into the soil to a depth of 15 to 20cm (6 to 8in) immediately after application. Once the fine granules have been incorporated by a rotavator or by a deep-working power harrow, the treated area must be covered with a thin, photo-degradable polythene film, using a polythene-laying machine to lay the film and bury its edges to seal in the treated soil. The granules act by releasing methyl isothiocyanate fumes upon contact with moist soil to fumigate the ground. If the soil is below 50 per cent of its water-holding capacity, the ground should be irrigated before treatment. To ensure that sterilization of the soil is completed effectively and quickly, the soil temperature should be above 7°C (45°F).

Dazomet takes four to eight weeks to disperse fully. A 'cress-growing' test, using some of the treated field soil, should be used to check that the chemical has been dispersed fully before removing the polythene cover to cultivate the ground.

The treatment of nursery soils for tree seedbeds is undertaken in summer (July/August) to ensure optimum control in the short time before autumn sowing. The polythene covers must be removed and the ground harrowed following the treatment period to ensure full chemical ventilation before preparing the ground for sowing. If sowing is not to take place until the following spring, it is advisable to leave the polythene covers on as long as possible to reduce the risk of the ground becoming re-infected by weed seed blown in from adjacent land.

In recent years an 'organic' means of controlling soil nematodes has been developed following research work in Holland, by growing a crop of *Tagetes erecta*, more commonly known as African marigolds. These marigolds were grown as a cover crop in the year prior to planting a commercial tree crop, and they gave a very good control of soil nematodes without affecting other beneficial soil organisms. The marigolds are sown in early summer (late May/ June) into clean soil conditions, which must be kept weed free during the crop's full growing season. The presence of weed in the marigold crop would allow the soil nematodes to feed and thrive on the roots of the weeds present, so diminishing the control possible from the roots of the marigold crop, which are toxic to the nematodes feeding upon them.

This new commercial method of controlling soil nematodes may have an application where a new hedge is to be planted along the line of an old hedge, for which approval has been obtained to grub and replant. There may have been soil-borne diseases present in the old hedge that contributed to its demise, in which case every effort should be made to identify any such problems present before planting the replacement hedge. If harmful nematodes are present, the sowing of African marigolds along the proposed hedge line in the summer prior to replanting would be a simple and safe means of ensuring a clean and disease-free site, which in turn would give the new young hedge an excellent start.

Most new hedges are planted into fresh sites that are unlikely to suffer from damaging soil-borne diseases. The only concern is to avoid purchasing virus-infected planting stock. This can be achieved by purchasing the plants from a reputable nurseryman who has grown the plants himself. The planting stock can be inspected during the growing season prior to requirement. It is important to avoid buying plants direct from the continent without any knowledge of the conditions under which they were grown. The government system of 'plant passports' covers the movement of all trees and shrubs grown or supplied throughout the United Kingdom and Europe.

Every nursery has a unique registration number that enables government plant health inspectors to trace the movement of all plants sold throughout the country. Thus any infected plant material can be traced back to its origins, a policy that can help to eliminate the spread of any disease outbreak. The system has brought a new awareness of the consequences of supplying infected stock, as no reputable nurseryman wishes to have his reputation compromised by the knowledge that he has been found to be selling infected plants.

PESTS

An infestation by a particular pest is able to spread much more rapidly on a commercial nursery where individual plant species are grown together in much larger numbers, as compared to a good mixed species hedge or a woodland setting in the countryside. In a mixed species hedge an attack of aphids on wild cherry is unlikely to spread far because the aphid is often specific to *Prunus* species and so will not spread to other plant species; and there will not be large numbers of similar species in the vicinity. But a specific pest attack on hawthorn in a new hedge could be a problem, and should be controlled before it spreads along the hedge line that will certainly contain a high proportion of the same species.

Many aphids, caterpillars, mites and weevils can be indiscriminate in the subjects they choose to attack; but most are very selective, and it is important to be able to identify pests correctly before considering any control measures. Chemical control of insect pests in a hedgerow must be regarded as the last option if one is to preserve the fragile and developing ecology of a new hedge. Only resort to spot treatment with a selective insecticide if the offending pest is unlikely to be controlled by other predators, or is one that could spread amongst other species to severely restrict the growth of a young hedge in its formative years.

The table on page 122 lists common pests that can attack the different species found in hedges. Those that can cause serious damage are highlighted in bold type, and these must be controlled as soon as they are identified in any numbers.

Pests that can cause damage to hedgerow plants

Hedgerow Plant	Common Pests
Field Maple	Aphids, scale insects
Hornbeam	Scale insects, tortrix and winter moth caterpillars
Dogwood	Aphids, winter moth caterpillars
Hazel	Rust mites, leaf and nut weevils, spider mites
Hawthorn	Woolly aphids, button top midge, winter moth caterpillars, scale insects
Spindle tree	Black bean aphid, scale insects
Beech	Woolly aphids, scale insects, vine weevils
Ash	Ash bud moth, rust mite, goat and leopard moths
Holly	Leaf miner
Wild privet	Leafhopper, leaf miner, spider mite, tortrix moth
Crab apple	Scale insects, tortrix and winter moths, aphids and woolly aphid, weevils
Blackthorn	Aphids, scale insects, tortrix moth
Wild pear	Woolly aphids, leaf blister mite, scale insects, tortrix moth
Wild plum	Woolly aphids, red spider mite, scale insects, several moths
Oak	Aphids, leaf galls and mites, several moths, scale insects, several distinctive gall wasps, weevils – the oak carries the greatest number of insect 'pests' of all our native trees
Wild roses	Aphids, several moths, weevils
Wayfaring tree	Aphids, capsid bug
Guelder rose	Aphids, capsid bug

All hedgerow shrubs and trees are at risk from a wider range of pests than those listed above. A good mixture of species along the hedge will create a better environment for predators to colonize alongside the pests, and so maintain a balance between the two, minimizing the damage and spread from an outbreak of any particular pest. Allow predators a chance to eliminate any pest before resorting to the use of an insecticide.

Hedgerow pests fall into five categories, so you can select an appropriate insecticide according to the way the pest feeds upon the host plant:

Aphids: Sap-sucking insects that have a winged form enabling them to move and spread quickly from plant to plant.

Caterpillars: The larval stage in the life cycle of butterflies and moths. Caterpillars usually eat the leaves of plants, but can bore into the bark, roots or seeds of some plants according to the life cycle of the particular larva.

Beetles and weevils: They eat the leaves of plants. The larvae of some beetles and weevils eat roots.

Spider mites: They feed by sucking the sap from the leaves or from young tender shoots.

Scale insects: They are also sap-sucking creatures.

Control of Pests

The following insecticides control pests according to pesticide selectivity:

Contact insecticide: Kills the pest upon contact; often non-selective and harmful to other insects and wildlife nearby.

Stomach poison: The insecticide is sprayed on to the plant to be protected so that any caterpillar, scale insect or weevil is killed when it eats the 'poisoned' leaf. This group of chemicals is broad spectrum and thus fatal to other harmless insects with the same feeding habits.

Systemic poisons: The chemical is absorbed into the plant tissue, remaining in the leaf cells so that any sap-sucking aphid or mite is poisoned by the toxin in the plant sap.

In recent years great strides have been made in reducing the harmful side effects of pesticides on other insects living on plants that are being sprayed to control a particular pest; in other words, chemical selectivity has been improved to target only the insect pest and not to harm other insects with similar feeding habits on the same plant. The use of non-selective contact insecticides has been greatly reduced, and there is a continuing reappraisal of all pesticide usage to protect wildlife in general.

The following pesticides have been approved for use on hedgerows and in woodlands:

Deltamethrin: A contact and residual insecticide, based on pyrethrum for the control of aphids, beetles, moths, scale insects and weevils. It is harmful to bees and fish, so do not use near hives, ponds or watercourses. Follow the manufacturer's instructions carefully to avoid damage to wildlife.

Pirimicarb: A selective contact and fumigant insecticide for the control of aphids on a wide range of hedgerow and woodland plants. It has little adverse effect on bees, ladybirds, lacewing and other beneficial insects. Follow the manufacturer's instructions fully.

Diflubenzuron: A selective, persistent, contact and stomach acting insecticide for the control of a wide range of caterpillars / moths and rust mites on fruit and vegetable crops. It is also cleared for use on hedges. It is very toxic to aquatic organisms; so do not use near ditches, ponds or watercourses. Only one application each year is cleared for use on hedges. Do not spray when plants are in flower and keep away from livestock. Follow the manufacturer's instructions very carefully prior to use.

CHAPTER 11

Hedge Maintenance and Protection

The role of hedges in the landscape has changed in the past half century, but the need to maintain them has never been more in the public eye than in recent years because of widespread neglect, especially in arable farming regions. Every hedge must be maintained to ensure that it remains a hedge, and does not deteriorate into an overgrown thicket, or decline into a thin line of 'lifeless sticks'.

During the past forty years great changes have occurred in the countryside, mainly because food production is no longer the driving force of the rural economy. An increasing proportion of land is now used for such diverse interests as horse and pony paddocks, riding schools, golf clubs, shooting syndicates, farm and wildlife parks, nature conservation areas, plus the spread of out-of-town industrial parks and shopping centres. English Nature is also championing the restoration of downland, meadows and wetland sites; many of which had been brought under cultivation during World War II.

With a steady decline in agricultural profitability and its effects upon the diversity of individual farm crops, dairy and stock production has declined, retreating to higher rainfall areas and to the traditional livestock counties in the West Country and Wales. Cereal and related crop production, that can be harvested with a combine, has become the dominant use for a greater part of the lowland landscape.

All these factors have reduced the traditional role of the hedge, and have seen an increase in the use of barbed wire and wire fences for stock and security fencing. The hedge has had to 're-invent' itself, aided by the general public's alarm at the widespread removal of hedges in the latter half of the twentieth century. The government has stepped up its support for the revival of hedges, and provides grant aid for both their replanting and their restoration. Farmers and landowners are therefore now being actively encouraged to restore and maintain hedges, in their new role as a wildlife habitat, and for their contribution to the visual beauty of our landscape.

HEDGE RESTORATION

Many hedges had become neglected and overgrown, others had been over-trimmed to the point of extinction, and many had been allowed to become smothered in bramble and other choking weeds. Whatever the cause of the deterioration, there are several options for the restoration and subsequent maintenance of mature hedges:

- Brushing, or siding up
- Coppicing
- Laying
- Trimming with a mechanical flail or cutter bar

Each of the above will be dealt with in turn except hedge laying, which will be covered in following chapters.

Brushing, or Siding Up

Old hedges will need occasional trimming up to prevent side branches flopping out and possibly breaking. This will also let a little more light into the bottom of the hedge to encourage fresh growth. The removal of bramble, briar, old man's beard and other such invasive growth is necessary to prevent them from smothering the hedge, especially if it is young.

Older mixed species hedges should be allowed to grow on with less formal maintenance. A quick trim with a pair of loppers or a long-handled slasher will prevent branches from drooping too much. It may be necessary to cut out a few of the larger stems as necessary to encourage some new growth within the hedge or to remove invasive elder for the same reason.

Any species that becomes too dominant, such as field maple, wild plum or common elder, will need thinning out or cutting back to prevent them dominating their slower-growing and higher valued 'neighbours', such as common dogwood, spindle or wild crab.

New, mixed-species 'conservation' hedges will contain a much wider selection of plants: they can contain up to 50 per cent of non-hawthorn or blackthorn plants, and need to be treated differently to a traditional hawthorn enclosure hedge. The wider mix of species grows at different rates and will require less trimming, and may only need light trimming according to individual need; slow-growing species such as wayfaring tree, guelder rose and those mentioned above need to kept free from 'overbearing' neighbours, with a little individual attention to provide adequate space to enable them to maintain their rightful position.

The two main stock-proof hedge species, hawthorn and blackthorn, are both vigorous and thorny. Blackthorn is capable of sucker growth that can soon spread into adjacent land or become invasive within the hedge itself, characteristics that require them to be given regular attention to control their growth. It has been normal to trim or brush up hawthorn and blackthorn hedges at least every two to three years; however, new guidelines laid out in government funding to farmers and landowners now encourages trimming on a three-year cycle to improve the wildlife habitat value of hedges.

Coppicing

This is a severe, yet sometimes necessary means of restoring a hedge that has been neglected for so long that many plants have died out, fallen over or simply become stunted 'lollipops'; such hedges can only be revived by cutting them back to ground level and letting each stump put out new growth to rejuvenate the hedge.

Coppicing entails cutting the whole hedge-line back to ground level, clearing and burning all the debris, replanting any gaps with strong two-year-old transplants, and keeping the cleared hedge-line free of weed until the stump (stool) cuts have sent up new growth alongside the transplants in the gaps, to give a fresh start to the old hedge. Each stem of the old hedge must be cut back close to the ground – no more than 10cm (4in) – to ensure vigorous regrowth from the stools.

It is very important to put up notices to explain that one is cutting the old hedge down as a necessary method of restoring it. It is illegal to remove a hedge, and many local people will be very concerned at seeing a hedge being treated in this manner, and may not be aware of the longer-term benefits from coppicing. If coppicing is *clearly explained*, it will avoid risking local reaction against the person cutting down the hedge.

Trimming

Hydraulically operated, tractor-mounted flail trimmers now dominate the market for mechanical hedge trimming, and cutter-bar machines have been almost completely superseded. Saw-head trimmers are sometimes used to coppice a hedge or to cut back an overgrown, tall hedge.

Old and new hedges containing a high proportion of hawthorn or blackthorn are suitable for regular flail trimming, most being cut annually or biennially at present. Both species respond well to regular trimming by producing fresh, bushy, light growth to keep the hedge stock- and windproof. Hedges containing a greater number of slow-growing species such as holly, wayfaring tree and guelder rose should not be flail-trimmed regularly, and the same rule applies to new hedges containing stiff, brittle-stemmed species such as field maple, wild crab and spindle, which tend to produce upright, stiff growth.

Annual trimming is really only necessary on stock farms to keep new growth tight and dense for the containment and wind protection of livestock. It may also be necessary to trim annually in situations where the hedge has been grown up to the maximum height of the hedge trimmer in order to provide a windbreak and to improve spring soil temperatures for early-maturing, valuable horticultural cash crops. However, hedges on arable and cereal farms could readily be adapted to trimming every two to three years to reduce maintenance costs and improve the habitat for wildlife. Trimming should be carried out in the autumn or early winter so as not to disturb nesting birds. *Do not trim hedges between 1 March and 31 July*.

A Bomford Turner hedge trimmer shows its versatility by reaching over a thick hawthorn hedge to give it an annual trim. Only by trimming such a hedge regularly can it be kept bushy and stockproof. (Bomford Turner Ltd)

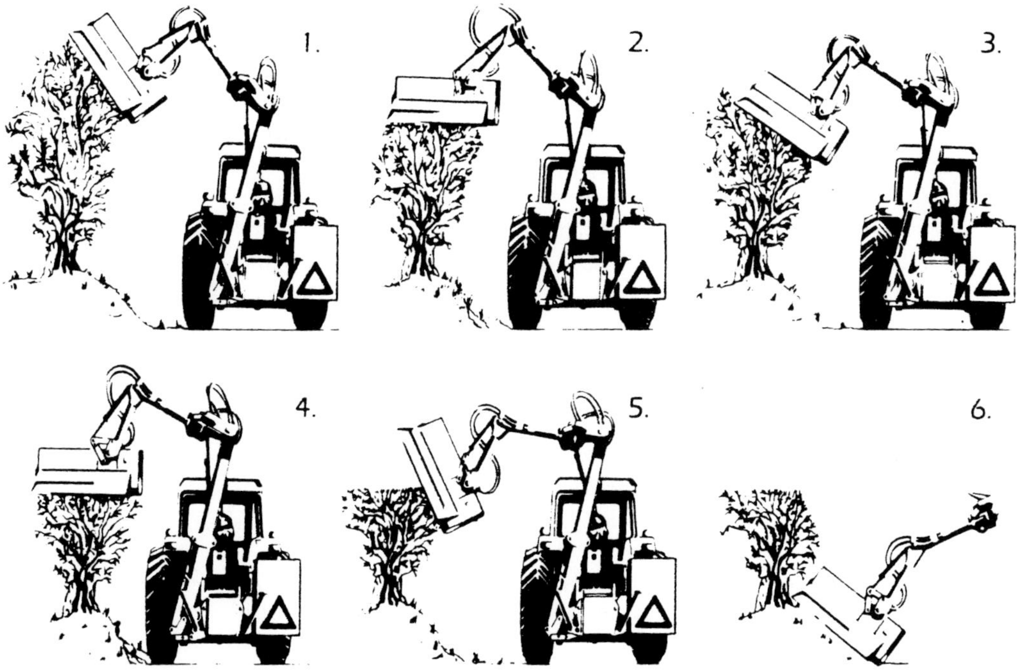

A Bomford Turner diagram showing a series of cuts to reduce an overgrown hedge. Start from the top and work down; in this way any trimmings that have fallen will be further cut up and mulched as the cutter head moves down the hedge. Cut off longer material in a series of passes, taking off layers of approximately 45cm (18in) at each pass to leave short trimmings that will decompose rapidly, and to avoid overloading the hedge cutter. (Bomford Turner Ltd)

The diagrams show the way to reduce an overgrown hedge using a flail trimmer. If a partial trim is adequate, only carry out lighter cuts using one or more of the angles shown.

Newly planted hedges for stock control or crop protection should be trimmed every two years to keep the new growth tight and dense. In the early years following planting it may be easier to walk the hedge-line, cutting off any excessive top or side growth with a pair of sharp hedge clippers or loppers. Do not use a mechanical flail trimmer until the growth is sturdy enough not to tear, rather than be cut by the flail. If the new growth is cut with a ragged finish it can cause die-back and reduce the vigour of fresh growth in the spring. Cutting with a flail trimmer can begin when the hedge is in its fourth or fifth year after planting. To prevent tearing when cutting, ensure that the operator does not drive too quickly along the hedge.

Points to remember when hedge trimming:

- Where possible, trim only every two to three years.
- Trim hedges in rotation to leave some untrimmed for nesting birds.
- Do not trim during the bird-nesting season, 1 March to 31 July.

Different hedge-trimming shapes. The choice of shape will be influenced by the way the hedge has been trimmed in the past, by personal choice, or by the lie of the land and its effect on access to the hedge, such as a ditch on one or both sides of the hedge. Physical factors often limit the scope to trim the way one might like. (Bomford Turner Ltd)

- Trim later in winter when most berries and seeds will have fallen.
- Increase the hedge height where possible.
- Trim hedges in an A-shape, or with a rounded top.
- Tie a marker tag on to any young trees in the hedge to avoid cutting them.
- Ensure the blades are sharp, and drive slowly to ensure a clean cut.

Rectangular cut: vertical sides and a flat top give a somewhat formal appearance.

HEDGE SHAPES

Rectangular

This is the most common shape of cut, and produces a thick hedge if trimmed annually. However, a flat top can cause problems with the trimmings lodging on the top, reducing spring re-growth, although most fall through to the bottom of the hedge where they build up a mulch. This can be a mixed blessing, because although the trimmings may control weed growth and conserve moisture, so helping the growth of the hedge, on the other hand, as the hedge matures there could be detrimental effects from the build-up of such a covering, for instance reducing the growth of wild plants in the hedge bottom.

A steady build-up of old trimmings in the hedge bottom can also harbour fungal infection and cause stems to rot, especially in high rainfall areas. And if the mulch prevents plant growth it will deny wildlife the

Chamfered cut: the sides and top are cut slightly at an angle to give a more rounded and natural appearance.

'A'-shaped cut: a mixed species hedge trimmed with a flat-topped 'A' shape, providing a thick wide base that is an ideal wildlife shelter.

opportunity to forage and feed on insects and suchlike. The mulch produces a sterile environment that may harbour a few mice and rats, which could provide a meal for passing raptors, but doesn't help to build up a broader ecology to provide a shelter and food source for birds and insect life.

Chamfered

This is a variation of the rectangular form, with angled cuts to the side of the hedge top; it is normally employed to give a neater finish to a tall hedge that has been grown to the maximum height of the hedge cutter. A taller hedge will attract more nesting birds, because they are able to build higher to avoid predators near the ground.

The chamfered top will improve the flow of air over the hedge, reducing the vortex effect of the leeward side. This shape also helps to deflect some of the trimmings away from the centre of the hedge.

A-shape

This shape exposes both faces of the hedge to more sunlight, and has an improved capacity to shed trimmings, and snow after a heavy snowfall. It provides a thicker base,

Rounded: although this hedge has been trimmed quite low, it has a wide base adjacent to the ditch, offering good protection for small mammals in the hedge bottom.

and encourages better regrowth in the hedge, especially if the hedge is aligned east to west: in this case it has a shaded north side, which does not grow so vigorously, and a south side that produces stronger growth because it faces the sunlight for most of the day. The angled side helps to let more of the sun's rays pass over the hedge top on to the shaded north side.

Care must be taken when trimming to keep the hedge in balance. The shaded north side should be trimmed lightly, whilst the sunny south side can be trimmed a little harder, thus reducing the likelihood of the hedge 'leaning' sideways towards the sunlight, as well as maintaining the balance of growth.

Rounded and Topped A-shape

These two forms have a greater ability to withstand the weight of heavy snowfall, and to deflect any sort of deposited material. Rounded old hedges are often seen growing on an awkward bank or on the far side of a steep ditch where trimming access is difficult. Both shapes help to retain a broad, thick base that is ideal for good wildlife cover for nesting birds.

Rounded tops are better for keeping a hedge stock-proof than tall rectangular or thin A-shapes. Suckering shrubs such as blackthorn, dogwood and crab benefit from the broader base shapes, which do not restrict the spread of sucker growth.

A-shaped forms will be more difficult to trim if they are growing close to a fence. The flail cutter head may not have adequate space to reach close to the ground if the base has grown out into the fence.

The FWAG booklet *Hedges and Field Boundaries* (*1991*) draws attention to areas where close trimming might be relaxed to favour songbirds. Junctions in hedges often occur where there is less concern for their competition with the adjacent crop. These corner sections can be allowed to grow out to form small bushy thickets, with a tree planted into the corner, adding a change in height to provide a lookout or songbird perch, as well as offering more wildlife cover.

PLANT PROTECTION AND FENCING

Individual Plant Protection

Good hedgerow plants are bushy and do not fit easily into the range of proprietary guards available. Besides, the cost of individual guards is nearly the same as the cost of the plant, so the first rule is: *don't fit guards unless there is a known threat* of damage to the plants from rabbits or hares. Where deer are a serious threat, the only safe option is to erect a wire-netting fence to both sides of the new hedge. If the cost of planting the hedge is being grant aided, you may be required to fit individual guards as part of the grant agreement. There is a choice of individual guards suitable for hedge plants: basically, the higher the cost, the better the product, and the easier it will be to fit.

Spiral Guards

These are flexible plastic spiral tubes, varying in height from 450mm to 750mm (18 to 30in) and in diameter from 38mm to 50mm (1.5 to 2in). The most popular size for sturdy two-year-old transplants is to choose a spiral guard that is 600mm (24in) high and 50mm (2in) wide; for one-year-old seedlings a guard 450mm (18in) high and 38mm (1.5in) wide will be adequate.

Fit the guard after planting by unwinding the spiral and recoiling it around the plant; once the guard is in place a bamboo cane is inserted between the plant and the inside of the spiral guard to support the guard, which may otherwise cause the plant to lean over due to its weight.

Other features of spiral guards are that they can be bought either with or without ventilation holes up the side. I prefer those with ventilation, so the plant can breathe in hot weather and even put out a little leaf growth from the holes. The guards are also available in clear or brown plastic. I recommend the use of clear plastic guards for

Hedge seedling protected by spiral guards, each with a stout cane to support both the guard and plant. Note the ventilation holes in the sides of the guards.

hedgerow plants to encourage some side growth. The brown plastic guards are better suited to wrapping around young trees, which will then be encouraged to have a straight and clean stem – the brown guard prevents the entry of sunlight, so discouraging any unwanted side growth on the lower part of the stem.

Net Guards

A selection of narrow, tubular plastic, open mesh net guards are available for hedge plants. Some are thin, cheap and awkward to fit; others are much more robust, wider in diameter and better suited for larger shrub species. They are usually 60cm (24in) in height, and supplied in nests of four similar tubes, ranging in diameter from 130 to 160mm (5 to 6in), 150 to 180mm (6 to 7in), and 170 to 200mm (6.7 to 8in). The different diameters allow choice according to plant size.

Tree Shelters

The straight stem of a young tree can best be protected in the early years of growth by a different selection of guards. All guards have the limitation that sooner or later the tree will grow out of the guard and become exposed to the rigours of the climate, and come within the reach of larger predators, such as cattle and deer.

Young trees planted into a new hedge should be protected by plastic tube tree shelters. These are made from corrugated polypropylene and come in the form of either an oblong box section, a triangle or a tube, which is placed down over the planted tree. The tree shelter needs a stake for support. Some are supplied with the required length of stake and two ties as a complete package. A range of heights is available: 60cm (24in), 90cm (36in), 120cm (47in), 150cm (60in) and 180cm (70in). In each case the appropriate length of stake is the same as the height of the guard.

A newly planted mixed species hedge with individual trees protected within tall plastic shelters, supported by a strong stake secured to the shelter by two ties.

The shelters can be made from an unventilated, plain corrugated sheet, or an open 'net' mesh, or a net mesh with an attached clear polythene lining. The options for ventilation and visibility in the guards allow for personal choice.

The open mesh will provide maximum ventilation, but will encourage side branches to grow out through the mesh squares, making it very difficult to cut off the guards at a later date.

Unventilated, plain tube guards provide a 'greenhouse' environment that stimulates vigorous growth. In some cases the growth is so vigorous that the young tree grows rapidly to the top of the tube, emerging into the open air in such a soft state of growth that its tender leader is vulnerable to wind damage or to being accidentally damaged by large birds perching on the rim of the shelter. I prefer the open mesh option, so long as the guards are removed before any shoots either branch out through the side, or the developing tree becomes so thick stemmed that the guard begins to throttle its main stem. The young trees grow at a more moderate rate and are less prone to the soft growth damage mentioned above.

All good quality guards will have a fluted top to prevent the young stem of the emerging tree from rubbing on a straight-cut rim in windy conditions. The fluted rim also helps to improve the tube's rigidity.

It is important to ensure that the base of the tree guard is pushed into the soil to a depth of at least 50mm (2in) to prevent mice or rats from getting inside the tube to damage the stem, or simply to form a nest in the shelter and warmth of the tube. The value of the shelter provided for the young plant inside the guard can best be shown by quoting from Forestry Commission trials undertaken to assess the efficacy of the guard in promoting growth, in comparison with an unguarded control.

Transplant oak trees 22cm (8.6in) in height grew unprotected to a height of 34cm (13in) in two growing seasons. Similar transplant oak trees (22cm) fitted with an enclosed mesh guard grew to a height of 53cm (21in) in the same two-year period on the same site. But where the same oaks were fitted with an unventilated plastic tube guard, they grew to an impressive height of 132cm (52in) – *three* times the growth rate of their unprotected trial neighbour!

Trials continue to demonstrate the growth benefits from fitting tree shelter guards. I have used the word 'plastic' to describe what is, in fact, an opaque, twin-walled, polypropylene material from which most tree guards are made.

Very good growth responses have been recorded for ash, sycamore, sweet chestnut, crab, oak and lime. Variable growth responses have been noted on alder, horse chestnut, beech and whitebeam. Some species respond better than others according to site variations, so do not expect all species to grow equally well in the tubes. *Young* beech should be protected by an open mesh guard; they don't like the greenhouse effect of a fully enclosed tube guard because young beech normally keep their leaves on for most of the winter, losing them as the new leaves emerge in the spring. This process is upset inside an unventilated tube due to the absence of natural alternating wet and dry conditions, which can result in the leaves rotting on the plant, so inducing fungal infection to the stem.

I have avoided mentioning the names of individual makers of tree guards because of variations in local availability. Be aware that there are variations amongst the types of guard that I have described, according to the manufacturer, and there are marked differences in quality and thus cost. Having spent good money buying and planting healthy young plants, it is a folly to cut corners with the quality of their protection if one wishes to see good results from one's efforts.

Protective Paint

This is a dithiocarbamate (ZIRAM) bird and animal repellent. Apply the undiluted chemical as a paint on to the dry stems and thicker branches of young trees and shrubs. Ziram can also be use as a diluted spray on the thinner branches. The diluted spray will not give as much protection as the paint form. Follow the manufacturer's instructions carefully for safe application and to obtain the best long-term results.

It must not be applied to foliage or fruit buds.

Repellent Sprays

If one wishes to protect plants for a short period and avoid the cost and limitations of individual guards, the use of a repellent spray on the stem and vulnerable parts of each plant can deter rabbits, hares and deer.

Spray the plants with aluminium ammonium sulphate, which can be purchased as an approved short-term inorganic bird and animal repellent. The chemical is mixed with water according to the instructions, and sprayed on to the plants when they are dry. The spray must dry fully on the plants, when it makes a coating that is distasteful to potential 'diners'. The addition of an approved wetter (coating agent) will enhance the spray cover and prolong its protective activity.

FENCING

The best way of keeping deer, hares and rabbits from damaging a new hedge is to enclose the hedge line within a fence. This is the most expensive form of protection, but it is the only way of ensuring that a young hedge will grow unmolested in areas where deer, in particular, are known to be a serious threat to its survival.

If short-term protection is necessary for the start of the first growing season, it may only be necessary to borrow or hire some electrified sheep netting to place along both sides of the hedge until the growth of fresh spring grass and young shoots of other plants provides a more accessible alternative food source. A galvanized wire-netting fence is adequate protection against hares and rabbits. Use 19-gauge wire netting made to BS 443 standard with a 31 to 38mm (1 to 1.5in) mesh size in 50m (164ft) rolls. The height should be 105 to 120cm (41 to 47in) to allow for 20cm (78in) of the netting to be buried, to deter rabbits from burrowing under the fence.

Firstly, dig or plough out a 150mm (59in) deep trench at least one metre (40in) away from the planted hedge-line, to mark the fence line and for burying the base of the netting; this space will allow for future growth of the hedge.

The problems resulting from placing the fence too close to the young hedge are that it will eventually grow through the netting and make it difficult to trim. This problem is exaggerated where blackthorn is one of the species used in the hedge, because of its tendency to sucker and spread rapidly through the fence to become a difficult problem to control in the absence of livestock who will graze off the sucker growth.

A widely spaced, double row hedge protected against deer, hares and rabbits on the Berkshire Downs by a good wire-netting fence.

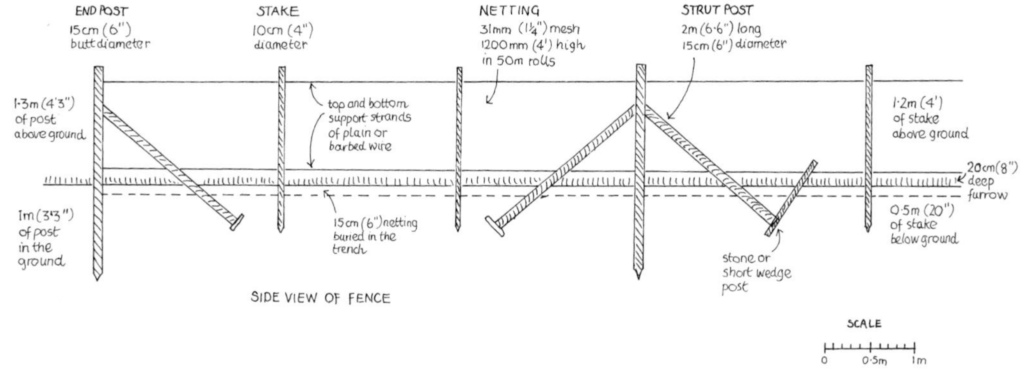

Diagram showing the position and sizes of posts, stakes and wiring necessary for a good fence that will protect a new hedge until it has grown to maturity, or until the fencing is removed to enable trimming to be carried out safely. The eventual removal of the fencing will allow small mammals into the hedge bottom.

Use stakes that are 1.5m (5ft) tall, 50-80mm (2-3in) in diameter, and pressure-treated for length of life. Space the stakes at 5 to 6m (intervals, and drive them into the ground to a depth of 0.50m (1.6in) for good stability.

Use 2.30m (7.5ft) tall end posts with a minimum diameter of 100mm (4in), dug into the ground to a depth of 0.75m (30in). Stabilize the end posts with a diagonal strut post 2m (6ft 6in) long and 80—100mm (3—4in) in diameter, braced into the ground with a wedge stone or a short wedge post. For long stretches of hedge, use intermediate strainer posts with a strut on each side every 50-100m (165-330ft), or at any change of direction. All fence corners must be treated similarly.

Erect the end post and any corner posts as well as the intermediate stakes along the line of the open trench before attaching the netting.

Fix a tensioned single strand of barbed or plain wire just above ground level, and another at the top of the post to hang the netting on and to give it adequate support. Hang, tension and fix the wire netting with staples, ensuring that 150—200mm (6—8in) of the netting is well buried in the ground, with the bottom bent over in an 'L'-shape, facing outwards. Replace the soil or turf into the furrow once the netting has been fixed to the posts.

A maturing hedge protected by a pig-netting fence. The fence was placed a little too close to the hedge, making it difficult to trim the hedge without damaging the fencing. The large mesh netting would not have protected the hedge from rabbits and hares when it was younger, but it does allow access for smaller mammals into the shelter of the hedge bottom.

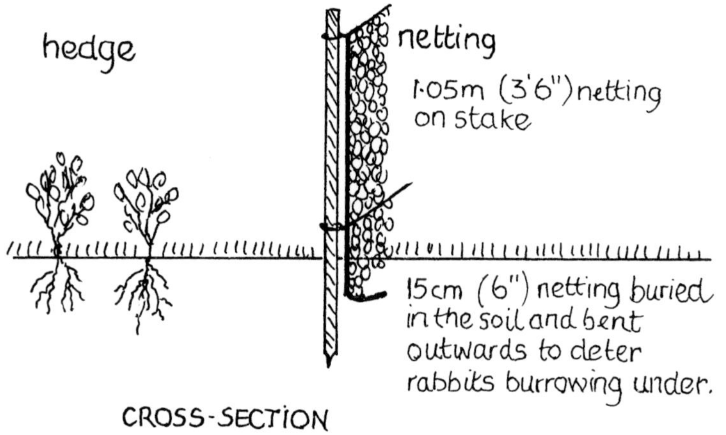

Diagram showing how the netting is buried 15cm (6in) into the ground with the wire bent outwards to discourage rabbits from burrowing under the wire. They will have to burrow deeply to get under. Normally when they encounter the wire they give up and try to do the same elsewhere, so 15cm of buried wire is sufficient in most instances.

Fencing can be done by one's own staff, assuming they are supplied with all the correct tools. A fencing contractor may be able to do the work nearly as cheaply because of his ability to buy the materials at keener trade prices, and he should have the skill to do the work both to a higher standard and more quickly because of his experience.

In situations where the fence is only needed to keep stock at bay and there is little risk of rabbit damage, a square-mesh cattle or pig netting may be adequate. Fencing to prevent deer from getting at the hedge will need to be from 2.3 to 3m (7 to 10ft) high, with a corresponding increase in the dimension and size of all materials used. There will be few cases where a hedge can justify this level of protection, and such fencing is reserved for special woodland sites.

Badger gates should be incorporated if they are known to be in the vicinity, to allow them to forage freely. Badgers make well-worn tracks along their regular foraging routes, which one would notice should it cross the line of a proposed hedge fence. To enable the badger to continue to use its usual track and yet not let vermin pass, fit a flap gate at the points where the tracks cross the hedge.

Attach a wooden frame, 300mm (12in) square, to the fence netting and peg it into the soil. Cut out the piece of netting within the frame and mount on to this a smaller 'door' frame to hang within the outer frame. The netting door can be fitted to the top rail of the outer frame with a piece of thick plastic, and nailed on so as to hang down as a hinged flap, like a domestic cat flap. It should be free to swing in both directions, according to the direction of the badger's travels. Upon approaching the gate the badger will put its nose under the lower lip of the door and push its way through.

Those wishing to fence their own hedges or woods can find more detailed information by purchasing a copy of *Fencing*, published by the British Trust for Conservation Volunteers, Conservation Centre, Balby Road, Doncaster DN4 0RN.

Footpath gates or stiles must be incorporated if the proposed hedge-line crosses a public footpath. Fit either a simple stile made from planks and posts, or a sprung gate that will swing closed once the walker has passed through, so maintaining the vermin-proof requirement of the fencing.

Fencing may be a requirement of grant aid for the new hedge, in which case the fencing or other forms of plant protection will also be grant aided.

CHAPTER 12

The Development of Hedge Laying

Hedge laying is the method by which an overgrown hedge is cut back to reduce its bulk and height to restore it to a state where it can again act as a compact, stockproof barrier and screen for the retention of livestock within a hedged field. Dead and older wood is removed to leave selected straight stems, called 'layers' or 'pleachers', along the hedge-line, which are then partly cut through near the base so they can be laid over at an angle to form a thick barrier about 1.20m (4ft) high. The cut stems are supported by stakes driven in at intervals; the laid stems and support stakes are finally bound together along the top by weaving long, supple rods of hazel called 'binders' or 'ethers/ hethers' between the stakes.

In the opening chapter covering the evolution of the hedge, it was noted that the earliest references to hedges date back to c. 55 BC, during the time of Julius Caesar and his campaign in Gaul (Northern France) where he encountered 'dead hedges', formed to contain stock and to keep out unwelcome intruders. These are the earliest references to the management of hedges; most early records relate to their position or use, such as those found in Anglo-Saxon charters and manorial records.Landscape archaeologists and historians continue to

A fine example of a laid hedge, showing the selected 'pleachers' (cut stems) cut and laid over at 40 degrees; these are supported by the stakes driven through the line of laid pleachers. The stakes are held firmly in position by long thin hazel rods woven between the stakes to complete the laying of the hedge.

improve their techniques for interpreting the evolution of land use; however, in the absence of documentary or other proven evidence, some of their views must remain well reasoned speculation. There are very few direct references to the practice of hedge laying until the Middle Ages, when the pattern of settled agriculture attracted the attention of early writers on rural affairs, such as Thomas Tusser, who mentions hedges in his book *Five Hundred Pointes of Good Husbandrie* written in 1580.

In Chapter 22 Tusser states: 'When frost will not suffer to dike and to hedge, then get thee a heat with thy beetle and wedge'; by which he means that when it is too cold to obtain firewood from the work of ditching and hedging, cut and split timber instead. Thus we are aware that hedge laying in some form was a common practice by the mid-sixteenth century. Later, in Chapter 23, he discusses wood cutting and recommends: 'In lopping and felling, save edder and stake, thine hedges, as needeth, to mend and make,' and he instructs us to save binders and stakes for hedge repairing and laying. No description is given of how to do the work, because Tusser would not have been acquainted with the intricacies of manual skills; he simply observed and recorded the daily tasks that had to be done throughout the year by all good farmers and landowners.

Moses Cook, writing in 1724 in his book *The Manner of Raising, Ordering and Improving Forest Trees* does provide us with some instruction on how to lay hedges, because his book was directed at those who would be carrying out the work he described. Moses was gardener to the Earl of Essex, himself a 'great encourager of planting'. In Chapter 33 he states:

> First, at every laying, lay down some old plashes (pleachers), or young ones if your hedge be thin; but let them point with their ends to the ditch side of the bank: they will the better thicken the bottom of your hedge…
>
> Do not cut your plashes too much, but just so much as they will bend down; and do not lay them so upright as some of our workmen do, but lay them near to a level, the Sap will break out at several places the better, and not run so much to the ends as it will when they lie much sloping. If you have wood to spare, cut up most of those that grow near the ditch; but hang the bank then with bushes (brushwood), to keep the cattle from cropping them the first year…
>
> Lay your hedge pretty thick, turning the 'beard' [light brushwood] on the ditch side; but do not let the beard hang uncut…but cut off all the straggling boughs within half a foot of the hedge on both sides, then it will shoot strong at these places, and thicken your hedge much the more…….
>
> If you would have a good hedge for a fence, you must 'fell' [lay] it often, doing it as is foresaid, and take care at every felling to root out elder, traveller's joy, briony, etc and also leave not too many high standard trees or pollards in it.
>
> Do not use too much dead wood in the bottom of your hedges, for that choaks your Quick (Hawthorn); but if you have a gap, make your dead hedge at a distance…

All sound advice that is as relevant today as it was nearly three hundred years ago.

The portrait of a hedger in the possession of Lord Saye and Sele, painted in first half of the eighteenth century. His tailcoat and hat are torn from encounters with thorn hedges, against which he is well clothed with a thick coat, long leather gloves and substantial leggings. In his hand is a billhook, somewhat like a slasher with a straight blade on the back, associated with the Stafford or Yorkshire styles. (Lord Saye and Sele)

The importance and value of hedge laying came to the fore with the extensive planting of hedges during the enclosure movement that began during the early eighteenth century and continued until most arable land in lowland Britain had been enclosed by the mid-nineteenth century. The planting of hedges on such a scale brought with it the need to formalize the way hedges should be controlled from becoming overgrown and a hindrance to the efficient management of the newly enclosed fields, formed to give farmers the chance to grow better crops, freed from the time-consuming problems of managing their former scattered strips in the old open field system.

By the end of the eighteenth century, with the enclosure movement well under way, there were differing opinions on how best to manage hedges, and the respected writer William Marshall lent his views to the debate in an excellent book entitled *Planting and Ornamental Gardening* published in 1795. He describes several ways to manage both new and older hedges:

> 1. It is some time before a young hedge becomes an absolute fence against resolute stock; and the shortest way to making it *blind* (a good screen) is, by encouraging its upward growth, to raise it high enough to prevent their looking over it; and by trimming it on the sides, to endeavour to render it thick enough to prevent their seeing through it; giving it thereby the appearance, at least, of a perfect fence.
>
> 2. A *pruned* Hedge requires a different treatment to perfect it as a fence. As soon as the stems have acquired a suitable stability, they should be cut off hedge-height; and, in order to give additional stiffness, as well as to bring the live stakes into line, some dead-stakes should be driven in here and there. This done, the whole should be tightly eddered (bound) together near the top. As an adequate fence against horned cattle, the stems are required to be of considerable thickness; but as a sufficient restraint to sheep only, strong plants may be treated thus a few years after planting...

3. The After Management. There is one general rule to be observed in this business; *cut often* (lay) for the countryman's maxim is a good one; 'Cut thorns and have thorns '

The proper length of time *between the cuttings* (laying) depends upon the plant, the soil, and other circumstances: seven to eight years may be taken as the medium age at which the Hawthorn is cut in most counties.

In Norfolk, however, the Hedges are seldom cut under twelve to fifteen years... In Surry and Kent seven to eight years is the usual age at which the Farmers cut down their Quick (thorn) Hedges: and in Yorkshire they are frequently cut so young as five to six. There may be one reason for the excellency of the Yorkshire hedges; for under this course of treatment every stem, whether strong or weak, has a fair chance; the weak ones are enabled to withstand so short a struggle, whilst the large ones are rather invigorated than checked by such timely cropping......

4. The usual *time of cutting* (laying) is during the spring months of February, March, April. The Hawthorn, however, may be cut any time in winter; and it is observable, that the shoots from the stools of Hedges cut in May, when the leaves are breaking forth (note that the time of bud burst was later in 1795 than it is today) have been equally as strong as those from Hedges felled early in the spring.

5. The *methods of cutting* are various. In Surry and Kent, the general practice is to fell to the ground, scour out the ditch, set a Stake-and-Edder Hedge behind or partially upon the stubs and throw some rough thorns into the ditch.

In Hertfordshire, Gloucestershire, and some parts of Yorkshire, *plashing* (hedge laying) is much in use. This is done by cutting the larger stems down to the stub, and topping those of a middling size Hedge-height by way of stakes, between which the most tender are interwoven, in the wattle-manner, to fill up the interspaces and give an immediate live-fence. If live stakes cannot be had, dead ones are usually driven in their stead: and in order to keep the plashes (pleachers) in their places, as well as to bring the stakes into line and stiffen the whole, it is customary in most places to edder (bind) such Hedges...

...many good Hedges are spoiled by plashing (laying).

The plashes should be numerous and should be trimmed to naked rods, in order that their spray (spread) may not incommode (shade) the tender shoots from the stools below: they should be laid in an ascending direction (uphill), so that they may be bent without nicking at the root, if possible: such as will not stoop (bend) without breaking, should be nicked with an *upward* not with a *downward* stroke: that, if properly done, gives a *tongue* which conducts the rain-water from the wound;...

However, where the *stems* stand regular, and are of themselves stiff enough for a Fence, or where they can be readily made so by driving large stakes in the vacancies and weak places, plashing and every other expedient ought to be dispensed with: where, upon examination, the stems are found insufficient, it is generally the best practise to fell the whole to the ground and train a set of new ones.

> In cases of gaps or vacancies too wide to be filled up by the natural branches of the contagious (adjacent) stools, they should be filled up by *layering* (laying) the neighbouring young shoots, the first or second year after felling; being careful to weed and nurse up the young layers until they are out of harms way....
>
> The fittest instrument for the purpose of trimming and weeding is a long hook, or rather a long straight blade with a hooked point... (see the billhook in the hands of the 18th c. hedger in the above illustration).

William Marshall goes on to describe every possible aspect of, and the problems with, both new and old hedges, giving very sound advice to the reader. However, it is safe to deduce that hedge laying was far from being the preferred method of maintaining or restoring hedges, as will be further illustrated below.

Henry Stephens' *Book of the Farm*, published in two volumes in 1850, provided detailed descriptions of all farming operations in an almost dictionary-like format with numerous illustrations. It would have been an invaluable reference book for all good farmers, and was typical of the very informative writings on agriculture during this period of prosperity. Stephens provides extensive descriptions on all aspects of planting and maintaining hedges.

Hedge laying is referred to as 'plashing', and his opening paragraph is quite direct in presenting his personal view on the subject!

> 'Plashing' hedges is much practised in England, where it is frequently very neatly executed; but I cannot help thinking that many a good hedge is needlessly cut down for the sake of plashing. Plashes are laid at all possible angles, and twisted into all possible forms, as if to prove that the thorn plant can withstand every possible torture....

He goes on to quote from Kames' *Gentleman Farmer*:

> A cat is said among the vulgar to have nine lives. Is it their opinion that a thorn, like a cat, may be cut and slashed at without suffering by it? A thorn is a tree of long life. If, instead of being massacred by plashing, it were raised and dressed (trimmed) in the way here described, it would continue a fine hedge for 500 years....

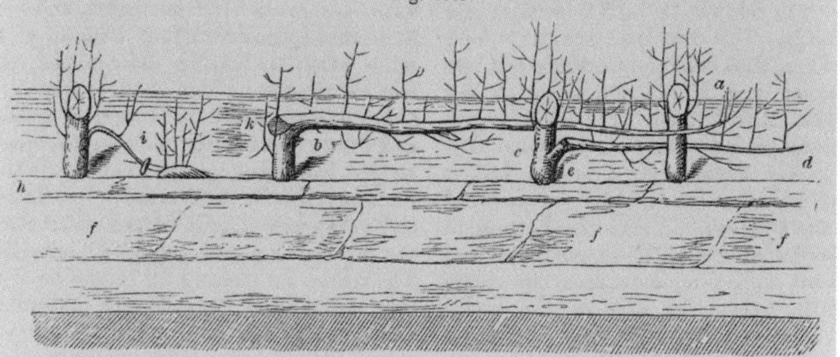
nce there is no means of fastening it of the stem *a*; but had there been a m
own at *c*, and its end is wattled in front of fastening it at *c*, it should have

Fig. 466.

THE PLASHING, AND LAYING OF AN OLD HEDGE, AND THE WATER-TABLING OF A DITCH.

it off there. It will also be observed, continue a fine hedge perhaps for
at the stem *e d* originates at *e* and not at years."*

Stephen's illustration of his form of hedge laying, or 'plashing'. A very severe version that verges on coppicing, with only one pleacher left on each old stool.

Stephens' description and illustration of laying old hedges show a severe form of the art, with few pleachers left and these laid very low and parallel with the ground. He does not provide a possible reason for such low pleachers, with the odd one being pegged down to encourage regrowth from layering, which is clearly indicated in the diagram that accompanied the text. Henry Stephens is recorded as having farmed successfully on a large scale, and thus would have known the best way to carry out the tasks he describes so fully in his book. Once more we are faced with differing opinions and techniques, which do not equate exactly with our present-day understanding of this 'ancient craft'.

With the arrival of early plate photography it was popular in the mid-Victorian era to take pictures of craftsmen dressed in their working clothes as a social record of the time. There is no date on the wonderful shot of 'old John Brinkworth of King's Stanley', (near Stroud in Gloucestershire) complete with his axe and slasher. He is well protected from thorns with leather knee pads, a strong leather mitt, and a very rough sacking waistcoat. Even his wide-

The caption written on the original photograph describes John Brinkworth as 'an honest, hardworking Hedger and Ditcher – hale and hearty at 81 years of age'. He does not look very hearty at being photographed in his ragged attire; he bears a striking resemblance to the earlier picture of his eighteenth-century counterpart. (The Museum of English Rural Life, The University of Reading)

brimmed hat shows signs of being snagged by thorns. He probably could not afford better clothing, and was not embarrassed to be seen working in such ragged attire. The photo would have been taken in the late nineteenth century.

W. J. Malden wrote an article for the RASE journal in 1899 entitled 'Hedges and Hedge-making', which described his recommendations to a railway company for the planting and subsequent maintenance of their hedges to border new track lines. He is an advocate of hedge laying as being the best method of treatment for mature hedges, stating:

> In the first place, all decaying stumps should be cut off level with the ground, and rods for wattling (laying) and stakes chosen from the most vigorous stools......Wherever practicable the wood should be cut with an upward stroke, as the cut is then smooth, so the water runs off easily...but when cut with a down ward stroke there is vibration, which causes the wood to splinter, so the rain and frost ... cause considerable decay. When the wood is thin, a single stroke, as shown at *C* (fig.7) is sufficient.
>
> It is important to cut it so far through that it may be bent without splintering; the angle at which wood is to be laid in the wattle regulates the extent of the stroke, for the lower it is to be laid the further through is it necessary to cut. Where thicker, as at *A* (fig7), an upward cut should be taken, after which a downward cut may be made without splintering, a chip being taken out, so that the rod may be laid down as at *B* (fig7). So long as there is only a small amount of wood adhering to the bark, the sap will flow to the upper part, and it is often advisable to cut out a long slice of wood, as shown at *D* (fig7).

Here we see a different method of cutting pleachers to that practised today. He goes on to describe all the other elements of laying, including details of differing finished hedge heights according to the different animals that the hedge is to contain:

> It is usual to fence (hedge) from 4 feet to 4 feet 6 inches [1.20 to 1.60 m] against cattle, and 3 feet to 3 feet 6 inches [90cm to 1.10m] against sheep and pigs, but deer require 6

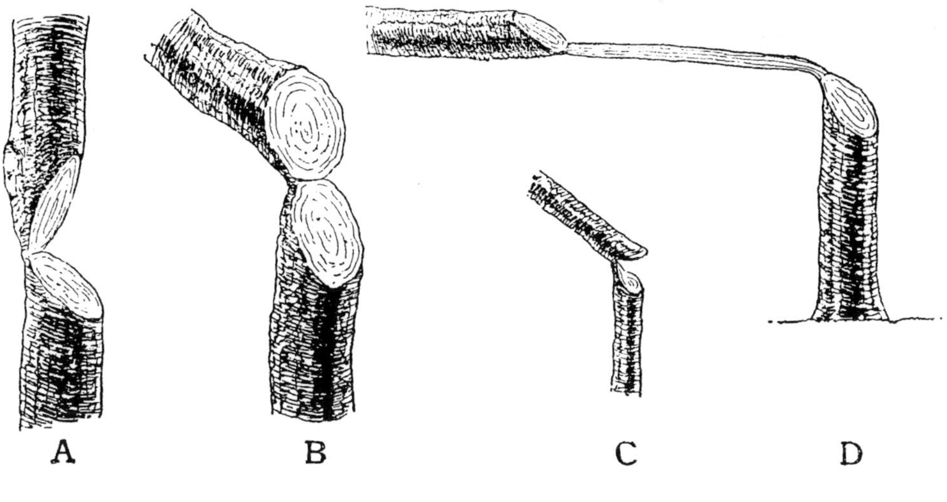

Fig 7. *A, B, C, D: the four methods of cutting growing 'rods' (stems) for laying, as described in the text.*

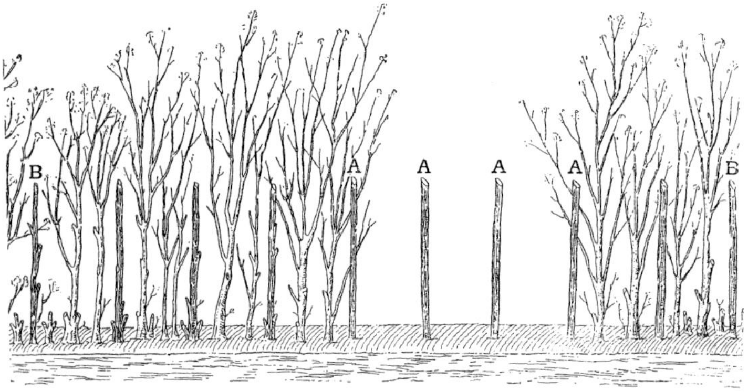

Figs 9 and 10 show the thinning out and trimming up of pleachers in a hedge either side of a gap. Support stakes (A) are driven into the ground at equal intervals, and then the pleachers are laid left and right to fill the gap. The completed laid hedge is finally bound at the top with hazel binders.

Fig 9

Fig 10

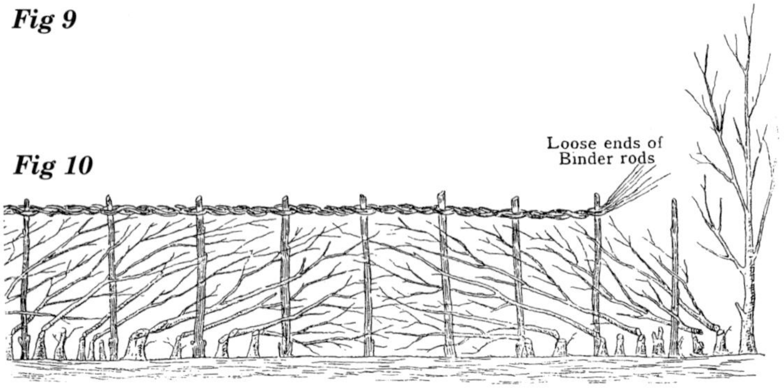

feet to 6 feet 6 inches [1.83m to 2.0m]. Hares and rabbits may be kept back by fencing 3 feet high, but they prefer going through instead of over!'

The illustrations, figs 9 and 10, show the mode of preparing and laying a hedge, a portion of the brush being cut off to show the method of wattling (laying); at the same time the filling in of a gap is illustrated. The hedge layers were not constrained by the requirement to lay in one direction only, and so were able to fill gaps by laying in both directions, if necessary, to achieve a living hedge at all times, rather than filling such gaps with deadwood, which will not provide a stock-proof hedge in the longer term.

Laying the pleachers in both directions according to personal choice is well illustrated by the photograph taken at a much later date, between 1920 and 1940. The hedge layer has removed a lot of wood and then laid the remaining pleachers in both directions, as he felt this was the best way to make a strong hedge that would retain stock effectively.

I will be bold enough to say that modern hedge-laying competitions do not foster the *living* hedge as much as they might. The use of dead wood to make a 'thin' competition hedge look better is not going to provide a good, long-term barrier against inquisitive cattle. In the days before the advent of barbed wire, hedge layers were very aware of the immediate requirements of their handiwork; their work was judged by the reality of more demanding circumstances.

An article written for the monthly *Journal of the Ministry of Agriculture* by J. S. Featherston on how to lay hedges,

The pile of debris behind the hedge shows that a lot of wood has been removed, yet the laid hedge looks robust and stockproof. The pleachers have been laid in both directions, well bound into one another, and stakes driven in where the hedger felt the pleachers needed additional support. Note his small, curve-bladed billhook. He has taken off his gauntlets to finish off his work in the West Country style by digging turfs and placing them along the bottom of the hedge. (Museum of English Rural Life, University of Reading)

dated September 1929, offered practical advice to farmers, with the added value of several photographs to illustrate his recommendations.

Farming was in a severe depression, with many hedges neglected because farmers could not afford to carry out any operation that did not relate directly to bringing in income. He starts by recommending the grubbing out of old, neglected or gappy hedges to form larger fields, but he is keen to lay hedges that are valuable as shelter for dairy or stock farmers.

The terms used to describe the work are the same as those still in use: 'laying, or plashing, with the use of stakes and binders to hold the pleachers in place…' will be familiar terms to all modern hedge layers. He recommends a wide choice of timbers for stakes: ash, oak, elm (though not any more, following the ravages of Dutch elm disease), hazel, fir and hawthorn. He also recommends using willow, but is quick to advise that the base should be peeled to prevent it re-growing when driven into the ground. Live stakes can be left every five yards in a grassland hedge, provided they are chosen from young growth and that they are cut at the base to promote growth.

To quote: 'In districts where binders cannot be obtained, sawn "banisters" are sometimes used. They are long strips of deal, 2 inches by 1 inch, of varying length and are nailed to the top of the stakes. These can be

The range of tools used by a hedger in 1929, before the advent of the chainsaw; from left to right: a slasher to trim up the hedge at the start of work; a rake for clearing out the hedge bottom before and after laying; a Stafford-style billhook for cutting and laying pleachers; a pruning saw to cut out light wood and tidy up cuts; a felling axe for cutting out larger stems, and for cutting and laying heavy pleachers; a grappling hook to pull out and draw down tall stems and for disentangling others; and finally, leather mits for hand work with blackthorn and hawthorn.

purchased from timber merchants or sawn out on the farm.' He continues to describe the work in the same way as it is done today, with more brushwood left on a grazed field-side and less left on an arable field.

The photograph shows that the tools used will be familiar, except for the absence of a chainsaw!

In an earlier edition of the *Journal* (October 1925) there is an article by G. H. Hollingworth, who covers much of what has been said above; but there is an excellent photograph showing the use of live stakes at close intervals, and their

Living 'stakes' are cut at the front of the hedge and laid to the left, while the hedge pleachers are laid to the right. There are other rough-cut stakes driven into the hedge at normal spacing to provide support for the binders. Mr Sykes, from Deddington in Oxfordshire, stands proudly beside his work holding a long-handled 'Bristol'-style billhook in 1925.

being layered in the opposite direction to the rest of the laid hedge; one of the live stakes appears to be a shoot from a high stump. The author accepts that the use of live stakes is a matter of opinion, an argument against their use being 'that they throw out a bunch of growth on the top'. The arguments in favour of using live stakes are:

- 'They are firm and rigid if the right growth is selected.'
- 'If they do throw out some shoots at the top in the first year, the young vigorous growth from the base soon gets the upper hand.'
- 'By using the material that is in the hedge for stakes, considerable labour is saved in cutting and carting material from elsewhere.' (This last point would seem to have practical merit in the present cost-conscious age.)

The smartly attired hedge layer, in the same photograph, complete with his black waistcoat and pocket watch with chain,

A hedge in 1939, simply maintained by cutting it back to chest height and laying in trimmed poles across any thin sections to keep it stockproof; no barbed wire is used here to supplement the hedge. The shallow ditch will discourage stock from getting too close to the hedge. (The Museum of English Rural Life, The University of Reading)

was a Mr G. D. Sykes from Deddington in Oxfordshire, an expert hedger and thatcher. He is seen standing beside an example of his work.

In the text there is a description of the binding at the top of a similar hedge which states that:

> As the work of laying proceeds, an outlook is kept for long, straight and not too thick growth, a few yards apart on the ditch side, or the opposite side to which the brush is carried through. When the laying is finished, these binders (or hethers) are cut partly through at the bottom, bent the reverse way to the layers, and interlaced between the stakes along the top of the hedge, thus completing an entirely living fence.

Again, every effort was made to keep the costs down by using material available on site; the fully living laid hedge did not require the use of any 'imported' stakes and binders. To be able to achieve this would require the hedge to be laid when it was young, vigorous and thick enough to offer the hedger the choice of selecting all these necessary living components! Many hedges today are laid when they are nearly too overgrown to be fit for anything short of coppicing; unfortunately, only a few are in a condition to offer all the components to lay an entirely living hedge, especially if they have been subject to flail trimming!

The laying of farm hedges was always an important winter maintenance task that would be undertaken whenever the weather prevented arable cultivations or when other routine winter tasks had been completed, such as the daily feeding of stock or when the threshing gang had visited the farm. But however important the task was, there were hard times when farmers simply could not afford to do any hedge laying.

The fortunes of farming have ebbed and flowed over the decades, and so whenever the price of corn or the value of livestock fell, farmers would tighten their belts by laying off staff, and this would result in the less pressing work of

Mr Vernon Hall from Little Milton, near Oxford, stated in 1942: 'it was 14 years ago that I last dealt with this hedge... I laid just over one mile that season.' He went on to state that he aimed to lay a chain and a half a day, equivalent to 30.5m / 33yd. (The Museum of English Rural Life, The University of Reading)

hedge laying being put off until finances improved a few years later. During times of depression hedges would become neglected, and the minimum would be done to keep them stockproof.

Before the invention of barbed wire in the late nineteenth century, farm workers would have patched up gaps in hedges by cutting down some brushwood and stuffing it into the gaps, probably using a few stakes and some binding to make the patch more secure.

The two earlier references to hedge laying from Ministry of Agriculture journals in 1925 and 1926 coincided with a period of severe depression in farm incomes. The price of wheat following the end of World War I peaked at 80s per quarter in 1920, and then fell rapidly to 49s by 1927, but it continued to fall steadily until reaching a low point of 22s in 1935. Thereafter, as the clouds of war began to gather, the price steadily revived to reach 42s by 1940, following the formation of the County War Agricultural Executive Committees (WAEC) in 1939 to coordinate agricultural production.

A photograph taken in March 1939 shows that many hedges were renovated simply by cutting the overgrown stems back to normal hedge height, and then laying in trimmed poles to fill gaps or thin sections along the hedge. The shallow ditch has been dug out by hand, and selected elm and other hardwood trees have been trimmed up to complete a tidy job.

A wartime edition of the *Farmers Weekly*, dated April 1942, carried a short article describing the way an Oxfordshire hedge layer went about his work. Again we see the use of selected pleachers being laid in the opposite direction to the rest to act as a living support in addition to the stakes, which have been cut from the wood removed in laying the hedge; such articles would have encouraged other farmers to have a go themselves.

The formation of the Agricultural Committees was the foundation of a long-lasting commitment by successive governments to support agriculture and encourage farmers to produce the food needed to reduce the nation's dependence upon a very wide range of imported foodstocks. With a close involvement in the fortunes of farming during and after World War II, many changes took place that are now regarded as having been detrimental to the fabric of the countryside.

Among these changes, the removal of thousands of miles of hedges to accommodate the ever-increasing size of farm machinery would change the landscape for ever and result in the near extinction of the hedge layer until the cries of anguish, which began with the likes of Rachael Carson in her book *Silent Spring* (1962), awoke the general public to what was happening in the countryside.

The government became concerned with the costs of supporting farmers, who had become so efficient that grain was being exported to dispose of ever-increasing crop surpluses. The scale of farming had become a highly mechanized industry, but it was losing touch with the fragile ecology of nature in the countryside. Something had to be done to halt the decline in wild bird numbers, address the increasing pollution of water sources, and reverse the wholesale removal of hedges as well as the conversion of ancient downland and meadows into larger arable fields.

During the past decade great strides have been made to redress the balance of nature in the countryside. Hedgerow removal grants have been replaced with planting and maintenance grants. A wide range of initiatives has resulted in the formation of conservation groups offering advice, grants and training in all aspects of regenerating natural habitats for every mammal, from the lowly vole to the lofty owl: field margins for butterflies, moths and small insects; hedges and woodland for birds and wildlife in general; and ponds for frogs and rivers for fish: every aspect of the fabric of the countryside is now under scrutiny.

Hedge laying has witnessed a welcome revival, and many newly trained hedge layers are now able to earn a modest living during the winter months thanks to training courses organized by The National Hedge-laying Society, as well as many local conservation groups throughout the country, set up with funding from a variety of sources. (Details about the National Hedge-laying Society appear at the end of the last chapter.)

CHAPTER 13

Hedge Laying

In the first part of this book the evolution of the hedge was described; the plants to be found in them; how to plant and maintain them in the early years; and the annual trimming of mature hedges. Before mechanical hedge trimmers, hedge laying was regarded as the established method of rejuvenating older hedges that could no longer be kept bushy and stockproof with an annual trimming up of the hedge sides using a light 'brushing' hook or 'slasher'.

In the previous chapter the development of the craft over recent centuries has been described. This now brings us to the present renewed interest and revival of this valuable rural craft, which has gone hand in hand with government encouragement and grant aid to replant and restore hedges throughout the country.

Most of the reasons for planting hedges, as listed at the beginning of Chapter 2, apply equally to hedge laying, because a laid hedge restores an overgrown or neglected hedge to the condition and potential use for which is was originally planted. Ideally hedges should be laid every ten to

A neglected and 'tired' nineteenth-century hawthorn enclosure hedge that is too small and sparse to lay. Such a hedge should be coppiced back to ground level and all the gaps filled by planting healthy transplants, which would grow away alongside the re-growth from the coppiced stools. The benefit of such a restoration is that within a few years the hedge could again become stockproof and of much greater value to wildlife.

fifteen years to keep them in good condition; however, not every overgrown or neglected hedge is suitable for laying. If the old hedge has become very sparse, the best recourse is to coppice (cut) the remains back to ground level, replant in the gaps, and protect the new plants and the regrowth from the stools until the restored hedge is fit for trimming, or until it has grown up to a height suitable for laying.

So what is a suitable height and state for laying? Ideally the stems should be between 2.5m and 3.5m (8 and 12ft) tall and with adequate side branching to provide a bushy pleacher when laid. In reality the state of neglected hedges will vary considerably; many will be very overgrown and will require a great deal of preliminary clearance to reveal the basic hedge, others will be thin and 'tired'. A competent hedge layer will be capable of making the best of the material that is available, hopefully without the need to put in too much dead wood to compensate for the lack of suitable living stems. If an adequately thickly laid hedge can only be achieved by the addition of a lot of dead wood, it is worth considering coppicing the whole of the old hedge and starting again, as mentioned above.

Before even contemplating laying a hedge there are a number of procedures and preparations that must be carried out to ensure that one is able to undertake the work safely and with equipment that is both suitable for the task and in sound condition.

An East Anglian farm hedge being prepared for laying: a good job for a cold winter's day. The men are removing all the brambles and other vegetation from the hedge bottom prior to laying. The man in the foreground wears thick leather gloves and is using a sickle to clear the base of the hedge. Beside him is his slasher, leant against the hedge, which he will use to 'brush up' the sides of the hedge. In the background the second man is doing such a job in his section. Where the tidying up has been completed, it is easy to see that there are plenty of good, bushy pleachers to choose from, making it possible to lay a thick, stockproof hedge. (The Museum of English Rural Life, The University of Reading)

PERSONAL SAFETY

Enrol for a course on hedge laying that provides plenty of 'hands-on' practical training, and preferably one that ends with a beginners' competition to show that the instruction and practice can translate into students being sufficiently competent to lay a section of hedge unaided, within the time allotted. Thereafter it will be a case of obtaining as much further experience as possible on hedges of varying ages and condition.

An important part of any training will focus on personal safety. The tools used are very sharp, and thus capable of causing serious injury if not handled with care and due respect for their correct method of use. It is worth attending a basic first aid course so you can deal with an injury to yourself or to others.

The correct clothing for working with power tools and thorny hedge plants are further aspects to taken into consideration.

EQUIPMENT

Avoid buying any tools of your own until you have had adequate basic training to be able to appreciate what is required from each of the following pieces of equipment. Don't be too proud to ask a professional hedge layer for his advice on any point that you don't understand, especially when it comes to the choice of equipment and tools that are going to make the work easier to carry out; you don't want to be doing any unnecessary extra hard work. Hedge laying is hard manual work that can be significantly eased by the choice of good equipment, which is then maintained in safe, sharp and sound order for every working day.

Clothing

Overalls and all other working clothes should be a good body fit. Avoid any loose clothing that could catch in the hedge or your equipment. If you are using a chainsaw it is a legal requirement that special chainsaw trousers and boots are worn, together with a safety helmet that incorporates both ear defenders and a visor. It is possible to buy chainsaw 'bib and brace' overalls to provide extra cover and protection for the upper body, which still allows good freedom of movement for the arms and shoulders.

Boots are an important item, and are especially recommended in preference to wearing trainers, heavy shoes or Wellingtons. If a chainsaw is being used it is imperative that chainsaw boots with steel toecaps are worn. In view of the variable winter weather conditions it is advisable to choose boots that are waterproof. Wet feet are cold feet, and working with cold feet in winter is no pleasure.

Gloves that are thick enough to resist thorns are essential. Choose good quality leather or waterproofed material gloves that have sleeves to protect the wrist. It may be necessary to have two pairs of gloves: first, a light pair for use with all the tasks that do not involve direct contact with the thorny hedge timber, such as clearing out before starting and binding at the conclusion of work. Then for the hard work of cutting and laying the pleachers, use thick, soft leather gloves, such as welding gauntlets, that are robust enough to resist long thorns yet supple enough to allow adequate free movement of one's fingers to hold the tools and grasp stems firmly and safely.

Leggings provide a valuable protection against thorns, and help to keep you dry in wet conditions. These are

A well attired hedge layer, wearing all the correct safety clothing necessary when using a chainsaw. He wears a safety helmet to which is fixed a wire mesh visor to cover his face when sawing; the helmet is also fitted with ear defenders. The jacket and trousers are made from a special material that will protect his body from accidental chainsaw cuts or snags. The most vulnerable parts of the body are protected by extra padding – on the shoulders and upper arms of the jacket, and down the front of the trousers. The material used for padding protects by snagging in and stalling the chainsaw. His feet are protected by waterproof, rubber chainsaw boots incorporating protection down the front, together with steel toecaps. Only purchase equipment that is manufactured to the correct BSI standards, and wear all the protective clothing recommended by the Health and Safety Executive.

made of plasticized or waxed canvas, and can be hung from a belt; some are available with internal padding at the front to give greater protection when kneeling down.

Arm protectors help to keep the lower arm dry, and offer protection for the wrists against thorns in the absence of long-sleeved gloves.

A good **hat** will keep out the wet and shade the eyes from the sun or from possible scratches. It is said that up to 15 per cent of one's body heat can be lost from an exposed head.

A heavier **coat** may be necessary for working in cold or wet conditions – but take care when using a chainsaw to ensure that the coat tails do not hang down and risk snagging in the chain.

Wellington boots may be necessary for working in wet weather or if clearing out a damp ditch beside the hedge. Never use a chainsaw when wearing such boots, but always change to the correct boots, as mentioned above.

A **first aid kit** that complies with current health and safety regulations should always be to hand, and any items used should be replaced as soon as possible. For outdoor use the kit should be in a robust, waterproof container that is clearly marked. Remember to have the first aid kit close to the working area for quick access.

Always take adequate **food and drink** according to the length of the working day. Plenty of liquid should be a priority to prevent possible dehydration when working hard.

Professional hedge layers often work on their own and so must take particular care for their own safety while working, because there is every likelihood that no one will be about to help them should they get into difficulties or injure themselves; so carry a **mobile phone**

A selection of gloves for outdoor work:
Top row, left to right: lightweight cotton gloves with rubberized, dotted palms for light use offering some protection, but better suited for simply keeping the hands clean and warm. Fully waterproof, robust, rubberized, cotton-based gloves for working in wet conditions. Chainsaw gloves with protective material in the back of the left hand, fingers and thumb. Hide leather fronts, water-repellent nylon backs, and elasticated knitted wrists.
Bottom row, left to right: Two styles of 'gristle' gloves; soft rubber impregnated cotton gloves that are both waterproof and robust for hard use in wet conditions. Supple and tough leather 'welding' gauntlets with a cotton lining, ideal for handling thorny pleachers. The open fingers provide a better grip and feel.

with all the relevant numbers recorded on it, to be able to quickly contact the necessary emergency services.

Learn the correct way to handle all the tools, and never take risks. Don't rush at the work, or rush to get a job finished; it is under these conditions of stress and reduced concentration that mistakes, and injuries, occur. It needs to be mentioned that if you are unable to work through injury, you are also unable to earn money, so the old expedient of 'more haste, less speed' needs to be remembered.

TOOLS OF THE TRADE

Slasher

A long-handled, two-handed trimming hook is the ideal tool for cleaning away all weed, brambles and other vegetation that needs to be removed to expose the bottom of the hedge on both its sides before starting to cut and lay. The most popular shape is one with a curved blade that makes it easier to 'cut and

The slasher, or trimming hook (nearest to the camera) can be used to cut out brambles and other vegetation at the bottom of the hedge.

The Southern Counties billhook (second up from the bottom), with a wooden 'pistol' handgrip, has a lightweight, single blade that has a curved end to give a good cutting action.

The Yorkshire billhook: the only double-sided cutter in the photograph. It has a longer handle for double-handed use. The blade is heavier because it is used to make deeper cuts into heavier pleachers.

Two axes are shown at the top of the photograph: one short-handled, lighter-weight axe of approximately 1kg (2lb) in weight. The larger, long-handled felling axe will weigh about 2 to 3kg (4 to 7lb) according to choice.

pull' with, so you can reach up to trim off overhanging branches as well as rake out debris.

Billhooks

There are numerous regional styles that will be mentioned later. At this point there are two styles that are most commonly used, the 'Southern Counties' and the 'Yorkshire'.

Southern Counties

This is the simplest, single-bladed, curved billhook that can still be purchased new (see illustration above). Choose one that is light to handle and well balanced in the hand. Professional hedge layers are often on the lookout at jumble sales, farm sales or country shows to try and buy old billhooks, many of which were made of better quality steel that can retain a sharpened edge longer for a full day's work. There are a few manufacturers still making a small range of quality billhooks, so choose carefully once aware of what a sharp, well balanced billhook should feel like. The billhook shown in the photograph has had its blade reduced in weight by grinding metal from the body of the blade to thin it down, making it lighter to handle. The thinner, very sharp blade makes cutting much easier and less tiring, which should be borne in mind when using such tools all day long.

Yorkshire

A heavier, double-sided billhook with a longer, metal and wooden handle (see illustration below). It has a full length blade with a curved end on one side, and on the back is a shorter straight blade, so providing different options for cutting according to the thickness of pleachers to be cut. This billhook has also had weight removed by thinning the blade with a grinder, and filing down to ensure a smooth and very sharp blade edge on both sides. The strengthened, longer handle is of particular value as a lever to open up pleacher cuts and to help lay over the cut stem. Its extra weight is invaluable for making cuts into thicker stems, and helps add to the momentum of cutting, especially if the stems are thick, old, hard hawthorn. This style is one that is keenly sought after in the old tool market. The Yorkshire can be found in different sizes, from 1 to 4.

If the overall weight of the billhook is too heavy on the wrist and forearm for your own liking, it is possible to carefully file or grind off some of the thickness of the main body of the blade to lighten it. The reduction in the thickness will improve the ease of cutting by reducing the resistance of the blade's entry into the wood. When faced with the reality of using these tools all day long, you quickly realize the need to have a sharp, balanced billhook that does not tire the user within the first few minutes; select a billhook according to the thickness of the stems to be cut. Use the single-bladed Southern Counties style for thin, lightweight stems, and the heavier Yorkshire on thick, older wood.

The 'Stafford'

A compromise between the two preceding styles of billhook is the 'Stafford', a short-handled, lighter-weight version of

The Stafford billhook (second from the right). This is a short-handled and lighter-weight form of the Yorkshire billhook, on the right. It has a gentler curve on one side, and a shorter, straight blade on the back. As with all billhooks, personal choice and regional preferences become an important factor in deciding which tools to use. The photograph shows the three styles of handle to be found. The Yorkshire billhook on the right has a longer handle for two-handed use, but can be used by one hand. The two billhooks on the left have slightly differing versions of the 'pistol' grip, whilst the Stafford billhook, third from the left, has a 'tang' handle, which is smaller and rounded. Once again it is a matter of personal preference; try out all possible blade and handle styles at work, and choose the one that you find most comfortable after sustained use.

The leather holster for holding a single-bladed billhook is hung from the waist in a position that is easy to clip into, and out of, for quick and safe use. Its use prevents losing sight of the billhook, or putting it down where it may be damaged or cause injury.

the Yorkshire style. It has a gentler curved blade for cutting and laying, and a shorter straight blade on the back that is handy for pointing stakes or trimming binders; but beware the hook end of the curved blade when using the straight-edge side, and don't let it catch or cut into clothing or oneself. It is a compromise between the two billhooks already described, and has the advantage of being a medium-weight cutter, allowing heavier stems to be cut and laid, without having to resort to the greater bulk and weight of a Yorkshire billhook. It will be a case of personal choice, taking into account one's own physique and the amount and type of work to be carried out. It is important to choose the style of tool that you feel comfortable using, and with which you can achieve the best results.

These billhooks should be available with different styles of handle, either a rounded (tang) handle or a pistol grip. The photograph shows the three styles of handle to be found. The Yorkshire billhook, on the right, has a longer handle for two- handed use, though it can be used one-handed. The two billhooks on the left have slightly different versions of the 'pistol' grip, whilst the Stafford billhook, third from the left, has a 'tang' handle, which is smaller and rounded. This shape may be more comfortable for those with a small hand. Once again, personal choice will decide which one offers the most comfortable hand grip, according to the size of one's palm.

Try out all possible blade and handle combinations to find the ones that suit you, and which ones remain comfortable after sustained use. It cannot be stressed strongly enough the need to select tools that are comfortable, well balanced, sharp, and as light a weight as possible for the proposed use. Using hand tools all day long needs careful thought to ensure that you do everything possible to reduce the effort input, so making a long day less tiring than it will be anyway!

A leather billhook 'holster' with its metal hanging hook is a very useful and safe means of carrying a billhook while hedge laying. It is hung from the waist in a position that is easy to clip into, and out of, for quick and safe use. Its use prevents losing sight of the billhook, or putting it down where it may be damaged or cause injury.

With the increasing use of chainsaws for many aspects of hedge laying, it is still useful to have a compact 'D'-shaped bowsaw for making small or awkward cuts in confined positions.

Bowsaw

A small, 'pointed-nose', tubular-framed saw is a necessity if a chainsaw is not available. Bowsaws come in a range of shapes and sizes, with replaceable blades, from 53cm to 90cm (21 to 35in) long. A small pointed-nose saw is very handy for getting in amongst tightly bunched stems to thin them out prior to laying. Many hedge layers who rely on the use of a chainsaw will still have a bowsaw handy to make the odd cut and to save starting up the chainsaw.

Axes

Usually hedgers will have two axes, a light 1kg (2lb) felling axe with a short handle, suitable for cutting across the grain of the small wood to point stakes, and a heavier 2 to 3kg (4 to 7lb) wedge, or splitting axe, with a long handle for cutting down the grain of heavy stems and for levering open the cut made to lay a heavy pleacher. The larger axe head with its longer shaft offers greater leverage for laying over larger pleachers. (See illustration on page 146.)

Fencing Maul (Wooden Beetle)

A metal fencing maul with a wooden handle is robust, but may prove to be somewhat bulky and heavy to use; so many hedge layers have made their own short-handled wooden maul, fashioned from a short section of ash or wild crab log that has a convenient branch stem to act as a handle. (See the illustration on page 171.) A 'home-made' beetle has the advantages that it is more compact and, being made of wood, will reduce the chance of damage to the tops of stakes or to the binders when it is used to tap them down level.

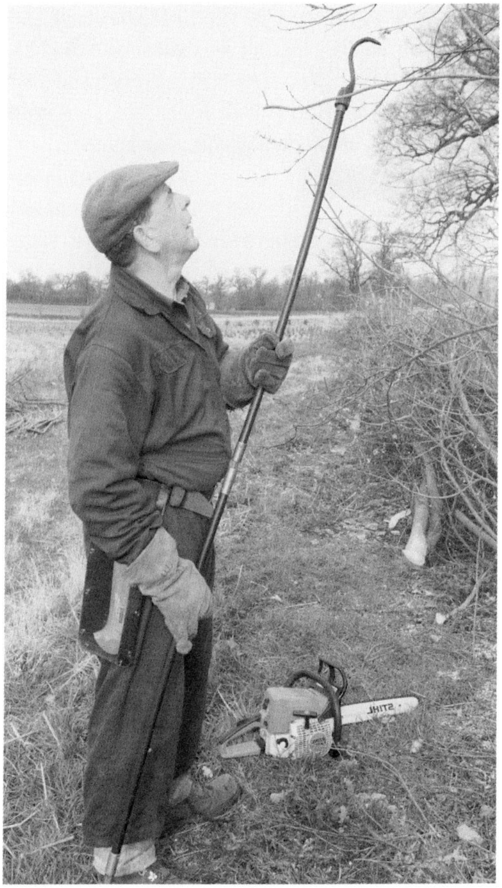

The pole hook is a very useful tool for untangling high branches when laying pleachers or removing cut wood from the hedge. It can be simply made by a blacksmith, or adapted from some other shaped metal hook and fixing on to a long wooden pole.

Hedge-Laying Terminology

Stem The individual trunk of a small bush or tree within a hedge.

Stool The rooted stump of a felled tree, from which new shoots spring.

Pleacher, or Layer/ Sleeper The partly cut stem, which is laid over at an angle to form the laid hedge, usually between 35 to 45 degrees from the vertical.

Heel The uncut stub (or 'tongue') at the base of the stem left after making the pleacher cut. This is cut off after laying the pleacher.

Stake The light wooden post used to support the laid hedge, usually hazel.

Binder The thin pliable rods of hazel or willow used to weave between the stakes along the top of the laid hedge to give a firm finish to the staked stems (also called 'ethers' or 'heathers'); thus the work is called 'binding'.

Brushwood The young bushy growth along, and at the top of, each stem.

Single brush The presence of brushwood on only one side of the laid hedge.

Double brush Brushwood present on both sides of the finished laid hedge.

Laid off The angle at which the pleachers are laid away from the centre line of the hedge towards the field.

Pole Hook

A long wooden or fibreglass pole with a metal hook at the top to pull down or untangle a high branch or stem. It is an item that can be made up from salvaged bits, and it should be possible to take it to pieces for compact storage. It is an item that is not essential, but which can prove to be very handy for dealing with tall hedges.

Sharpening Stone or File

There are several types of carborundum (silicone carbide) stones for sharpening tools. Some people will resort to the use of a grinding wheel or small hand-held electric grinder, which can be too coarse a cut. Diamond dust files are much finer, yet can be expensive for good quality long life use, but will give excellent results. Metal files come in different grades, so there is a wide choice of sharpeners that will put the necessary keen edge on to hedge-laying tools. Whichever form of sharpener you choose, ensure that it is capable of providing a sharp edge that will last most of the day.

THE PHYSIOLOGY OF HEDGE LAYING

An awareness of the way a laid hedge regrows, and the reasons why any particular hedge has been selected for laying, will help the hedger in his evaluation of the proposed work before starting.

When a pleacher is cut and laid over at 45 degrees from the vertical it is important to ensure that an adequate thickness of bridging contact remains to provide enough strength to withstand the process of bending it over, and subsequently enabling plant nutrients and water to flow up from the roots the following spring.

The bark of a tree is its protective outer layer, or skin. Directly underneath the 'corky' outer layer lies the newly forming 'inner' bark, called the phloem, that carries nutrients up and down the plant according to the time of year. This is separated from the soft, water-carrying sapwood, called the xylem, by gossamer-thin tissue that creates new cells to build up both the sapwood on the inner side and maintain the living outer bark cells. This soft cell tissue, called the 'vascular cambium', utilizes the plant sugars and water provided by the phloem and the xylem, enabling the cambium to do its work of forming new plant growth cells to add to the sapwood and to the inner bark. The newly formed sapwood matures each year, and hardens to form the next annual ring of heartwood.

The vital importance of this thin remaining link between the rooted butt of the stem and the laid pleacher must never be forgotten. If this contact is broken, then the stem will die and become nothing more than another bit of dead wood left to rot in the hedge, no longer able to provide new growth to help rejuvenate the hedge.

A number of pleachers have been cut and laid with an axe; all are showing a good contact remaining with the stem. Note the long, clean cuts that have allowed the pleachers to be laid over close to the ground. This is only possible by making a long, pliable cut through the stem. If the cut were too short it could result in the stem breaking at the cut when trying to lay the pleacher down close to the ground. The cleanness of the cut will help water to run off, reducing the risk of rotting and die-back.

When a clean cut is made to lay a pleacher, all the above productive tissues are exposed; there must be adequate outer bark, cambium and inner sapwood remaining to provide for the future growth of the pleacher, which is laid over in such a way that the most vigorous new growth in the following seasons will be stimulated to come up as new shoots from both the butt and from the sides of the stem in preference to growth coming from the ends of the smaller branches as they would have done if the stem had remained intact and upright.

Earlier it was noted that the optimum thickness and height of stems for laying are those found in a hedge of between ten and twenty years' growth. Unfortunately, the hedger is often called in to rescue a tired old hedge that has become thin from a combination of age, decay and neglect, or a hedge that has become dense and overgrown from lack of maintenance. In both cases he accepts that there will be some heavier, tree-sized stems that will have to be laid to provide enough material to form a thick hedge. The larger diameter, older trunks may not send out quite as many vigorous new side shoots as younger stems, but there will be plenty enough to reclothe the laid hedge in a short time.

CUSTOMER RELATIONS

Always explain fully to the hedge owner what is going to happen. If the hedge is in a public place it is a good public relations' exercise to put up a sign explaining that the hedge is being laid to ensure its revival as well as its future health and vigour – it is most important to avoid the impression, found in some uninformed circles, that laying a hedge is little short of destroying it. The majority of the population now live in an urban environment, away from the countryside, and do not understand the sound principles of hedge laying and coppicing.

Examine the hedge carefully, noting aspects of the proposed style of laying in relation to the age and condition of the hedge, the presence of any adjacent ditch, fence, path or roadway, overhead power lines, and the lie of the land. All these factors must be evaluated in making decisions on the correct regional style of laying, the direction of laying, the choice of side from which to work, and the collection and subsequent disposal of surplus brushwood. Most work will be done to a quoted price, so make sure that every contingency has been allowed for.

Grants may be available as part of an existing Countryside Stewardship agreement, from a local authority or from the district council. A few quick telephone calls may lead to a grant that will either reduce the cost of the proposed work or enable more work to carried out than was originally planned. Whether the work is for oneself or for a customer, a little time spent on fully evaluating the job will help to reduce costs and time wasted correcting mistakes.

Don't assume that all the timber and brushwood to be cut out of the hedge will end up on a bonfire. Check to see if any of the heavier wood has a value for firewood or turnery work, and the lighter wood for walking sticks, runner bean supports and so on. In the past, much of the wood cut from laying or trimming hedges had a value locally. In Wales, brushwood was used for 'gletting' or filling in gaps in other hedges. The photograph on page 88 taken before World War II, at Penn in Buckinghamshire, shows a horse-drawn cart being loaded with bundles of faggots, while further bundles remain beside the hedge that has been cut back. There is no record of where the faggots were going, but there would have been a ready market from the local baker and households for these as kindling for fire lighting. Bundles of faggots were also used in place of tiles for field drainage work. We have become a very wasteful society, and would do well to be become more aware of any potential use for so much that we now burn or throw away.

HEDGEROWS AND THE LAW

There is an old saying that states 'Good fences make good neighbours'. When this saying evolved, the word 'fence' was the name given to what we now call a hedge, so it is very important that one is aware of, and acquainted with, all the current legal requirements relating to hedge ownership, boundary regulations, maintenance, trimming, and especially laws regulating hedgerow removal. For instance, the Highways Act 1980 contains regulations relating to trees, hedges, hedge-banks and their related ditches.

Anyone working with hedges should obtain a copy of the *Hedgerow Regulations 1997*, introduced to conserve the nation's depleted number of hedgerows. These regulations effectively ban the removal of any hedge without prior permission from the local authority.

A hedgerow is defined as 'having a continuous length of, or exceeding, 20 metres; or if it has a continuous length of less than 20 metres and, at each end, meets another hedgerow'. Any gap resulting from a breach of the *Hedgerow Regulations*, and any gap of 20m (65ft) or less, will be treated as part of the hedgerow.

The rules do not apply to hedges within the curtilage of, or marking the boundary of the curtilage of, a dwelling house. The 'curtilage' is the area attached to a dwelling house as part of its enclosure.

No part of any rural or farm hedge can be removed without meeting all the requirements of the *Hedgerow Regulations 1997*, a brief summary of which is set out below:

- If you wish to remove a hedgerow, or part of one, you must send a hedgerow removal notice to your local authority, who will consult with the local parish council. Their decision will be based upon criteria such as the age of the hedge, the species within it, as well as its historical or landscape value.
- The local authority will either:
  a. Grant permission in writing for the removal of the hedge.
  b. Not reply within the required forty-two days (or a longer period that you may have agreed to).
  c. Issue a hedgerow retention notice, if the hedge is important.
- You may only remove the hedge if you have the written permission of the local authority, or if the local authority has not responded within the agreed time limit. Only the work set out in the removal notice is permitted.
- You are permitted to remove a hedgerow in a limited range of situations, as listed in the *Hedgerow Regulations*. More information can be found by contacting DEFRA, local conservation organizations such as FWAG, or from your local authority.

The Wildlife and Countryside Act 1981 contains regulations relating to the protection of wild birds, among which are obligations concerning the season in which coppicing and hedge laying should take place to protect nesting birds.

Farmers now have to meet certain requirements (called 'cross compliance') relating to hedges and their maintenance as part of the Single Payment Scheme (introduced in 2005). There are restrictions on the season in which hedge trimming and laying may be carried out. If farmers have also signed up for the Entry Level Stewardship Scheme they may opt to allow their hedges to grow taller and to be trimmed on a two- to three-year cycle.

It requires time and patience to keep up to date on the ever-changing regulations that govern the management of the countryside. Ignorance of the law is no excuse in a court of law, so acquire copies of all the relevant acts and regulations outlined above to ensure that you work within the law at all times.

PREPARATIONS FOR LAYING

All the necessary tools and equipment have been discussed, and the site will have been examined in advance to size up the work, provide a quotation where necessary, and to determine how long the work should take, especially if laying hedges is one's profession, because each job will be a part of a full winter's programme of work. Experience will enable the hedge layer to estimate how many metres he will be able to complete each day according to the condition of the hedge.

Variable weather, unforeseen problems on site, or simply underestimating the amount of work to be done, can all lead to delays, which will put the whole winter's schedule behind and soon result in customers ringing up to find out when you will get to them. This puts one under pressure to work faster, skimp on the quality, or simply worry about the problem, all of which can lead to mistakes and possible injury. So we are back to the importance of good preparations, and arriving at each hedge fully aware of the task in hand.

The hedge-trimming season starts in late September and ends at the beginning of March. The new farm grant scheme states that hedge laying and coppicing, as opposed to 'trimming', may continue up to the end of April, so long as no nesting birds are present in the hedge. The earlier a start can be made, the better, to gain every advantage of better autumnal weather before the harsher winter months of January and February. In northern regions there will be a greater risk of severe frosts, and in these conditions you should avoid laying because the wood will become more brittle, and pleacher cuts may tear.

No one likes working in wet conditions, but it will be unavoidable during the course of the season, so remember to take waterproofs and extra clothing to keep both dry and warm throughout the working day.

LAYING A MIDLAND OR 'STANDARD' HEDGE

The Midland style originated in the mixed farming counties, in the Midland shires, and, as with all hedge laying, was required to keep stock safely in the chosen field before the advent of barbed wire and wire netting. It is now the style most commonly associated with the craft of hedge laying. The main features are as follows:

- The brushwood of the laid hedge is left untrimmed on the inner, or stock, side of the field so the hedge is better able to resist any attempt by the stock to push their way out. The thorny brush of a well laid hedge is impenetrable. The younger brushwood also allows for some light grazing by bored animals in a dry summer, without causing any long-term damage to the hedge.

A laid Midland-style hedge showing the 'brushed' side. Some brushwood has been left to protect the newly laid hedge from browsing by livestock in the field.

A laid Midland hedge showing the trimmed side. This side faces the road or an arable field that does not require protective brushwood to be left in place. It presents a much tidier side for public view.

- The thickness of the brush should make it harder for inquisitive stock to see out of their field and so minimize their interest in getting out of the field into the next one.
- The 'outer' side of the hedge, facing a road, lane or an arable field, is trimmed back, removing the brushwood to reveal the laid pleachers. This side looks much tidier and reveals the skill of the hedge layer for all to see.
- The brushwood of a laid hedge must be high enough to prevent cattle looking over the top, so is set at approximately 1.20m to 1.30m (4ft to 4ft 6in).
- The width of the finished hedge will vary, but the stake line is generally 'set off' 20 to 30cm (8 to 12in) towards the field side to expose the base of the pleachers to light, so encouraging vigorous new growth in the bottom of the hedge.
- The Midland style is found in counties stretching from North Yorkshire, south into Lincolnshire, across into Shropshire and Hereford, and down through Buckinghamshire, Oxfordshire and Berkshire.

- This style is the one that is now most readily associated with the craft of hedge laying because it covers the basic requirements in a straightforward manner, and covers the largest area. Once this style has been mastered, it is easier to understand how the differences in cropping, climate and topography have influenced the development of regional styles.

Starting Work

Regardless of the selected cutting style, most of the preparatory work is common to all styles. First you must decide which side to start work: a Midland hedge may, or may not, have a ditch on the outside of the field, and if the brushwood is to be left untrimmed on the stock side (to reduce damage to the newly laid hedge from cattle browsing) one has to work standing in the ditch. This reduces the amount of bending necessary when cutting the pleachers. If there is no ditch it is still preferable to work from the front side because of the absence of brushwood, which is trimmed back on this side.

A Southern Counties hedge has the brushwood trimmed back on both sides, so you can work from either side. Your choice will relate to whether you cut right- or left-handed, or because of sloping ground. Furthermore each regional style has variations in the finishing of the work that may influence the initial choice of which side to work. Also you will have to investigate where it is easiest to pile up and eventually dispose of the rubbish and trimmings, and this may influence your decision as to which side to start laying – as will any of the other possible site restrictions mentioned earlier.

With the above decisions made, work can start.

Some hedge layers prefer to clear away weed and bramble growth at the base all along a stretch before starting to lay; others will clear only a few metres in front of their work. Prior clearance should include the removal of all old wire, stakes or barbed-wire fencing that may be embedded in the hedge. It is imperative that all possible wire is removed to prevent damage to chainsaws as well as other cutting tools.

With all the rubbish removed, turn your attention to clearing out elder, brambles and other 'foreign' climbers such as clematis or old man's beard. Dead and diseased wood can be removed at this stage to reveal the true quantity of usable living timber left, from which a choice can be made for laying; though it is advisable to leave some in, so as to retain a degree of choice as the work proceeds. (See illustration on page142.)

Selecting Pleachers

With the hedge cleared of all 'diversions', it is easier to concentrate on the selection of pleachers to lay, and those which can be removed, assuming there are still too many left. Often the removal of all rubbish and deadwood can leave little from which to choose, and in such a case greater care must be taken not to lose any more by poor cutting.

If there are still too many stems left, select and cut out those that:

- grow out from, or off the centre line of the hedge;
- prevent access to good potential pleachers;
- are non-thorny species, such as smooth-stemmed ash, because they will not contribute to keeping stock at bay. However,

if any straight young ash, beech, chestnut or oak are present in a form that would make a good tree, these could be left in place and trimmed up to encourage their retention; make them visible to prevent later accidental trimming.

You should also cut out:

- crooked or misshapen stems that would be awkward to lay in line;
- multi-stemmed bushes: these can be reduced to a selected single stem;
- thick, heavy stems that do not have adequate bushy side growth to maintain the thickness of the laid hedge.

Cutting and Laying

With the selection process completed, you are ready to start laying. The direction of laying is influenced by a few simple rules:

- Always lay uphill unless the slope is marginal.

A long, clean cut down the stem reduces its original rigidity, allowing it to be bent over without breaking, so retaining the vital living contact bridge at the base.

- Lay in the same direction as the hedge was laid previously if it has been laid before.
- If you are right-handed it is easiest to lay from left to right, and the opposite way if left-handed.
- When laying a hedge beside a main road, consider laying in the same direction as the flow of the traffic so that the draught caused by passing vehicles blows along the lie of the pleachers, minimizing disturbance.

Cut each selected pleacher with a clean angled cut downwards across the grain, starting at a height equivalent to three times the diameter of the stem, and finishing as low as possible. The exact point at which you start the cut depends on the thickness of the stem: the thicker the stem, the higher you start the cut to ensure that you obtain the necessary flexibility in the stem to be able to lay it over without it breaking off. If the wood is brittle, err on

A longer, gently angled cut is required to be able to lay this thicker and brittle wild plum stem. A chainsaw has been used to make the cut in the awkward forked stem. Once the left-hand half has been laid, the same treatment will be applied to the right-hand half.

The slim pleacher has been cleanly cut through and laid with a billhook.

This shows the thin, living 'tongue' that remains connected to the stem. The stump, or 'heel', will now be cleanly trimmed off in line with the angle of the tongue.

the side of caution, leaving a slightly thicker connecting 'hinge'.

Use a billhook for all cuts up to a stem thickness of 7.5cm (3in); thereafter use an axe or a chainsaw. It will take several clean strikes into the initial cut to reach the full depth of the required cut, so practise the art of making the minimum of correctly aimed strikes into the cut, thinning the stem as you go; and take even greater care not to cut too deep, to avoid leaving the living hinge too thin to withstand the bending over.

Try and practise pleacher cuts beforehand on stems that have been selected for removal from the hedge, or even practise on a length of stem cut from the hedge and stuck into the ground to gain confidence in making a sequence of strikes at the same angle into the same cut position.

If the pleacher is so thick that it has to be cut with an axe or saw, use an axe in the completed cut as a lever to carefully bend it over. Don't let it drop heavily or it

The axe that has made the cut is now used as a lever to carefully position the pleacher, and lay it in the required position. Clive Leeke, hedge layer, pulls the cut stem on to the hedge line, levering it into position with his axe.

could break its living hinge. If it snaps upwards, the stem was not thinned enough, so start higher next time.

As the cut is made, so the stem loses its rigidity and will need to be supported with the left hand as it is lowered gently down into its position on the laid hedge.

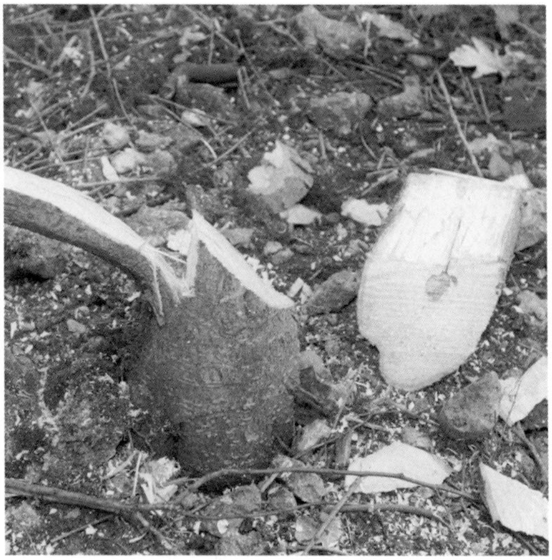

The heel of the stem is cut off cleanly in line with the tongue. Take care not to damage the delicate tongue connection.

As the cut pleacher is gently laid over, guide it down slightly off centre towards the field side.

After laying each pleacher, trim off the heel in line with the angle of the pleacher cut. Either use a bowsaw or a billhook to ensure the cut is straight and clean, taking care not to damage the hinge.

Continue to cut and lay an adequate number of selected pleachers to provide an even thickness of brushwood along the hedge.

Thick or bushy pleachers may not lay easily or neatly into each other, and may require further little 'nicks', or shallow cuts, so that parts of them can be tucked into the required position; this is known as 'nick and tuck'. In the illustration on page 169 two cuts have been made, the upper one to let the thicker upper part of the stem lie down into the lighter brush below, and the lower one to enable the side branch to be tucked inwards. Cut off any heel made by the nick.

A deep cut has been necessary to bend the thick stem inwards to fill a

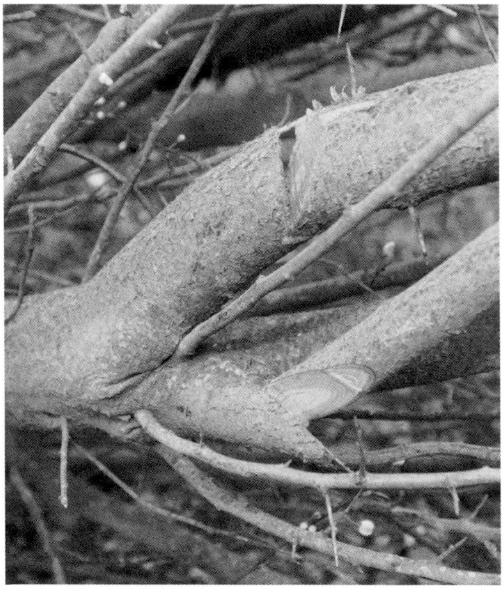

Note the two cuts made with a billhook to enable the respective branches to be bent into the required position within the laid hedge. The 'nick and tuck' process takes the rigidity out of a straight branch, giving it the necessary flexibility to be bent or twisted into a specific spot to fill a gap or simply to keep the laid hedge compact.

The above cuts viewed from a distance show how they have enabled the hedge layer to reposition the branches to thicken the hedge.

hollow within the brushwood. This work is best done with a billhook. The two cuts viewed from a distance show the effect of the cuts.

With the cutting and laying under way, it is now time to start putting in stakes to support the laid pleachers, and to define the line of working to ensure that it is kept straight.

Staking the Hedge

Stakes are usually cut from hazel, ash or sweet chestnut, but any straight young wood is acceptable, except willow, which must not be used because it will regrow very readily, unless its bark has been removed.

Hazel and sweet chestnut are probably the most commonly used species because they are capable of being cut in sufficient numbers from a coppice woodland. 'Coppice' refers to the tradition of establishing a close plantation, which is cut back to ground level after the first eight to ten years to encourage the regrowth of further numerous shoots from the base to form a 'stool'. The new shoots grow very vigorously and can be re-cut on a continuing eight- to ten-year cycle – this is called 'coppicing'. The photo shows the author (left) with professional hedge layer John Savings, who is about to cut more straight hazel stakes from a good coppice stool; some trimmed hazel rods, for making into stakes or binders, lie at their feet.

The author (left) stands with John Savings, a professional hedge layer, beside a good coppice stool from which several rods have been cut and lie on the ground. This stool will yield thick rods for cutting into stakes, and thinner flexible ones for trimming up to provide binders to finish off the hedge.

Two bundles of hazel stakes, trimmed up and cut into 1.5m (5ft) lengths before bundling. They are not usually pointed until the time of use.

Pointing the hazel stakes ready for use. Practise pointing stakes so that you can do it with the minimum of single clean cuts. This exercise will develop the ability to make swift and sure cuts when laying pleachers.

When pointing stakes, as hedge laying proceeds, experienced layers will trim each stake with a billhook, resting it on their thigh. Take care not to cut your trousers or, worse, into your leg.

Knocking in a stake with a flat-topped sledge hammer. A wooden maul, or beetle, is to be preferred, as they reduce the risk of splitting the top of the stake. Some hedge layers make their own maul from a hard piece of crab or oak, preferably with a branch attached to form a convenient handle.

Side view of a Midland hedge, from the exposed pleacher side, showing the stakes placed centrally in the hedge at 50cm (32in) intervals. The binders, coiled and running from one stake to the next, finish off and strengthen the top of the hedge. Note the brushwood visible on the far (field) side, and the long sloping cuts at the base of the larger pleachers, making the hedge dense and stockproof.

The hazel stakes need to be 1.50m (5ft) in length, straight and about 4 to 6cm (1.5 to 2.5in) thick.

The thicker end of the stake is then pointed with a billhook. Stand the end of the stake on a big block of wood to do the pointing; this will spare your back and provide a chopping block to get a good point on every stake with three to four clean cuts. Practise pointing stakes as an exercise in handling the billhook, and improve your ability to cut pleachers with a minimum of clean strokes.

Experienced hedge layers may point stakes by resting the thick end to be pointed firmly on their thigh, and making

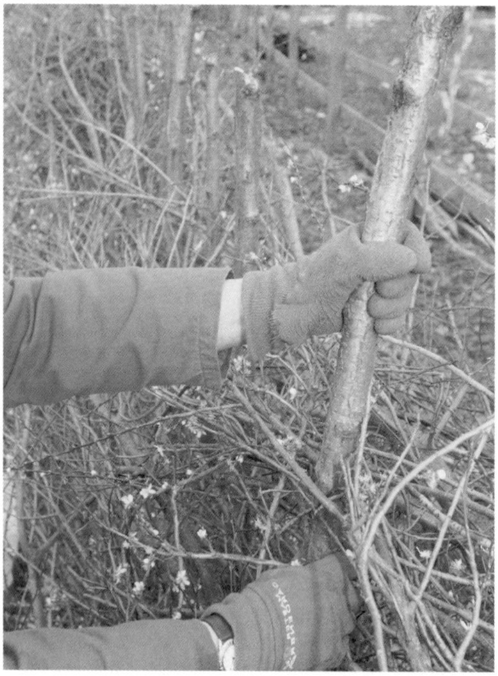

Turning a bent stake so that it is correctly aligned in the hedge. Sometimes it will be necessary to reposition stakes as the work proceeds.

The 45cm- (18in-) finger-tip to elbow measurement between stakes is an accurate measure for the average person.

clean downward strokes. Novices should not attempt to do it this way, however, because of the danger of missing the stake and cutting into their leg. The thinner (top) end of the stake must be cut square (flat-topped) for knocking in later.

The Midland style requires two stakes and two binders for every metre of hedge. The stakes are placed at 50cm (20in) intervals, and set 22 to 25cm (9 to 10in) off the centre line, towards the field side.

Push the stakes in firmly, and lightly knock them in with a wooden mallet or a flat-headed sledgehammer; it may be necessary to reposition some of them as work proceeds. Some stakes will not be perfectly straight, so twist/turn them round so that the bend does not affect the line of the hedge.

A simple measure for putting in the stakes at an even and correct spacing is to position each one at a 'finger-tip to elbow' distance apart. Only knock the stakes in finally, and firmly, when a section of hedge has been laid satisfactorily and you are about to start binding the top.

Binding

With the hedge laid and partially supported by the stakes, it is now time to bind along the top, weaving thinner, longer rods of hazel, willow or ash between the stakes to give the hedge a firm and secure finish. Willow can be safely used for binding because it does not come in contact with the ground and thus cannot take root. The rods used for binding need to be at least 2.5m (8ft) long, and should not be any thicker than 2.5cm (1in). Select thin pliable rods where possible because these will be easier to twist and weave around and between the stakes. The rods must be free of any side shoots, so trim them up with a billhook.

Bundles of thin, trimmed hazel rods suitable for use as binders along the top of the laid hedge.

Two pairs of binders have been tied together at the start of the hedge, one pair in front and one pair behind the first stake. Each pair is twisted together and passed alternately behind, then in front of, succeeding stakes as shown.

Start binding the top once a length of hedge has been laid and staked.

The binding is woven around the stakes at a height of about 1.20 to 1.30m (4 to 5ft) – see the illustration of a Midland hedge on page 155 – starting at the beginning of the laid hedge.

When binding a Midland hedge take two binders, tied together, and place them behind the first stake.

Twisting them to form a 'barley-twist rope', pass the pair in front of the second stake, twisting a little more as they are then passed behind the third stake, ending up in front of the fourth stake. Now take a second pair of binders, tie the ends alongside the first pair, but placed in front of the first stake. Twist them, 'rope-like', and pass them behind the second stake and then in front of the third stake, ending up behind the fourth stake.

Return to the first pair; take a fresh binder, place the thicker end behind the second stake, and weave it in and around the thickest one from the first pair.

Cut out the remaining (shortest) binder in front of the fourth stake, and pass the new twisted pair behind the fifth stake and then in front of the sixth stake.

The pairs of twisted binders are shown passing alternately in front and then behind succeeding stakes, one pair passing in front while the other pair passes behind, to then reverse their role at the next stake.

A fresh, pointed binder is about to be pushed in behind the stake and between the two binders to lock it in position, before twisting it in, with the longer remaining two binders coming out in front of the next stake.

Return to the second pair; cut off the shortest in front of the third stake. Weave in a fresh binder, with its thickest end placed behind the second stake and under the previous binders. Twist the new binder around the remaining one, and pass the twisted pair behind the fourth stake and then in front of the fifth stake.

Return once more to the first pair; again trim off the shortest in front of the sixth stake. Take a fresh binder, place its thickest end behind the fifth stake and under the previous binders, twist it around the remaining binder, passing the pair in front of the sixth stake, behind the seventh stake to end up in front of the eighth stake.

The process continues in the same way, moving from one pair to the other, each time 'locking' a new, full-length binder in place behind the last stake and under the previous ones, trimming off the shortest of the remaining pair at the front of the join, twisting the new binder around the remaining one, and passing the new pair behind and then in front of succeeding stakes to work along the line of stakes, weaving with one pair then the other and continuing to introduce a fresh binder at each change to the alternate pair.

Introducing a fresh, pointed binder behind the stake and between the two pairs of twisted binders.

Pushing in, and then weaving in each new binder, one behind each stake, to continue an unbroken 'barley-twist' along the hedge top. The end of each binder should not hang down behind each stake as shown here: it should be tucked in neatly into the barley twist above. The photo was chosen to illustrate the introduction and twisting in of each new binder behind each stake.

Knocking in the stakes after completing the binding to strengthen the completed work. Also tap the top of the binding down so that it, too, is level.

This looping in front of, and then behind succeeding stakes, combined with the regular introduction of a fresh binder to each pair in turn, maintains a continuity of the 'rope' binding along the hedge top.

Once a stretch of binding is completed, check that it is level and at the correct height of 1.20 to 1.30m (4ft to 4ft 6in). The stakes can be knocked in firmly.

The bindings can now be tapped down level with the wooden maul or a flat metal sledgehammer.

Trimming the Stakes

Trim off the tops of the stakes to a height equivalent to the width of a hand or fist above the bindings. Trim each stake at a 45-degree angle, ensuring that the cuts are facing forwards on the outer side of the hedge, and are all neatly in line. The cuts can be made with a bowsaw (see the illustration on page 147), or with a pair of stout long-handled loppers.

For competition work it is preferred that the stakes are trimmed with a billhook. Take a stout stick, place it behind the stake to be trimmed to support it, and wedge the

Trimming off the tops of the stakes with a pair of loppers. Note that the cuts are all at the same height above the binders, and are at the same angle to one another.

This method shows the true skill of an experienced hedge layer, a person who can make a series of perfect cuts along the hedge top, all at the same angle.

end of the stick behind the next stake to give leverage support for the required clean cut.

The cut must slope upwards at the correct angle and should, ideally, be achieved with one clean blow from a sharp billhook. The slope should match the direction of the pleachers.

The neatest cut is one made with a single cut from a billhook. A stout stick is held in the left hand, and placed behind the stake to give support for the clean cuts made with a billhook at the correct angle.

Tidying Up

Walk the hedge removing any remaining bits sticking out from the trimmed outer side. Trim off any protruding binder ends or rough stubs at the base of the pleachers. Rake up all remaining bits to leave both sides of the hedge looking tidy.

The disposal or burning of all the surplus material removed during hedge laying will need to be dealt with, or other arrangements made for their satisfactory clearance. A tractor and foreloader is ideal for this work.

MAINTENANCE OF A NEWLY LAID HEDGE

Once a hedge has been laid it is important that every care is taken to ensure that it is protected and maintained to grow away steadily in the following years.

- If the livestock grazing density is high in the field adjacent, the laid hedge may need to be protected by erecting some electric stock netting or by putting up a single strand of barbed wire and/ or netting.
- Check the hedge during the follow summer to remove any aggressive weed regrowth from such weeds as brambles, cleavers and old man's beard.
- The following autumn, trim back the new growth to a point above the top of the stakes, and also trim back any vigorous side growth from the base. In effect, cut half off each new shoot from the top or bottom of the hedge.
- Check and trim the hedge for the first three years following laying, removing aggressive weed competition. The trimming should allow the hedge to grow up by about 10 to 20cm (4 to 8in) each year; this will help to keep the body of the hedge tidy and dense, as it steadily grows back up to the chosen final height.
- Don't forget that the trimming should only be done during the winter period from late October to early March, to avoid disturbing nesting birds.

The National Hedge-laying Society

'Committed to conserving hedgerows through traditional skills'

The society aims to:

- Encourage the craft of hedge laying, and keep local styles in existence.
- Train newcomers to the craft.
- Encourage landowners to manage hedges by laying.
- Encourage competitions of a high standard.

The society works with other countryside organizations in order to promote the preservation of hedges nationally, and organizes an annual 'National Hedge-laying Championship' each year in the early autumn. The championship event moves around the country to different regions each year.

The society has a display stand that can be found at many of the large agricultural and countryside shows around the regions in the summer months.

Full details of the society can be found on its website: **www.hedgelaying.org.uk**

The secretary and other committee members will be pleased to help anyone wishing to become involved with the craft, or who requires more information on any aspect of hedge-laying.

CHAPTER 14

Regional Styles

THE MIDLAND OR 'STANDARD' STYLE

This style is set out in detail in the previous chapter on hedge laying, where it is used to describe all the aspects of the craft. A brief resume is given here, for comparison with the other styles mentioned. It is sometimes called the Midland bullock hedge because it evolved for the specific need to keep livestock in fields that were often bounded by a ditch beside the hedge. The hedge is laid away from the ditch with brushwood exposed on the field side to protect the newly laid hedge from browsing damage by the cattle. The ditch, or outer side of the hedge, is trimmed to expose the laid pleachers and to encourage fresh growth. Keeping this side clean-faced also provides an opportunity to dig out the ditch, and it presents a neat finish to passers-by.

The pleachers are laid over at a 30-degree angle towards the field (and away from the ditch), with stakes driven in at 45cm (18in) intervals, placed behind the

The Midland style: the laid hedge viewed from the 'road or ditch' side with the pleachers exposed, free of brushwood cover. The brushwood can be seen at the top of the far side of the hedge. Note the thick, coiled binders along the top. This is a young hedge that was 'block' planted, where the mix of species was planted in groups, of ten in this instance. In the foreground is a block of ten hawthorn plants that have excellent, long pleacher cuts. Next is a block of thin-stemmed dogwood that has not made much growth, so the hedge layer selected longer hawthorn pleachers that have been extended to cover over the thin growth of the dogwood. Further along is a close-planted block of thick-stemmed field maple that is very evident from the visible white pleacher cuts. Note the sloping cuts at the top of each stake all pointing in the same direction and at the same angle.

The tight 'rope'-twisted style of hazel binding along the top of a laid Midland hedge, that will strengthen the laid hedge against any livestock or windy weather buffeting.

line of stems. The top of the hedge is bound with hazel binders.

At the end of the description of each of the following regional styles of hedge laying, the scale of points awarded at the National Hedge-Laying Championships are set out to indicate the importance attached by the judges to the key aspects of each style. Thus:

Midland style, competition points scale:

Cut and pleach	35
Stake and bind	25
Back of hedge	20
General appearance	20

SOUTH OF ENGLAND STYLE

This style is now found as far north as Buckinghamshire, down into Oxfordshire, Berkshire and south into Hampshire, Surrey, Sussex and Kent. It is the latter southern counties where it is practised universally; the northern counties should be using the Midland style.

The main differences over the Midland style, which has been described in detail, are that it is 'double brushed' and centrally staked. The double brush refers to the presence of light brushwood left showing on both sides of the hedge, so that cattle and sheep can be grazed, simultaneously, in the fields on either side of the laid hedge, which is more likely in livestock farming regions.

Because the hedge is laid with brushwood left on both sides, it follows that it will be necessary to place the stakes along the centre line to balance the lay of the pleachers.

The pleachers are cut and laid over at an angle of about 40 degrees. If young lambs are to be in the fields, the pleachers can be laid lower, at 35 degrees, to give better re-growth protection for the base of the hedge from low-level nibbling.

Two stakes per metre (50cm/ 18in centres) are used in the normal manner, but placed along the centre line of the hedge. Stakes are approximately 1.7m (6 to 7ft) long, and usually cut from hazel or sweet chestnut, both of which are to be found locally, in abundance, either from commercial coppice plantations or old woodlands.

The binding is different, and simpler, than the barley twist of the Midland style. Take one binder, place its thickest end behind the first stake, pass in front of the second stake, behind the third and end up in front of the fourth.

Take another binder, placing its thickest end in front of the first stake, pass it behind the second stake, in front of the third to end up behind the fourth. This is the reverse action to that taken with the first binder.

Repeat the sequence with a further binder.

The South of England style: a view along the work of several competitors showing different amounts of brushwood left on the sides. For this style brushwood is left on both sides of the hedge, so the other side should look the same. The top brush is packed down below the line of the binders, with the stakes showing a couple of inches above the binders. The cut base of the pleachers should be just visible to allow adequate light into the bottom of the laid hedge and so ensure good re-growth from the base of the pleachers and from low in the hedge. The section on the left is very bushy low down, so hiding the pleachers; whilst in the distance the base of the pleacher cuts is visible and the sides are less bushy.

Return to the end of the first binder. Cut it off either behind, or in front of the stake closest to where it ends, and introduce a fresh binder. Place the new binder's thicker end behind the second stake and below the second binder. Continue to weave in each succeeding binder in the same pattern as before, weaving along the line of stakes introducing a fresh binder at each stake. At some points there will be as many as four binders passing in front of, or behind each stake. Repeat this process by moving forwards one stake at a time.

Use a wooden maul or the flat side of a billhook to tap the binding down tight and to check that it is level at a height of 1.10m (3ft 7in).

Tidy up the brushwood on both sides and make sure that it is kept clear of the binders at the top.

South of England style, competition points scale:

Height	15
Pleaches	25
Thickness	25
Binders	20
Stakes	10
General appearance	10

LANCASHIRE AND WESTMORLAND

This style is found in South Cumbria, Lancashire and parts of Yorkshire.

It is a dense, double-brushed hedge with the pleachers laid down at an angle of 45 degrees. The stakes are staggered either side of a centre line, at 60cm (24in) intervals, to accommodate a wider hedge; thus their

Lancashire and Westmorland: stakes are placed alternately on both sides of the hedge at 60cm (2ft) intervals. The hedge is laid quite low at a finished height of 90cm (3ft). It is also 90cm wide, giving it a neat box-like shape that looks very natural. The pleachers are laid at a low angle, and a little brush is left to stick out if desired. The centre of the hedge is left fairly open to encourage re-growth. There is no binding along the top of the hedge.

Derbyshire style: the pleachers are woven in thick and tight to give the hedge adequate support in the absence of binders along the top. The stakes are placed behind the line of the roots. The pleachers are exposed on the near side, while the brush is left on the field side, similar to the Midland style. Sawn, soft-wood stakes are used in the absence of suitable local material, such as hazel or other coppiced stakes. Once again the young hedge was block planted, with blackthorn on the left followed by the thin long stems of dog rose in the centre.

spacing is 1.20m (4ft) apart when viewed from either side. It is not possible to use binders along the top.

The laid hedge looks 'box'-like, being 1m (39in) wide and about 90cm (3ft) high to give it a natural look. The stakes are cut from local sources of hazel, ash, sycamore, birch and even beech, if no other more suitable light stake material is readily available. The stakes are cut to a normal length.

The thick, double-brushed hedge is designed to contain sheep and their inquisitive lambs, so the pleachers need to be well covered at a lower level to protect them from browsing and to keep the lambs in the field. Heavy wood can be pushed well down to give a thick base. The centre is open, like a tramline, to allow light into the bottom of the laid hedge to encourage good re-growth in the centre. Some of the brushwood is pulled out from the centre to the outside, partly for protection of the pleachers, and to help give more rigidity to the hedge in the absence of any binders.

In upland areas the harsher climate results in stunted hedge growth, which makes it a more difficult task to select and lay the pleachers in a narrow band. The stunted growth is bushier and shorter, so the laid hedge reflects this by being up to one metre (3ft 3in) in width and just over a metre in height.

In Westmorland there are banked hedges, the banks of which can be as high as 1.20m (4ft) on the roadside, but only 60cm (2ft) high on the (inner) field side.

Lancashire and Westmorland, competition points scale:

Choice and distribution of wood	30
Axework	25
Staking	25
Finish (including bank, ditch)	20

DERBYSHIRE

This upland county does not have an adequate local supply of hazel or other vigorous softwoods suitable for cutting into stakes and binders, so other ways of hedge laying have been adopted; although it is somewhat similar to the Midland style.

Stakes are made from sawn 5cm square timber and placed a little off-centre yet close to the brush side of the stools; any sort of timber will suffice for the stakes, as long as it will last for two to three years. The pleachers are laid down and woven in tighter and firmer around the stakes to compensate for the absence of binders.

Brushwood is left on the field side of the hedge, and trimmed down to the top of the stakes.

The laid hedge is 1.20m (4ft) high and 60cm to 75cm (2ft to 2ft 6in) wide, with a flat top; it is a solid hedge capable of withstanding wet and windy conditions.

Derbyshire style, competition points scale:

Cut and pleach	35
Stake	20
Back of hedge	20
General appearance	25

Yorkshire style: the photograph shows that the finished hedge is both thin and low. Brushwood is not evident and the pleacher cuts are exposed to view, which means that the hedge should be laid when livestock will not be in either of the fields bordering the hedge for at least one year. Note the use of sawn softwood stakes and top rail, the latter being nailed to the stakes. The stakes have been sawn off, with an angled cut, just above the top of the wooden rail.

YORKSHIRE

This is another upland county with plenty of moorland and a harsh climate that stunts the growth of hedges. The style of laying is influenced by the climate and the need to have a low hedge for grazing sheep.

The pleachers are laid low at an angle of 45 to 50 degrees angle along the centre of the hedge to give a thick bottom, with an overall height of only one metre. Side branches are nicked to tuck them in tight to give a narrow hedge that does not have any brushwood showing.

Square softwood stakes are set at 60cm (2ft) intervals, and then a single softwood rail is nailed along the top of the stakes.

Strangely this style has to be protected from grazing livestock for at least one year by laying the hedge during the part of the farm's rotation when the adjoining fields are in arable cropping, which may not always be possible. In the absence of an arable break crop on both sides of the hedge, the newly laid hedge will have to be protected from livestock browsing by an electric fence, or sheep netting.

Brecon style: there are several Welsh styles of hedge laying, but this is one of two styles for which there are classes in the national championship. Note how the sawn stakes are driven into the laid hedge in the opposite direction to the lie of the pleachers, which are laid over at a low angle. A little side brush can be seen, as well as the use of 'half crops' (short sticks) driven into the bottom of the hedge to help keep the pleachers tightly held in place. The top is bound simply with hazel rods in the same manner as the South of England style.

Yorkshire style, competition points scale:

Cut and pleach	40
Stake and rail	40
General appearance	20

WELSH

There are numerous local variations of a central theme for hedges designed to contain and withstand sheep. In many areas stone walls and hedge-banks add to the variety of local styles, especially when a small hedge is planted on top of both.

The local feature of stone-faced or earth hedge-banks do not always feature a formal hawthorn hedge along the top. In many cases gorse, bramble and other mixed shrubs, including hawthorn, have developed and can now be easily contained by mechanical flail trimmers, which would not have been possible fifty years ago.

Laying a hedge on top of a bank presents added problems for the hedge-layer, particularly when a barbed wire or netting fence has been erected to prevent livestock damage to the hedge-bank. Access to the hedge and disposal of rubbish become more difficult, especially with much smaller field sizes.

The Brecon style: This is generally used for national competition work, and so this is the style selected for description. A lot of the brushwood growth is removed to leave a limited number of carefully selected

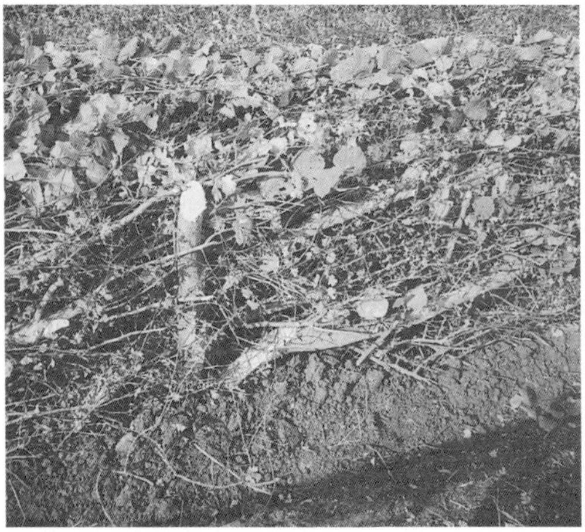

Montgomeryshire style: the other Welsh style with a class in the national championship. With no binders to support the top, the pleachers are woven in tightly at the top of the hedge. It is a thick hedge, again using half crops to help keep the hedge firm and tight; these are more substantial and evident in this photograph. Brushwood is added as necessary to give the finished hedge a solid, stockproof appearance.

With no turfs to dig and line along the bottom of the hedge, this competitor has dug over a strip along the bottom of the hedge to leave it looking tidy and well finished off.

pleachers for laying, giving an initially thin-laid hedge. These are laid over at an angle of 35 degrees, and the stakes are driven in at 60cm (24in) intervals, at an angle of 60 to 75 degrees; but in the opposite direction to the pleachers. The pleachers are laid down the middle of the hedge line.

Each angled stake is spaced so that the top end of one stake is directly above the bottom end of the next stake in the row; they are spaced at approximately 60cm centres. The stakes are made from 8cm- (3in-) diameter straight timber, which is then split to provide two half-round, 4cm (1.5in), stakes.

The pleachers are woven between the stakes to end up at the front and back, alternately, giving a double-brush finish to the sides of the one-metre (39in) high hedge.

Devon and Somerset style: the West Country hedges are often found growing on the top of earth banks of varying height and breadth. If the bank is high and narrow, it follows that the hedge will be laid narrow and low along the top; whereas if the bank is lower and wider, the hedge can be laid wider to suit. This photograph shows how to lay a hedge on top of a narrow bank.

In the low and narrow option the pleachers (stretchers) are laid very low and tight. They are held down and in place by 'crooks', short stakes cut from the waste material removed during laying, each having an angled crook at the top to pin down the brushwood. The crooks are positioned alternately on either side of the hedge at 60 to 90cm (2 to 3ft) intervals.

Close-up of a 'crook', driven in to hold down the stretchers and brushwood in place.

Some of the smaller brushwood, which was removed at the start, is then put back into each side of the hedge as the laying proceeds to protect the thin line of living pleachers in the middle. The finished hedge is quite narrow.

The top is bound in the same way as a South of England hedge, but the binders have their side feathering left on to provide greater protection against sheep browsing.

A final light trim is given to ensure a tidy rectangular shape.

The Montgomeryshire style: This version is similar in most aspects except that, in the absence of binders along the top, the pleachers are closely woven into one another, especially at the top. Sometimes 'half crops' (short stems cut from the hedgerow material) are driven in at the side of the hedge to add extra support for the bottom of the hedge.

Some hedge layers like to dig up a row of turfs and line them, upside down, along the bottom of the hedge to act as a marker to keep a straight laying line.

Welsh Border styles, competition points scale:

Front and pleach	20
Back of hedge	20
Bank	20
True to style	20
Stake and top	20

DEVON AND SOMERSET

Devon is famous for its high earth or walled hedge-banks that surround and protect the small fields from wind and storm, allowing the grass to grow lushly in this dairy and livestock area.

Somerset has both traditional hedges grown on the 'Levels' and other flat land, but in common with Devon, some areas feature high and, often, wide hedge-banks around small fields, and this has influenced the style of the way their hedges are laid. In national competitions one style now covers the two counties' banked hedges, and that style has been chosen for description.

How to lay a thick hedge on the top of a low and/or wide bank.

In the low and wide option, the lie of the pleachers (stretchers) and brushwood is similar, but because the finished hedge is much wider, cross stretchers are pushed in below the pinned pleachers on a diagonal across the hedge to hold the brushwood down tight. The centre of the laid hedge is fairly open to encourage new growth, protected by its surroundings.

The hedges have a rich assortment of up to thirteen or fourteen shrub and tree species present, which adds to the skill of laying; sycamore, ash and elder are among the more vigorous species that have to be accommodated. With such vigorous species present it is common to have to lay pleachers (locally called 'stretchers') that can be up to 20 to 25cm (8 to 10in) in diameter.

If the hedge at the top of the bank is wide enough it may be possible to lay the pleachers in two closely spaced lines a few inches apart (called the 'double Devon' style). This style is of benefit to wildlife, which can move easily along the hedge in the shelter of the gap between the two lines of pleachers. In many cases, however, it is more usual to lay one line of pleachers.

The width of the hedge will vary according to the width of the bank top, and can be from 45cm to 60cm (18 to 24in) wide.

The pleachers are laid very low and held down with crooks to ensure that high winds or horned livestock do not lift them. The crooks are cut from branches in the hedge, their length being the same as the finished height of the hedge and the depth of soil on top of the bank into which they are driven. Each crook has a hook top to be driven in, on the outsides of the hedge, at an angle to pin down the laid pleachers at 90cm (36in) intervals.

With short, crooked stakes to hold down the pleachers, it follows that there will be no upright stakes and binders as commonly used in most other styles, because the hedge is on top of an earth or stone-faced bank.

Where the laid hedge is particularly wide short stakes, cut from the hedge wood, are laid across the top of the hedge to keep the pleachers tightly down; these are called 'wands' or 'spreaders' and are pinned down by the crook side stakes.

A young beech tree has been allowed to remain standing within a newly laid section of a Derbyshire-style laid hedge. In Chapter 4, Wildlife Conservation, the value of hedgerow trees as song posts or vantage points for different bird species was discussed.

Devon and Somerset, competition points scale:

Cutting and laying; quality of cutting stool, lack of splitting	30
Selection and best use of crooks, leading to overall strength	30
General appearance, quality of finished hedge, effectiveness of the hedge as a stock barrier, tidiness of site	40

IN CONCLUSION

Whichever style of laying is practised according to regional, or personal preference, always aim to preserve any well shaped hedgerow trees to add to the beauty of the countryside and for the benefit of wildlife. Trees are an important feature of our unique landscape, and who better than the hedge layer to select and save any suitable young trees as he works along the hedgerow.

APPENDIX

British Imperial and Continental Metric Measures

OLD IMPERIAL MEASURES

Length

In 1101 AD, Henry I commanded that the length of his arm should define 'the yard'. From that date until the introduction of metric measurement in Great Britain, the yard remained the British unit of length.

12 inches (in)	= 1 foot (ft)
3 feet (ft)	= 1 yard (yd)
5.5 yards (yd)	= 1 pole, rod or perch (p)
22 yards (yd)	= 1 chain
20 chain or 40 poles or 220 yards	= 1 furlong
8 furlongs or 1,760 yards	= 1 mile

Surface Area

144 square inches (sq in)	= 1 square foot (sq ft)
9 square feet (sq ft)	= 1 square yard (sq yd)
30.25 square yards (sq yd)	= 1 square pole, rod or perch
40 square poles or perches	= 1 rood (r)
4 roods or 4,840 square yards	= 1 acre (a)
10 square chain	= 1 acre
640 acres	= 1 square mile

METRIC MEASURES

Length

10 millimetres (mm)	= 1 centimetre (cm)
100 centimetres (cm)	= 1 metre (m)
1000 metres (m)	= 1 kilometre (km)

Surface area

100 square metres (sq m)	= 1 are (119.6 sq yards)

100 ares	= 1 hectare (ha) (2.47 acres)

OLD FIELD SIZES

On old enclosure award maps, deeds or old farm maps, fields are often given a name or a description to define each parcel of land. Below the name or description will be written the size of the field or piece. For example:

a	*r*	*p*
83	1	27

This piece of land measured 83 acres, 1 rood and 27 perches.
83 acres (multiply by 0.4047 to convert to hectares)
1 rood (divide by 4, and then multiply by 0.4047 to convert to a fraction of a hectare)

Seedling and transplant tree sizes – metric to imperial conversions:
Some English nurseries continue to use metric height measurements that relate to the old imperial categories, to make the conversion easier for those who still think in imperial measurements.

10–20cm	= 4–8in
20–30cm	= 8–12in
30–45cm	= 12–18in
45–60cm	= 18in–2ft
60–90cm	= 2–3ft
90–120cm	= 3–4ft
120–150cm	= 4–5ft
150–180cm	= 5–6ft

References and Further Reading

Chapter 1

Curtler, W. H. R. (1909) *A Short History of English Agriculture* (Oxford at the Clarendon Press).

The Harmsworth Encyclopaedia (circa 1910) (The Amalgamated Press Ltd and Thomas Nelson & Sons, London).

Hoskins, W. G. (1955) *The Making of the English Landscape* (Hodder & Stoughton Ltd, Sevenoaks, Kent.)

Malden, W. J. (1899) *RASE Journal.*

Orwin,C. S. (1930) *The Future of Farming* (Oxford at the Clarendon Press).

Rackham, Oliver (1986) *The History of the Countryside* (J. M. Dent & Sons Ltd)

Tusser, Thomas (1812, Mavor Edition) *The Five Hundred Points of Good Husbandry*

Chapter 2

Beddell, J. L. (1950) *Hedges* (Faber and Faber Ltd).

Godet, Jean-Denis (1986) *Trees & Shrubs of Gt. Britain & Northern Europe* (Mosaik Books, Basingstoke, Hants).

Maby, Richard (1996) *Flora Britannica* (Sinclair-Stevenson, London).

Marshall, William (1785) *Planting — A Practical Treatise* (Dodsley, London).

Phillips, Roger (1978) *Trees in Britain* (Book Club Associates).

Prockter, and Noel, J. (1960) *Garden Hedges* (W. H. & L. Collingridge Ltd).

Sinclair, Sir John (1808) *General Report on Enclosures* (The Board of Agriculture, London).

Chapter 3

Beddall, J. C. (1950) *Hedges* (Faber and Faber Ltd, London).

Irrigation Management Services (1985) *Soil Survey for M. Maclean*, Frilford, Oxon.

Ordnance Survey (1968 & 1967) Soil Survey of England and Wales.

Chapter 4

Campbell, Bruce and Watson, Donald (1964) *The Oxford Book of Birds* (Oxford University Press, Oxford).

FWAG booklets: *Farming and Field Margins; Hedges and Field Boundaries.*

MAFF Bulletin No. 140 (1948) *Wild birds and the land* (HMSO, London).

Porter, Valerie (1990) *Small Woods and Hedgerows* (Pelham Books).

RSPB *Farming & Wildlife A practical management handbook.*

Chapter 5

Brooks, Alan and Agate, *Elisabeth Hedging – a practical handbook* (BTCV Enterprises Ltd, Doncaster)

Chapter 6

The American horticultural magazine (1970) *Handbook of Hollies* (Fall issue/ Volume 49/ No.4, a special issue on ILEX).

Hillier Nurseries (1981) *The Hillier Colour Dictionary of Trees & Shrubs* (David & Charles, Newton Abbot, Devon).

Hume, H. H. (1953) *Hollies* (The Macmillan Company, New York).

Newsholme, Christopher (1992) *Willows – the genus Salix* (B. T. Batsford Ltd, London).

Stott, K.G. (1971) *Willows for Amenity, Windbreaks and other Uses* (Reprinted from the Report of Long Ashton Research Station, University of Bristol 1971).

Stott, K.G. BSc (2002) *Cultivation and use of basket willows* The Basketmakers' Association and IACR Long Ashton Research Station.

Chapter 7
Godet, Jean-Denis (1988) *Trees & Shrubs of Great Britain and Northern Europe* (Mosaik Books, Basingstoke, Hants).
Mitchell, Alan (1996) *Trees of Britain* (Harper Collins Publishers Ltd, London).
Pontey, W. (1809) *The Profitable Planter* (J. Harding, London).
Phillips, Roger (1978) *Trees in Britain* (Book Club Associates, London).
Stokes, Jon and Hand, Kevin, The Tree Council (2004) *The Hedge Tree Handbook* (The Tree Council, London).

Chapter 8
FWAG (1991) *Farming and Field Margins* (printed for Monsanto Agriculture Company).
Smith, H. and MacDonald, D. W. (1989) *Brighton Crop Protection Conference Report* (Weeds Section).
Wye College (1994) *Hedgerow Management and Nature Conservation* (edited by Watt, T. A. and Buckley, G. P., Wye College Press).

Chapter 9
ADAS (1988), Leaflet P3172 *Weed control in Field-grown Nursery Stock* (MAFF)
British Crop Protection Council (2005) *The UK Pesticide Guide 2006* (edited by R. Whitehead BA MSc (CABI Publishing, Wallingford, Oxon).
Forestry Commission (1990-91) *Information Notes 171, 201 and 203.*
HDC (2001) *Practical Weed Control for Nursery Stock* (Horticultural Development Council and ADAS).
Stouts, R. G. and Winter, T. G., for the Forestry Commission (2000) *Diagnosis of Ill Health in Trees* (HMSO for the Department of the Environment, Transport and the Regions).

Chapter 10
ADAS/ MAFF (1983) *Leaflet on fireblight* CL39 (MAFF).
BCPC *The UK Pesticide Guide 2006* (edited by R. Whitehead BA, MSc (CABI Publishing, Wallingford, Oxon).
Stouts, R. G. and Winter, T. G. for the Forestry Commission (2000) *Diagnosis of ill health in trees* (HMSO for the Department of the Environment, Transport and the Regions).

Chapter 11
Bomford Turner Ltd *Hedges & Hedgerow Management* (booklet).
BTCV (1986) *Fencing* (BTVC, Wallingford, Oxon OX10 0EU).
FWAG (1991) *Hedges and Field Boundaries* (booklet).

Chapter 12
Cook, Moses (1724) *The Manner of Raising, Ordering & Improving Forest Trees.*
Curtler, W. H. R. (1909) *A Short History of English Agriculture* (The Clarendon Press, Oxford).
Featherstone, J. S. (1926) *The journal of The Ministry of Agriculture* (September).
Hollingworth, G. H. (1925) *The journal of The Ministry of Agriculture* (October).
Malden, W. J. (1899) *Hedges and Hedge-making* RASE Journal, article.
Marshall, William (1795) *Planting and Ornamental Gardening.*
Stephens, Henry (1850) *The Book of the Farm* 2 volumes.
Tusser, T. (1812 Mavor edition) *Five Hundred Points of Good Husbandry.*

Chapter 13
Brooks, Alan & Agate, Elisabeth (1998) *Hedging* (BTCV, Wallingford, Oxon).
Greaves, Valerie (1986) *Hedge Laying Explained* (The National Hedge-laying Society).

Chapter 14
Brooks, Alan and Agate, Elisabeth (1998) *Hedging* (BTCV, Wallingford, Oxon).
Greaves, Valerie (1986) *Hedge Laying Explained* (The National Hedge-Laying Society).

Index